'After reading this book, my first reaction was: what a positively written book. It reflects my opinion and experience as an autistic person. Nowhere is it absolutely stated that people with autism cannot do something at all. This innovative book radiates a lot of strength, hope and optimism.'
— **Sam Peeters**, *Autistic Self-Advocate, Author, and Blogger, Belgium*

'Translating cutting-edge research and complex theories into clear and useful information is challenging. Reading Peter's book is not. It offers opportunity to understand human thinking and behaviour in new and thought-provoking ways. In the context of autism, it provides new insights that can support autistic people, parents and professionals to deal with the everyday challenges of autism.'
— **Dr. Marita Falkmer**, *Associate Professor, School of Education and Communication, CHILD, Swedish Institute for Disability Research, Jönköping University, Gjuterigatan, Sweden, and*
Dr. Torbjörn Falkmer, *Emeritus Professor, Curtin University, Perth, Australia*

'Peter Vermeulen does it again! Vermeulen, more than most any other professional in the field of autism, has changed how we understand the autistic neurology. I thought it impossible that he could surpass the brilliance of *Context Blindness*, but I was wrong. This book on prediction provides new and much needed insights into how individuals on the spectrum react to and understand the world. To say this book is a "must-read" may sound trite, but this book is essential if you want to understand autism!'
— **Brenda Smith Myles, PhD**, *Speaker and Author*

'Peter Vermeulen has written another game-changing work that is sure to fundamentally shift how we understand autism. Just as he did in *Autism as Context Blindness*, Vermeulen makes an important but complex theory accessible, relatable and even often entertaining to read about. Drawing from the latest findings in neuroscience, he demonstrates the startling differences in how autistic and non-autistic people's brains respond to predictions and explores the dramatic implications of these findings for better understanding the incredible strengths and also very real challenges for autistic people living in a complex and ambiguous world. Readers are sure to look at social, sensory and communication differences in a whole new light, and will be equipped with autism-friendly approaches of offering greater predictability and certainty to reduce "uncertainty stress" and increase well-being for the autistic people in their lives.'
— **Aaron Lanou, MSED**, *Special Educator, Inclusive Education Consultant, and Former Director of ASD Nest at New York University's Steinhardt School, New York City, US*

'In this fascinating, accessible and fitting sequel to *Autism as Context Blindness*, Peter Vermeulen discusses how the autistic brain anticipates and processes uncertainty, and how this contributes to the "characteristics" of autism. In juxtaposing established theories of autism, and the psychology of human biases, important questions are raised about the prevailing autism narrative and the way autism is framed. In so doing, Vermeulen challenges many of the common heuristics about what is helpful to autistic people, and even of the nature of autism itself.'

         – **Richard Mills**, *Associate Consultant and Adviser to the Board, AT-Autism*

'This book uses established, innovative research about the human brain and relates it to real world experiences. Peter applies his wealth of knowledge to focus on areas that range from navigating the social landscape to providing insights into sensory issues. If you are a person who wants to learn more about neurological processing and how it relates to the autistic experience, this book will undoubtedly assist you. I wholeheartedly recommend this book as it provides another step towards demystifying autism, and helping us as practitioners, family members and friends to better support the autistic community to thrive.'

         – **Andrew McDonnell, PhD**, *Clinical Psychologist and Director of Studio3 Training Systems*

Autism and the Predictive Brain

What if our previous teachings and beliefs regarding processing stimuli, reading emotions and understanding human behaviour are all untrue? In this book, Peter Vermeulen investigates new findings on the predictive brain and what these insights mean for autism and current interventions.

Recent research has shown that the classic ideas about how the human brain first needs to process incoming information about the world before it can react are no longer tenable. Rather, to survive in the volatile, uncertain, complex and ambiguous environment of modern society, what we need is a brain that predicts the world quickly and unconsciously, while taking proper account of the context. This book explains the new theories relating to the predictive brain, summarising some of the more recent highly technical research studies about the predictive mind and autism into as accessible and understandable language as possible. Shedding new light on the predictive brain and its relation to autism, the chapters lead readers to the inevitable conclusion that many of the current interventions used in connection with autism urgently need updating and outline possibilities for revising.

This approachable book synthesises advanced research for professionals across disciplines working with people with autism spectrum disorder along with readers who have or have family members with ASD.

Peter Vermeulen, PhD, is an internationally respected lecturer/trainer in the field of autism and has written several books. In 2019, Peter received the Passwerk Lifetime Achievement Award for his more than 30 years of work in the autism field in Belgium.

Autism and the Predictive Brain

Absolute Thinking in a Relative World

Peter Vermeulen

This book was first published by Pelckmans Publishers in 2021

Routledge
Taylor & Francis Group

LONDON AND NEW YORK

Cover image: From Getty

First published 2023
by Routledge
4 Park Square, Milton Park, Abingdon, Oxon OX14 4RN

and by Routledge
605 Third Avenue, New York, NY 10158

Routledge is an imprint of the Taylor & Francis Group, an informa business

© 2023 **Pelckmans Uitgevers nv,**

British Library Cataloguing-in-Publication Data
A catalogue record for this book is available from the British Library

Library of Congress Cataloging-in-Publication Data
Names: Vermeulen, Peter, 1962-author.
Title: Autism and the predictive brain: absolute thinking in a relative
world/Peter Vermeulen.
Other titles: Autisme en het voorspellende brein. English
Description: Abingdon, Oxon; New York, NY: Routledge, 2023. |
"This book was first published by Pelckmans Publishers in 2021"–
title page. | Includes bibliographical references.
Identifiers: LCCN 2022025698 (print) | LCCN 2022025699 (ebook) |
ISBN 9781032374918 (hardback) | ISBN 9781032358970 (paperback) |
ISBN 9781003340447 (ebook)
Subjects: LCSH: Autism spectrum disorders–Treatment. |
Decision making–Psychological aspects. | Autism–Treatment. |
Asperger's syndrome–Treatment. | Cognitive neuroscience.
Classification: LCC RC553.A88 V4613 2023 (print) |
LCC RC553.A88 (ebook) | DDC 616.85/882–dc23/eng/20220629
LC record available at https://lccn.loc.gov/2022025698
LC ebook record available at https://lccn.loc.gov/2022025699

ISBN: 9781032374918 (hbk)
ISBN: 9781032358970 (pbk)
ISBN: 9781003340447 (ebk)

DOI: 10.4324/9781003340447

Typeset in Bembo
by Deanta Global Publishing Services, Chennai, India

For Det who makes my life exciting by treating me to prediction errors at irregular intervals.

Contents

Foreword

Peter Vermeulen is a world-renowned expert in understanding the thinking processes that help people to develop insights into autism. He has written a vast array of books on the topic, which focus on attempting to understand how people think and feel by trying to see the world from their perspective. Peter's work has been instrumental in understanding the autistic brain and has informed practice across the globe. In his book *Autism as Context Blindness* (2012), Peter noted that autistic individuals were often trying to make sense of a world that appeared to them to be 'chaotic and confusing.' In these situations, there is a strong desire for individuals to seek out predictability and 'an oasis of calm.' Whilst these behaviours have been largely misunderstood by society, Peter's work has shed light on the neurological mechanisms underpinning the stress and sensory overload often experienced by autistic people on a day-to-day basis.

As a practitioner, his interests are also reflected in practical approaches to supporting individuals in light of what we know about the predictive brain and context blindness. This book, *Autism and the Predictive Brain*, uses established, innovative research about the human brain and relates it to real world experiences. As Peter states, the brain is not a passive recipient of information, but an active processor as well:

> Although we feel that our brain is an organ that reacts to what happens in the outside world, that is not the case. In reality, the brain predicts what it thinks is going to happen in the world, so that we can better react to events when they occur.

Understanding the workings of the predictive brain is, I believe, a crucial factor in empathising with the 'autistic experience,' and enabling the best possible support and interventions for individuals struggling in a world that is often a volatile, uncertain, complex and ambiguous (VUCA) place.

In this book, Peter applies his wealth of knowledge to focus on areas that range from navigating the social landscape to providing insights into sensory issues. If you are a person who wants to learn more about neurological processing and how it relates to autism and the autistic experience, this book will undoubtedly assist you in explaining why people sometimes see the world differently. My colleague Damian Milton often refers to a 'double empathy' problem, whereby people sometimes struggle to empathise with the autistic experience of the world. Peter Vermeulen's work encourages empathic understanding within a logical, scientific framework, and has aided understanding and influenced practice for individuals throughout my organisation and across the globe.

This book is intended for a broad audience of individuals, and I would highly recommend it to anyone who is interested in the neurological processes of the autistic brain:

> Most people with autism, as well as the parents of autistic children, teachers, therapists, helpers, carers and autism-coaches, have never even heard of the theory of the predictive mind and know nothing about what it can mean for our understanding of autism. It is for these people that this book is intended.

In summary, I wholeheartedly recommend this book as it provides another step towards demystifying autism and helping us as practitioners, family members and friends to better support the autistic community to thrive.

Professor Andrew McDonnell
Clinical Psychologist, Studio 3

Introduction

When talking about autism, you often hear people attribute the condition to the disrupted processing of sensory stimuli. But what if the brain does not process stimuli at all?

We teach children with autism to link particular emotions to certain facial expressions, but what if there are no emotions to be read from the human face?

What if the understanding of human behaviour is primarily a matter of unconsciously predicting what people are going to do? Would the classic social skills training given to children, adolescents and adults with autism actually serve any purpose?

We read everywhere that people with autism require greater predictability in their life than people without autism, but is that really the case?

In the coaching of children, adolescents and adults with autism, use is often made of a five stage process: Events > Thoughts > Feelings > Behaviour > Result. But what if thoughts do not follow events but actually precede them? And what if feelings are actually predictions about how you need to react in the immediate future, rather than a response to what has just happened?

Many strategies, methods and interventions that are currently used for children, adolescents and adults with autism are based on classic ideas about how the brain functions, drawing on the 'computer' metaphor of input, processing and output. In other words, a brain that works in accordance with the principle of stimulus → response or event → processing → reaction.

Recent scientific research has shown that this classic view of the brain's functioning is no longer tenable. We now know that the brain does not function in the manner we had previously assumed. The new insights about how the brain actually works are truly remarkable and shed a completely different light on what is happening inside our heads. What's more, these insights are not only remarkable but also slightly shocking, because they go completely against our intuition. Although we feel that our brain is an organ that reacts to what happens in the outside world, that is not the case. In reality, the brain predicts what it thinks is going to happen in the world, so that we can better react to events when they occur.

Although these neurological insights are relatively recent in scientific terms, they are by no means brand new. Scientists first made this breakthrough in the

DOI: 10.4324/9781003340447-1

1990s, more than 20 years ago. Since then, the theory of the predictive brain has been used to develop applications in various fields, including medicine. I will give examples of this in the chapter on sensory problems in autism. The theory of the predictive brain has likewise made its entrance into the world of psychology and psychiatry, where it has resulted in refreshing new ideas in relation to matters like emotional regulation and hallucinations, ideas that are applied to better understand and treat a variety of mental conditions, such as psychosis and post-traumatic stress. Yet although this new knowledge about the predictive brain dates from around the turn of the 21st century, it is only now starting to make its presence felt in the world of autism. Even so, the application of this knowledge still remains largely confined to research projects in university laboratories. As a Fleming, I am proud that Flemish research teams are leading the way in this field and setting their stamp on the study of the predictive brain in autism. However, it is disappointing that beyond these few teams knowledge of how the autistic brain makes its predictions is largely *terra incognita*: unknown territory. Most people with autism, as well as the parents of autistic children, teachers, therapists, helpers, carers and autism-coaches, have never even heard of the theory of the predictive mind and know nothing about what it can mean for our understanding of autism. It is for these people that this book is intended. I have tried to describe and explain the most recent insights relating to the predictive brain and its potential impact on our approach to autism.

This is my third book on autistic thinking and the mechanisms that function in the autistic brain. For more than 30 years, I have attempted to build a bridge between scientific research into autism (in particular, brain research) and actual practice. I have tried to simplify and translate the content of scientific articles that are often incomprehensible for the ordinary public, in the hope that this will inspire everyone connected with autism and provide them with new ideas that will allow them to look at and, above all, deal with autism in a different and better way.

Where does my interest (some people in my environment call it an obsession) in autistic thinking come from? It comes from my belief that autistic thinking is the key to understanding autism as a whole. Although autism can be diagnosed on the basis of behavioural criteria – in other words, how someone acts and reacts – in my opinion there is no such thing as autistic behaviour. Just as there is no such thing that we could meaningfully describe as Flemish behaviour, old-age behaviour, day-tripper behaviour, etc. I fully agree with Barry Prizant, one of the leading autism pioneers, when he says that the only kind of behaviour that exists is human behaviour. Barry is fully aware that animals also display behaviour, but what he means is that there is no form of behaviour seen in people with autism that is not also seen in people without autism. As a result, I am firmly convinced that the diagnostic criteria for autism do not actually relate to autism per se, but to the results of autism. What typifies autism most tellingly is the way the autistic brain works.

I wrote my first book on this subject a quarter of a century ago, in 1996. It was called *This is the title*. In that book, I tried to explain autistic thinking through the medium of jokes and artificial intelligence. At the back of the book that you now have in your hands, I have again reproduced the final table from *This is the title*, since the table in question is a kind of summary of the 1996 book as a whole. Back then, my description of autistic thinking was inspired primarily by the work of Uta Frith and her ideas relating to weak central coherence (a term that I replaced with the simpler 'coherent thinking'). The core argument of *This is the title* was that the autistic brain finds it difficult to see coherence, so it is less good at 'guessing' the essential nature of things and events.

Of course, science has not been standing still since 1996. Quite the reverse. Since the turn of the century, the number of publications relating to autism has increased exponentially. The result of this explosion of autism research led to cracks appearing in the three existing major theories about the autistic brain: theory of mind, executive functions and central coherence. I thought that I was able to see a red thread running through all these research studies, a thread that could help to paper over the cracks in the three major theories and even link them together. This was the concept of 'context.' Please do not get the idea that I believed I had made some kind of major breakthrough. The idea of a reduced sensitivity to context in people with autism had already been suggested by Uta Frith. In fact, it was part of her original theory about weak central coherence in autism. Frith thought that there were two key aspects to this weak central coherence: firstly, an inability to see the greater whole in a coherent way; secondly, an inability to sense and use context. Most research up to that time had concentrated on the first of these two aspects (detail orientation), but it was becoming increasingly clear that this was not where the core of the problem was to be found, but rather in context sensitivity. During a meal with Uta and her husband Chris in a London restaurant, her enthusiasm persuaded me to write a second book on this relatively unexplored second aspect. It took a year to complete, but in 2009 I was able to submit my manuscript for publication. The result was *Autism as context blindness*, a book that has since been translated into six languages and won a number of prizes in the United States. (Thanks, Uta!)

Once again, however, science continued to take great strides forwards. And just as well that it did! Less than three years after the publication of *Autism as context blindness* an article[1] appeared in a scientific journal, in which for the very first time the connection was made between autism and a new theory of brain function, which argued that perception involves the alignment of expectations with incoming sensory information. For me, the message was clear: I could start all over again...

As had been the case when I was writing *Autism as context blindness*, I started again to read all kinds of scientific articles on the subject of the human brain, but especially those that made *no* mention of autism. It often pays dividends to look beyond your own field of expertise and see what you can learn from other disciplines. After all, it is difficult to be truly innovative if you never move out of your comfort zone.

I was astonished by what I read in these new articles. My faith in my existing knowledge about the human brain was shaken to its foundations. Matters that my many years of study and practical experience had convinced me were true, were now shown to be false, or at least not in agreement with the new discoveries made by neurological scientists since the 1990s. Contrary to what I had thought and what I had written in my book *Autism as context blindness*, it now seemed that perception is not a process through which the world becomes known to us through the senses. More recent brain research had demonstrated that perception is a process for which 90% of the activity originates *inside* the brain itself, a process in which the senses do not play an initiating role, but only come into play in a more limited (but not unimportant) way at a later stage. In other words, I learned that perception is a construction of the brain, a kind of self-generated illusion. Perception is not therefore an attempt to obtain the most accurate possible image of the world, but is a double-check (sometimes thorough, sometimes rudimentary) of an image or model of the world that the brain already has. In short, the brain does not receive the world; the brain predicts the world.

As if this was not already enough to digest, the new theories about brain function also suggested that the distinction traditionally made between perceiving, thinking, feeling and acting was no longer quite so important as had previously been thought. Like many others, I had believed, for example, that emotion and cognition, feeling and thinking, were engaged in non-stop competition to determine the nature of our outward behaviour. Perhaps you are familiar with the theory of the three types of brain people are supposed to possess: the reptile brain, the animal brain and the human brain? Since it first emerged in the 1960s, this triune model was used to explain the sometimes surprising results of the interaction between these three different parts of the brain. But none of it is true! We now know that feelings, thoughts and behaviour are just three different techniques the brain uses to deal with its own prediction errors. All three serve the same purpose and they work together.

Fortunately, there was one element of brain theory that was not consigned to the dustbin by the new discoveries, and that was the importance of context. Even in the revolutionary theory of the predictive brain, context continues to play a leading – one might even say a starring – role. For that reason, I considered using *Context blindness 2.0* as the sub-title for this new book of mine, but eventually decided upon a more neutral term, a term that is synonymous with context blindness but is not a reference to a disorder or a handicap and is more neurodiversity-affirmative: *Absolute thinking in a relative world*. At the end of the book, you will be able to read why I now think that this is the correct definition of autism. In this sense, the present book is not an updated version of *Autism as context blindness*. Both books do, however, complement each other.

In our modern-day VUCA world, you will find it hard to survive with a brain that reacts passively; what you need is a brain that actively creates and predicts. VUCA is a term devised by the Army War College, a military academy in the United States, and first came into use towards the end of the Cold War era. The ending of this war between the supposedly free and capitalist West and the authoritarian and communist East did not make the world an easier place to live in. The simple distinction between 'the good guys' and 'the bad guys,' between friend and foe, had disappeared. International relations became more complex. This was reflected in the acronym VUCA, which stands for volatile, uncertain, complex and ambiguous. In other words, a world that is essentially unpredictable, at least to a significant degree. Nowadays, the term is not only known and used by politicians and military men, but is also a rising star in the firmament of management theory, particularly in books and training programmes that deal with strategic leadership. For this reason, the term VUCA can also be applied as a perfect metaphor to explain the functioning of the human brain. As you will read later in the book, the information about the world that the brain receives through the senses is always volatile, uncertain, complex and ambiguous. Put simply, the information provided by the senses to the brain is unreliable. The only way for the brain to deal with this unreliability and uncertainty is to take control of the process of perception and to become the director of its own experience. In other words, moving ahead of events instead of waiting for them to happen.

In the following pages, I have tried to explain the new theories relating to the predictive brain as simply and as understandably as possible. I have also made an attempt to summarise some of the more recent (and often highly technical) research studies about the predictive mind and autism. This was by no means an easy task. Of the three books I have written on the workings of the autistic brain, this is the one that has cost me the most blood, sweat and tears. The theory of the predictive brain is not easy to understand. In her column in *Trouw* (a Dutch language news magazine), Heleen Slagter,[2] a neuroscientist at the Free University of Amsterdam, referred to this theory as 'the relativity theory of the cognitive sciences.' This was a doubly appropriate choice of words. Like Einstein's theory of relativity, the theory of the predictive brain is an absolute 'game-changer,' a breakthrough that sheds a totally different light on the way the human brain works. And as with the theory of relativity, it is also fiendishly difficult to explain. For this reason, I have tried to steer a middle course between a clear and comprehensible summary and scientifically accurate explanation.

Even so, it is possible that some readers will still find some sections difficult to follow. To make certain things crystal clear, it was sometimes necessary for me to adopt a technical approach. My explanation of autism in light of the new theory is therefore not always a simple explanation. But that is hardly surprising. Autism is not – and has never been – a simple subject, and it is becoming increasingly complex all the time. In my book *Autisme is niet blauw, de smurfen wel* (Smurfs are blue, autism isn't), I referred to the trivialisation of knowledge relating to autism, which is often reduced to simple and banal one-liners like 'low-stimulus = autism-friendly.' I have now written *Autism and the Predictive*

Brain for readers who want more nuanced and more scientifically grounded information. If you are looking for ready-made autism 'recipes' and cute metaphors, you will be disappointed.

At the opposite end of the spectrum, scientists who read the book will no doubt occasionally sigh or even grumble to themselves at passages where I felt obliged to cut scientific corners in order to make a particular aspect more readily understandable. And they will, of course, be right. I have deliberately opted *not* to explain some elements of the predicative brain theory in full technical and scientific detail, preferring my own simplified version or omitting some things altogether. Readers who are interested in a more complete technical and scientific analysis will find references to the studies on which this book is based in the end notes.[3] These literature references are not only designed to indicate my gratitude to my many sources, but will also serve anyone who likes to know all the details and prefers to read the original material. I have reduced the current scientific knowledge about the predictive mind and its relationship to autism to the minimum that I thought was relevant for everyday practice and for the target groups I had in mind (which does not include scientists, but rather people with autism, the parents of autistic children and professionals). Although this book is not specifically intended as a practical guide, I have nonetheless tried to describe the new insights in such a way that they can help people to deal with the daily challenges of supporting people with autism. The discovery of the predictive brain not only sheds new light on autism per se, but also leads to the inevitable conclusion that many of the current interventions used in connection with autism urgently need revising. This opens the door for new interventions and strategies.

As I have already mentioned, understanding the theory of the predictive brain is not easy. Moreover, the theory also makes you feel uneasy. It goes radically against your intuition about how your mind works. Although I am now used to this new way of looking at the human brain, certainly after writing this book, there are still occasions when I find it hard to accept what the new theory is telling me, because it is so totally different from what my own experience is telling me. It is a bit like the way we view the sun and the earth. Although we all know that the earth moves around the sun (and not the other way around), we still see the sun rise each morning and set each evening on the horizon, as though it – and not the earth – was moving. And it is exactly the same with the predictive brain theory. Even though I know that my perception is a construction of my brain and not a reflection of reality, I still cannot shake the feeling that I first process images that I receive from the outside world, in order to subsequently give them meaning. I find it difficult to believe that my feeling of hunger is a prediction of the approaching exhaustion of my energy reserves and not a response to an existing shortage of fuel (glycogen) in my system. Given this reluctance, it is perhaps no surprise that the writing of this book frequently led to intense discussions over breakfast, lunch and dinner in the Vermeulen household, such as the time when my wife said to me: 'So you think you can predict everything I am going to say? What nonsense!'

After all the years we have been together, my wife knew exactly how I would respond. Which rather proved my point...

All I am trying to say is this: when you read the book, there will be moments when you are guaranteed to raise your eyebrows in amazement. Some of the things I write will seem incredible to you. They also seemed incredible to me, at first. But I can assure you that as time passes you will get used to this kind experience, although your intuition, like mine, will continue to offer stubborn resistance.

Finally: I wrote this book during a period of great uncertainty and unpredictability. As with most of you, a seemingly insignificant but ultimately vicious (and virulent) virus turned my life upside down. Instead of travelling all around the world as normal, from a congress here to a workshop there and back again, everything came to a grinding halt in the early evening of a Friday in March 2020. Friday the thirteenth, no less! My agenda changed from something that was predictable for months in advance into a series of almost empty pages, littered with question marks about the future. The VUCA world had arrived in my life with a vengeance! But every cloud has a silver lining. To my way of thinking, the pandemic is an autistic experience that we can all share, whether we like it or not. Suddenly, we are all faced with the kinds of things that the autistic brain has to deal with day after day: unpredictability, uncertainty, models of the world that no longer seem to function (home is no longer only home, but also a place of work and a school), complex situations (what is 'essential' travel and what isn't?), confusion and lack of clarity (how exactly does that system with household 'bubbles' work?), etc., etc. The theory of the predictive brain teaches us that 'uncertainty' is the key word when attempting to describe autism. I hope that all of us, having learned from the pandemic what it means to experience life in a truly VUCA world, will henceforth be able to show a greater understanding for autism and those who are affected by it. Above all, I hope that we will all realise that autism is much less 'different' than we think. None of us like uncertainty. We all want to live in a world where we can predict what will happen without making too many mistakes. How that works is something I will explain in the following chapter.

1   The predictive brain

I will get straight to the point: your brain does not know itself. And if the contention of the famous Dutch brain researcher Dick Swaab is correct – namely, that we are our brain – this means that you do not know yourself.

This is a bold assertion, but a necessary one, if an author wishes to convince his readers to continue reading a book of this kind. Of course, some people, having read the previous paragraph, might simply throw the book into a corner and never open it again. But that is a risk I am willing to take… If you are still with me, that's great. Thank you!

Why would you not know your brain? After all, you and your brain have been together for years. In other words, you should know everything that happens under that skull of yours. None of its many inhabitants should be strangers to you: your ideas, memories, emotions, thoughts, dreams, etc. Of course, it cannot be denied that you do indeed know all these things. But that is not what my opening assertion says. You might 'know of' all the inhabitants of your brain, but you do not 'know how' they order their daily existence and interaction. In other words, the claim that 'your brain does not know itself' means that your brain does not know how it works. Again, many of you who have reached this far might have serious doubts about the accuracy of this claim. If you are reading a book like this, there is a good chance that you have already read other books and articles about the brain and its workings. You have probably seen dozens of diagrams that explain how the brain processes information. If you haven't, you can find hundreds of them on Google Images. The vast majority look something like this:

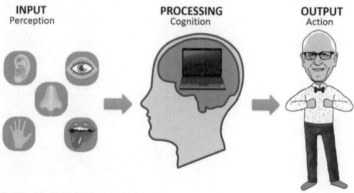

| INPUT | PROCESSING | OUTPUT |
| Perception | Cognition | Action |

DOI: 10.4324/9781003340447-2

When people want to use a metaphor for the brain, nowadays the computer is usually the most popular one. In this sense, the computer is a recent addition to the long list of 'machine' metaphors that have been used over the centuries to describe how the human body and its various component parts work. Think, for example, of the heart as a pump. In much the same way, the brain is seen as a kind of computer and we even use computer terminology to explain how it operates: input, processing, output.

Our senses provide the input: information about the world, from both outside and inside our body. The brain then takes this information and organises it, assesses it and stores it. This is the processing. The result of this processing tells us how we should react to the world: the output. And, to some extent, this is all true. The brain does indeed process information, as does a computer. But to say that the brain is like a computer is taking things too far.[4] It is like comparing a ball pool for your kids with a tin of tomato soup with meat balls, simply because they both contain balls. In recent years, brain science has undergone a Copernican revolution, which has turned our thinking about the brain and its functioning upside down.

A Copernican revolution? At the start of the 16th century, the Polish mathematician and astronomer Nikołaj Kopernik (now more generally known as Nicolaus Copernicus) sent shock waves through the society of his day by claiming that the world was not the centre of the universe, as people had assumed since ancient times. Copernicus proved that the earth revolved around the sun, and not the other way around. At the time, this was a troubling thought and one that most people found hard to accept, because it was the first time that science had dared to challenge what almost everyone believed intuitively. We all see the sun rise each morning in the east and set each evening in the west, but we have no real sense of the dazzling speed and complexity that this seemingly simple daily process involves.[5] And it was no different in the 16th century. As a result, many of Copernicus's contemporaries thought that his ideas were absurd. Pope Paul V even put his book on the list of publications banned by the Catholic Church. The few scientists who supported Copernicus's views, such as Galileo Galilei and Giordano Bruno, soon found themselves in serious trouble with the authorities. Galileo was confined to his home under house arrest, while the less fortunate Bruno was eventually burnt at the stake as a heretic by the Inquisition.

Although nowadays no one is likely to be burnt or cast into a dungeon (or so we hope!), brain science is currently in the throes of a revolution of equally dramatic and paradigm-shifting proportions. And like the discoveries made by Copernicus, the recent discoveries made about the human brain have also been met with disbelief, because they seem to go against what we intuitively believe. What the brain scientists have discovered simply does not square with our own idea of how we think our brain works. It makes us doubt our view of the world. Perhaps even more crucially, it makes us doubt our view of... us. For many, this is a worrying thought.

So what are these spectacular new discoveries? And what is so wrong with the computer metaphor?

In the first place, the use of the computer metaphor leads to the idea that the brain functions logically and rationally. The brain receives information from the senses (a process referred to as perception). It then organises and processes this information (a process referred to as thought or cognition) to generate 'meaning,' on the basis of which the brain tells the body how to respond to the outside world (our behavioural reactions). Or that is what we have always assumed. In reality, however, the brain does not work as logically or as rationally as we think. At least, not for most of the time. One of the many scientists who have demonstrated this is Daniel Kahneman,[6] an Israeli psychologist. For the past five decades, he has conducted research into how people make decisions. He came to the surprising conclusion that we make more mistakes when we think consciously about a problem, resulting in decisions that are far from being intelligent or well-founded. Kahneman's ideas had a huge and immediate public impact, especially in the world of economics. Up to that point, economists had always assumed that good economic performance was based on a careful assessment of possible risks and gains. Kahneman showed them that they were wrong – an act of enlightenment for which he was awarded the Nobel Prize for Economics in 2002.

In other words, the fact that our human species has managed to survive the dangers of the world for tens of thousands of years is *not* due to our brain's ability to reason and calculate in a logical manner. Brain scientists have not only demonstrated that the brain tends to get muddled when it is required to think logically, as shown by Kahneman and his colleague Tversky as long ago as the 1970s, but also that this kind of logical thinking is a slow process that takes a lot of time. And if you want to survive, you not only need to be smart; you also need to be fast.

Let's imagine that we are 15,000 years back in time, wandering the savannah with our hunter-gather ancestors in search of food. We are making our way carefully through the tall grass when we hear a noise ahead of us. We cannot see what is making the noise, but it is, in fact, a sabre-toothed tiger. What kind of brain would be of most use to you in these circumstances? Before you answer, here are two other factors you need to take into consideration. One: although humans are not at the top of the tiger's 'favourite food' list, they will never turn down the chance for a bit of human flesh when the opportunity arises. Two: when it comes to speed, the tiger is a hare and you are a tortoise. So back to our question: what kind of brain will help you to survive? Probably not the brain that says: 'Listen up, everyone. We can all hear the rustling in the grass ahead, but we can't see what it is. It might be a large and dangerous predator. But it might just as easily be the kind of small mammal or bird that we love to eat. So let's not be too hasty about this. Let's take some time to make the right decision. Let's gather all the facts, arrange them in the right order, assess the potential risks and gains, and only then take a decision that we can be confident will be well-grounded. This is the only logical way to know whether we should run for our lives or get the frying pan ready...' By the time you have completed this long-winded process, you will already be half way down the tiger's throat. In this kind of situation, our ancient ancestors simply did not have the time to make a detailed and time-consuming profit and loss analysis! The brains that survived were the brains that took the fast and unconscious decision to run away as soon as they heard the grass move. If we were in a position to ask them how or why they made this decision, they wouldn't be able to tell us. Because they wouldn't know. But evolution has demonstrated that by its own terms these unconscious 'let's-not-take-the-risk' brains were smarter than their more rational and contemplative counterparts.

And what was valid for *homo erectus* in the Pleistocene era is still valid for modern men and women today. True, we no longer have to worry about sabre-toothed tigers, but these have been replaced by other dangers. For example, cars approaching at high speed when we – or our children – want to cross the road in a hurry. Do you walk? Or don't you? Decisions of this kind not only allow us to survive, but also make it possible for us to do many other things that have nothing to do with survival. Like playing tennis. Playing tennis is impossible for beings with brains that need to process sensory information before they can adjust their behaviour.

> **❛Playing tennis is impossible for beings with brains that need to process sensory information before they can adjust their behaviour.❜**

The human body and its various senses contain millions of receptors and in the vast majority of situations there is simply not enough time to process the millions of stimuli with which these receptors constantly bombard the brain into a coherent whole that we can call 'meaning.' For example, the receptors in the eye convert the stimuli it perceives into electronic signals that are transported by nerves to the brain at a speed of between 70 and 120 metres per second. This might sound fast, but in reality it is too slow to allow us to react consciously to most of the things that happen in life. The length of time between the moment when light falls on the retina and the moment when the resulting electronic signals arrive in the area of the brain that recognises objects amounts to approximately 170 milliseconds (slightly more than one-sixth of a second). For these signals to be reconverted into a first tentative perception of what you see requires a further 80 milliseconds.

Most of the world's top-ten tennis players can serve a tennis ball at a speed of around 250 kilometres per hour. At the time of writing (anno 2021), the absolute world record is held by the Australian Sam Groth, who in 2012 produced a serve of 263 kilometres per hour at a tournament in South Korea. A tennis court is 23.77 metres (78 feet) long. This means that Groth's ball reached the other side of the court, where his opponent was standing, in about 325 milliseconds. The ball passed over the net in roughly 170 milliseconds, the same time that it takes for a visual stimulus to travel from the retina to the visual recognition zone in the brain. In other words, when Groth's opponent 'sees' him hit the ball, that ball has already covered half of the distance towards him. By the time he 'sees' it cross the net, it has already passed him – and Groth has scored another 'ace' (assuming the ball was 'in'). If the brain dealt with stimuli in the same way as a computer (input – processing – output), nobody would ever be able to hit a tennis ball in a competitive way, even when travelling at sub-Groth speeds. Many other sports where objects travelling at high speed are an essential part of the game – such as baseball or even football – would be equally difficult to play. And equally difficult to referee. Take, for example, the offside rule in football. In the 170 milliseconds that it takes for the visual image of a player to be transported from the retina to the linesman's brain, any decent striker will already be at least a metre and a half further on!

In short: to survive the dangers of evolution (and also to make offside decisions without the need for the Video Assistant Referee; VAR), the human brain has learnt *not* to wait for information or input before deciding what to do. In other words, our brain is not only active, but also – and primarily – proactive. There is only one way to compensate for the slowness and imperfections of our processes of conscious perception and thought, and that is the making of super-fast and unconscious predictions. Tennis players can return Groth's serve (sometimes, at least), not because they have followed the actual flight of the ball, but because they *predict* the flight of the ball, quickly, accurately and unconsciously. In much the same way, referees and linesmen who have a 'good eye' for spotting offside have above all learnt how to predict offside.

> **'The human brain is not only active, but also – and primarily – proactive.'**

In addition to speed and a better chance of survival, there is another important reason why the brain prefers not to wait for information from the senses before taking decisions and initiating actions. As well as being slow, the information provided by the senses is also highly unreliable. Our brain has no direct contact with the outside world. It sits trapped within the darkness of the cranial cavity. It cannot see, hear, touch, smell or taste. All it can do is receive and process electromagnetic signals. This is something that it does well, but there is a problem: there are many different and wholly unrelated events in the outside world that can generate the same electromagnetic signal. This is something that was discovered as long ago as the 19th century by the German physiologist Johannes Peter Müller. He shone a light onto the retinas of his test subjects and they told him that they were seeing 'light.' But people had the same sensation – that they were seeing light – when he did nothing more than apply a little pressure to their eyeball. Applying electrical stimulation to the optic nerve also created the same experience: the people concerned said that they saw light. Put simply, three signals were sent to the brain, each exactly the same, but each one the result of a totally different cause. The implication of Müller's findings is that the brain often needs to 'guess' the cause of the electric signals that it is constantly receiving. Our 'experiences' are therefore not a direct impression of the world, but are the brain's best assumption about the cause of the signals that flood our nervous system every hour of the day. And because there is no direct link between a stimulus and a sensory experience, it is possible for the same stimulus to generate a range of very different experiences. This can sometimes lead to spectacular discussions; for example, about the colour of things.

At the start of February 2015, Cecilia Bleasdale from Lancashire, in the northwest of England, went shopping to find a suitable dress to wear at the marriage of her daughter, Grace. At a shop near the city of Chester, she found three dresses that she quite liked. She was unable to decide which one to choose, and so she took a photo of each of them on her smartphone. Having thought about it a little while longer, she eventually decided to buy a dress in blue and black. When she arrived home, she sent all three photos to Grace, who lives in Scotland, adding in a text message: 'I bought the third one.' To which Grace replied: 'You mean the white and gold one?' To which a confused Cecilia now in turn replied: 'No, it's blue and black!' Grace then suggested that perhaps it was time for her mother to visit an optician, because the third dress was very clearly white and gold in colour. Seeking confirmation that she was not colour-blind or barmy, Cecilia showed the third photo to her husband. But he only confused matters further by answering 'Sorry, luv, but it looks white and gold to me as well,' even though he had actually held the dress in his hands in the shop, so that his wife could photograph it! Grace later posted the photo on her Facebook page, where it was seen by one of her friends, Caitlin McNeil, who said that she also saw the dress as being white and gold. Imagine Caitlin's surprise, however, when the day of the wedding finally arrived and she saw that Cecilia's dress was very obviously blue and black! Still puzzled by this curious phenomenon, Caitlin posted the photo on her own Tumblr blogsite on 26 February and asked her followers to tell her what colours they saw. The response was overwhelming, and within hours a new internet craze was born, which eventually became known as 'dressgate.' Millions of people viewed the photo, which at peak moments had more than 10,000 views per second. And it was not only on social media that 'dressgate' became a big hit: the question about why different people saw the same dress in different colours also made national newspapers like *The Guardian* and *The New York Times*, not to mention scientific publications and even the Ellen De Generes TV talk-show.

How is it possible that people experience something as basic to human visual perception as the identification of colours in such radically different ways? The explanation is actually quite simple – or at least sounds simple: we don't actually see colours; we fabricate them. Colours are a construction of our brain. The different colours that we perceive are different wave lengths of electromagnetic emissions. The receptors in the human eye are only capable of picking up a limited range of these wave lengths (for example, they are unable to perceive x-rays or radio waves). This limited range (wave lengths between 400 and 750 nanometres) is known as the colour spectrum. These different wave lengths all produce different electronic signals in the brain. Once again, the brain needs to 'guess' what might have caused these electronic signals. And to do this, the brain takes account of the wider context of the surrounding environment and, in particular, the fall of light.

A concrete example. We all perceive a ripe tomato as being red. However, in reality a tomato is not red. It has no colour. The skin of the tomato absorbs all different wave lengths of light, but reflects back the wave length that corresponds with what we call 'red,' which is roughly 700 nanometres. The wave lengths that the tomato reflects are dependent on the nature of the light that falls on it. These wave lengths will be different, for example, for clear white light than for blue or yellow light. In order to avoid becoming confused by all the various colour permutations that this can create, the brain applies a corrective process by 'guessing' the colour of things on the basis of the fall of light. If the brain failed to do this, we would experience the colour of tomatoes indoors on a shop shelf as being very different from the colour of the tomatoes hanging on a plant outdoors in our garden. In the same way, we would 'see' the skin colour of people change throughout the day, depending on the time (morning, midday, evening) because the light coming from the sun is different at different moments of the day. This would drive us crazy, since nothing would have a stable colour, transforming the world into a very unpredictable place.

It is because of this corrective process that people were able to see Cecilia's dress in different colours, even though the photo was the same for everyone. Some people assumed (unconsciously) that the photo was either overexposed or underexposed. Others made corrections to take account of the screen or the light on/in which the photo was viewed.

Which one is the palest, A or B?

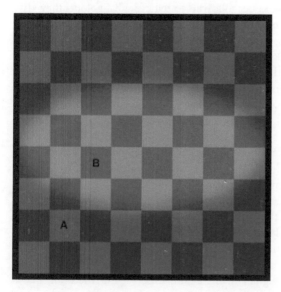

This automatic correction based on our assumptions also explains why in the chessboard above square A seems to be paler in colour than square B, even though both are exactly the same. Your brain "knows" that A is a pale square on the board, corrects for shadow and therefore sees the box as paler than square B.[7]

In other words, we do not see what is really there, but what we unconsciously assume should be there. This means that reality is something constructed by your brain. Chris Frith,[8] a well-known neuroscientist and husband of Uta, a world authority in the field of autism, expresses it as follows: 'Perception is an illusion that corresponds (in most cases, happily) with reality.' Another well-known brain researcher, Anil Seth, in a widely viewed TED talk[9] from 2017, even went so far as to refer to perception as 'controlled hallucination.' We do not perceive the world as it is; we perceive a model of the world created by our brain.

If that were not the case, we would start to panic every time we watch our loved ones walking or cycling away from us, because we would see them increasingly shrinking in size. The further away someone is from us, the smaller the image projected onto our retina. It is fortunate that we do not rely on the scale of that image to draw our conclusions about a person's size, but instead base those conclusions on the brain's knowledge that people do not suddenly get smaller once they start riding a bike!

At this point, some of you are probably asking yourself: how can we have a model of the world without first having sensory input on which to base that model? How can you recognise a dog as being a dog, unless you have seen one first? The answer to this question is complex. In fact, the answer is both 'yes' and 'no.' No, you do not first need to have seen a dog in order to recognise it as an animal. But yes, you do need to have seen a number of dogs in order to refine and improve your model(s) of dogs and other pets. This explains why toddlers sometimes refer to a cat as a dog or have the tendency to refer to all men as 'daddy' (much to the amusement of those present – except perhaps for the real daddy!).

When we are born, our brain is not empty. It is not a tabula rasa, but actually contains lots of 'pre-programmed' information. For example, you do not need to learn that the world is a three-dimensional (3D) environment. Or that light generally comes from above. This knowledge is gifted to you at birth. You can regard it as a kind of starter's pack for your survival mission on earth. What's more, this knowledge is so strongly present in your brain that you cannot act as though you do not know it. Well-known illusions make use of this. For example, our innate knowledge tells us that the world is 3D and that the human face is convex in shape and not concave, as is the case in the perplexing Hollow-Face illusion you see below.[10] The left-hand face is projected forward towards us (convex), whereas the right-hand face is actually pushed inwards away from us (concave), although both faces appear to be the same, because that is what our brain tells us should happen.

Convex face mask   ...turning into a...   concave face mask.

We do not know exactly how much or what kind of information is pre-programmed in this manner. But it is certainly more than we generally think. For example, Flemish researchers[11] have discovered that the categories used by the brain to group and make distinctions between what we see (Is this a face? Is this an object? Is this a landscape?) are already present inside our head at birth and do not need to be learnt on the basis of visual experience. The researchers allowed a group of visually impaired people – some of whom were born without sight or even without eyes, so that they had never had the opportunity to see anything – to listen to sounds from different categories, such as laughing or eating for the 'faces' category and a clock or a washing machine for the 'objects' category. The brain activity of the test subjects was measured and, in spite of the fact that they had never seen a face or a clock, the visual cortex in their brain reacted differently to each category, in precisely the same way as people who can see. In other words, visually impaired people seem to use the same visual 'map' as sighted people to make distinctions between categories. What's more, this map exists inside their head, even though they have never seen the outside world. Conclusion: we know certain things without the need for prior sensory input.

But it goes even further than that. When one of your senses is not functioning properly or not at all, you can acquire the information that this sense would normally provide through one of your other senses. Really? How is this possible? It needs to be remembered that the brain functions exclusively through the processing of electric signals. No matter which sense the signal comes from, they are all transmitted in the same electromagnetic form through the body's various neural pathways. For this reason, it makes no difference to the brain where these signals come from, as long as it continues to get the signals it needs to help us survive. This means that you can use your other sensory organs for seeing, although it takes a great deal of practice and patience. Erik Weihenmayer from Colorado (USA) is living proof of this fact. Erik suffers from a rare hereditary disease called juvenile retinoschisis. This is a condition that splits the retina in two, so that you either have very poor vision or – as in the case of Erik – eventually become blind. From the age of 13 onwards, Erik's sight gradually worsened, until he was no longer able to see at all. As he had been growing up, Erik had always been a big fan of sports like rock climbing, cycling and skiing, all of which are potentially very dangerous – if not impossible – when you cannot see. Even so, Erik did not want to give up these sports that meant so much to him. And so he didn't. At the age of 33, he became the first blind person ever to reach the summit of Mount Everest. He also continues to be a fervent cyclist and excels in acrobatic skydiving. And all without the benefit of normal sight. So how does he do it? The secret is that Erik now sees with his tongue. Erik wears a camera. This camera sends visual information that would otherwise be projected onto his retinas in a digital form (a series of ones and zeros) to a smart mini-device on Erik's tongue. From there, the tongue sends electrical signals to the brain through its own neural pathways in exactly the same way that the optic nerve would do in a sighted person. As far as the brain is concerned, information is information; it doesn't care where it comes from. And as with information transmitted via the eyes, the brain now needs to make a 'guess' about the cause of the electrical impulses it has received via the tongue. The experience of Erik and others shows that the brain learns very quickly to interpret the signals as visual information. Moreover, as time progresses the brain develops and improves its 'model' for the origin of these signals, so that it eventually interprets the signals as though they were received via the traditional neural pathways; in other words, from the eye and not the tongue. This sounds spectacular, and it is – but it is not new. It works on exactly the same principle as the cochlear implants that are used to allow aurally impaired and deaf people to hear: the implant converts sound into electrical impulses that stimulate the acoustic nerve, so that people who can hardly hear or hear nothing at all can perceive sounds and speech.

It seems hard to believe, but it is nonetheless true: although our brain certainly needs input and information to function, it is far less reliant on the senses to obtain this input and information than we think. In fact, it is no exaggeration to say that in the computer metaphor for the brain, the contribution made by the senses is grossly overestimated.

> *Our brain needs input and information but is far less reliant on the senses than we think.*

And that is not the only shortcoming of the computer metaphor. For example, there is also the problem illustrated by the diagram on page 8. This image shows both a static and a linear model. Everything begins on the left-hand side with a stimulus and ends on the right-hand side with a reaction. Somewhere in between, once the information has been processed, 'meaning' is generated. But where, exactly? At what point does perception end and cognition (thought) begin? Does cognition already start directly behind the retina in the optic nerve? Or does it only begin in the optical cortex inside the brain?

We know that there are various zones within this cortex, ordered in a kind of hierarchy that only allows the 'lower' zones to react to simple stimuli like movement, direction or contours, whereas the 'higher' zones react to stimuli with a more complex composition. But the question remains the same: where does a stimulus acquire 'meaning'? Is the 'seeing' of lines or movement – even though you do not know what or who this represents – a form of 'meaning'? Who can tell? In the final analysis, all we can say is this: the processing of information can never flow in just a single direction – which implies that there is no specific point where perception ends and cognition begins.

In reality, the way in which our brain helps us to understand and to react appropriately to the world is a dynamic story in which information moves in different directions: bottom-up and top-down. Bottom-up refers to the upwards flow (feedforward) of electrical signals from the senses to the higher regions of the brain. Top-down refers to the return downwards flow of processed information (feedback) from the brain to the lower-lying parts in the brain hierarchy and – ultimately - the senses. Both flows take place simultaneously. The senses feed the brain with information, to which the brain responds by only giving access to the information that is useful for further refining its model of the world. In other words, there is top-down control and correction of the bottom-up flow of sensory impulses. And a good thing, too! Just imagine what would happen if your brain allowed access to every sensory impulse. Your mind would be full to overflowing within minutes of your waking up each morning. By breakfast time, your head would already be on the point of exploding! If the brain were to work in the manner shown at the start of the diagram, you would not only find yourself constantly being hit in the face by unexpected balls while playing tennis, but would also fall victim in many other areas of your life to the tendency of your senses to continually overwhelm you with information for which you are not prepared. Your brain is not a fan of (too many) surprises.

Instead, it prefers to deal as economically as possible with the energy management of the body for which it is responsible, which means not wasting any effort on information that is not necessary for our effective functioning and survival. As a result, it blocks out anything that it doesn't need. It only lets through what is essential. In this way, for example, Japanese people cannot hear the difference between the letter R and the letter L, because that is not a useful distinction in their own language. Their brain therefore spends no time and energy on trying to differentiate between these two sounds.

What is useful and/or necessary for the human brain? Everything that helps us to function and survive. In this respect, the brain is not interested in 'truth.' Perception is not about seeking to obtain the most 'truthful' or most accurate image of the world. It is a check – sometimes thorough, sometimes cursory – of the image or model that the brain has made of the world. The brain does not want to know if its model of the world is correct and matches external reality. It only wants to know if the model it has created helps us to react quickly and appropriately to that reality. In other words, the model does not need to be an accurate reflection of the true nature of reality. That is the reason why illusions work. In an illusion, we see something that is different from what is real. But the brain is happy to accept these perceptual imperfections, as long as most parts of its self-created model of the world keep us alive.

Like the rest of our body, the brain functions in service of our survival (and our reproduction, if there is sufficient time and energy to do both). To succeed in this mission, the brain has developed into an organ that has taken control of our existence into its own hands. Or as Lisa Feldman Barrett puts it: 'We are the architect of our own experience.'[12] The brain does not want to be dependent on the unreliable and ambiguous information provided by the senses. If you can't even trust these senses to recognise something as simple as the colour of a dress, what use are they anyway?

Equally, the brain does not want to be swamped by the mass of useless information emanating from the senses. It has no intention of becoming a slave to these senses.

Last but not least, the brain does not like unpredictable surprises and the information provided by the senses is too slow to allow the brain to be well prepared in all circumstances.

In short, the whole idea of the computer metaphor – input - processing - output – simply does not hold water. So how do things really work?

The basic idea is simple: the brain does not like surprises and therefore wants to anticipate what will happen to the maximum possible extent. For this reason, the brain does not wait for the senses to provide information about the outside world, but prefers instead to make predictions about that world. This is something that has only recently been discovered by brain scientists working at the start of the 21st century. What makes this discovery so Copernican and therefore so revolutionary is the conclusion that perception does not begin as a result of a stimulus in the exterior world, but actually starts inside your head, in your own brain. The old idea of 'stimulus → reaction' is simply not true.

'The brain does not like surprises and wants to anticipate what will happen to the maximum possible extent.'

What Copernicus and his followers did with mankind's image of the universe, today's neuroscientists are doing with our image of the human brain: they are turning that image on its head.

In the old way of thinking about the brain, everything starts with a stimulus that is picked up by the receptors in one of the senses. This information is then forwarded via the neural pathways to one of the higher processing zones in the brain. Once processed, these zones give feedback on this incoming information to the rest of the body. That, at least, is how it seems to most of us. But that is not what actually happens. Before stimuli are picked up by the senses, the brain already predicts what the input of the senses will be. When you see a piece of chocolate, you already know (unconsciously, without thinking) what it will taste like before you pick it up and pop it into your mouth. The brain does not ask the senses for new information or input, but wants feedback on the information that it already has about the world. With this in mind, your brain will check to see whether the texture and flavour of the chocolate matches your (and its) expectations. In other words, what we used to call the feedforward of information (the bottom–up flow) is actually feedback, and vice versa! The brain uses the senses to check the continuing usefulness and survival value of its own predictions about the world. In neuroscience, this is known as the theory of the predictive brain or predictive coding.[13] The diagrams below help to clarify this. To make it easier to understand, I have used the example of visual perception.

What we thought until recently:

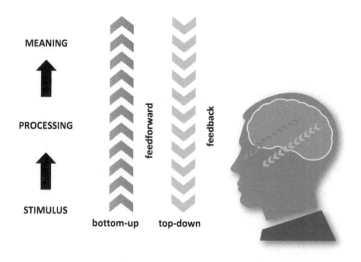

What we now think:

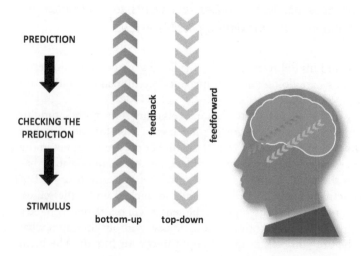

It is not easy to believe that perception begins inside our own head and is not the result of an impression received from the outside world. This goes against our intuition: we all have the feeling that we first get impressions from the world around us, and only then do we process and use them. The idea that the brain predicts sensory input on the basis of a model of the world that it has previously constructed sounds as incredible to the vast majority of people today as Copernicus's claim that the earth revolves around the sun must have sounded to men and women in the 16th century. And I must confess that I am no different! Even though I have spent the last dozen or so pages describing the new theory of brain functioning, my own gut reaction is still to feel that I respond to the world, rather than constructing it in the labyrinths of my own mind.

Of course, this leads on to a whole series of further questions. Is the brain clairvoyant? If it can predict the input of the senses, does this mean that it always knows what is going to happen? And if it does, why don't we win the lottery every week? To answer these and other similar questions, it is necessary to explain how the predictive processes in the brain actually operate.

If you already see the predictive brain as some kind of fortune teller, armed with a crystal ball and a pack of tarot cards, you should get that idea out of your head before we go any further. A predictive brain is not a brain that can predict the future. There is nothing paranormal about its predictions. To understand why will require us to explain the word 'prediction' in more technical detail.[14]

Once again, I will use the sense of sight as the easiest example to follow. Non-experts are often surprised to learn that the part of the brain responsible for the processing of visual information – the visual cortex – is not located immediately behind the eyes but is actually situated at the rear of the brain. In other words, we almost literally see out of the back of our head! This visual cortex is structured in a hierarchical manner. There are lower levels that have only a very limited range of vision and deal with the processing of relatively small and simple elements of information about the world, such as colours, lines, contours, movement and orientation. Higher up, there are more complex networks of neurones that have a wider range of vision that makes it possible for them to identify and 'see' objects, people and scenes. These different zones within the visual cortex have all been allocated a number that indicates their relative position in the cortex's hierarchy: V1, V2, V3, etc. So where does the predictive aspect come into all this? When we talk about the brain's predictions, what we are actually talking about is the predictions made by one hierarchical brain level about the brain activity of the level immediately beneath it. In concrete terms, this means that V4 predicts the brain activity of V3, V3 predicts the brain activity of V2, and so on down the chain, until the most primary groups of neurones in the cortex predict the electric signals that are to be generated by the receptors in the retina. On the basis of what then effectively happens in terms of brain activity at the lower levels, each group of neurones is given feedback about the predictions it made. In this way, V4 receives feedback on its predictions from

V3, while V3 in turn uses the brain activity of V2 to check whether or not its predictions were correct.

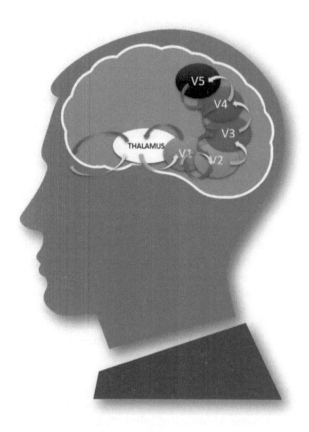

Groups of brain cells predict the activity of lower groups of brain cells. The lower groups send feedback that allows the accuracy of the predictions to be checked.

In short, the predictions made by the brain have nothing to do with clairvoyancy. Moreover, the predictions are not made in any single area or specific place in the brain. There is no zone that we can designate as 'the prediction zone.' No, the predictions are made simultaneously in many different parts of the brain, in what is effectively a self-organising system. What's more, this complex interplay of predictions and feedback on predictions takes just milliseconds to complete.

When the predictions turn out to be correct, nothing happens. The brain needs to take no remedial action and can therefore, metaphorically, rest on its laurels. Its model of the world is accurate. Hooray! It is a very different story, however, when predicted activity in the lower-lying zones and the sensory receptors does not match expectations. When this happens, the brain instantly moves into corrective overdrive. Why? Because its model of the world is no longer perfect. It faces what is known as a prediction error.

The brain does not like prediction errors. When they occur, the brain can do one of two things: it can update its model of the world, so that its expectations better match the feedback coming from the senses; or else it can take action in the real world and adjust it to better match the expectations of the model. Either way, our brain is constantly alert to the need to minimise the number of prediction errors and unexpected surprises.[15]

During the break at a major congress where I was one of the speakers, I was given a piece of chocolate along with my mid-session cup of coffee. It was plain chocolate, dark in colour, exactly the kind I like. As a result, I popped it into my mouth, almost without thinking. It tasted awful, and if I was not standing in the middle of a room full of other distinguished guests and speakers, I would have immediately spat it out. One of my colleagues noted my surprise and commented: 'It's an interesting flavour, isn't it, that chocolate made with sea salt.' It was the first time that I had ever eaten this kind of chocolate and my brain had not expected to experience the taste of salt. Salt did not have a place in my brain's model of what chocolate should taste like. This led it to encounter a prediction error; namely; 'Dear me, there is something very strange about this chocolate!' My immediate gut reaction to spit out the chocolate was a survival reflex triggered by my brain, because it thought that something was wrong. Salt is not what we were expecting! Spitting it out would have been a corrective action in the real world to eliminate the prediction error and keep the brain's model of chocolate intact. In this way, the bad taste would just disappear. But I didn't have the courage to do that in a crowded room. Besides, I not only like chocolate, but also like salt. As a result, my brain instantly adjusted its model of chocolate, so that salt is now one of chocolate's possible characteristics. This means that my brain no longer makes prediction errors whenever I eat a piece of salted chocolate. There is just the delicious flavour of both chocolate and salt.

This example shows that the brain does not respond to stimuli, but responds to deviations from the stimuli it had predicted. In other words, it responds to prediction errors.[16] We only become aware of our environment when the feedback we receive from our senses does not match our expectations. This is a good thing: as I have already pointed out, we would be driven mad if our brain had to process all the input it receives from all the senses. Thankfully, the brain only needs to start working when there is a difference between what it expected to happen and new information based on what actually did happen. For the brain to do otherwise would simply be an uneconomical waste of its limited energy resources. Why should it worry about things it already knows and expects? As a result, it relies instead on the system already outlined above: a constant stream of top-down activity in the form of predictions, with remedial action only to be taken in the event of it being made aware of prediction errors through bottom-up sensory input.[17] This explains why there are ten times more fibres leading from the visual cortex to the thalamus – the link between the brain and the optic nerve – than there are in the opposite direction.[18] It also needs to be remembered that just 10% of the information used by the brain to see actually comes from the eyes. The remaining 90% of information comes from other areas of the brain.[19] In other words, the senses are by no means the leading actors in the process of perception; on the contrary, theirs is just a supporting role. The real star when it comes to perception is the brain itself; that is where almost all the work is done.

The brain has a remarkable ability to adapt. It adjusts and improves its models of the world continually, and it does so at lightning speed. For example, your brain requires no more than a just few minutes to supplement its existing model of your body with a new false limb! This was proven by an experiment carried out at the end of the 1990s by Matthew Botvinick and Jonathan Cohen,[20] now generally known as the 'rubber hand' illusion. Botvinick and Cohen sat their test subjects at a table and asked them to put both forearms on the table's surface. They then positioned a partition on the table, so that the test subjects could no longer see their right hand. On the visible side of the partition, they placed a rubber hand. Next, the researchers stroked the rubber hand and the 'invisible' right hand with a soft brush. Result? By combining what they could see and what they could feel, based on all their previous experiences of seeing things and feeling things at the same time, the brains of the test subjects came to regard the rubber hand as an actual part of the body! People even flinched when the researchers pretended that they were going to hit the rubber hand with a hammer! What's more, this process of adjustment took just two minutes to complete. When the researchers asked the test subjects how they had experienced the experiment, most responded that it was as though their own hand had disappeared and the false hand had become real.

'The concept of the predictive brain is not simply a theory about perception, but is above all a theory about the way people learn.'

This all suggests that the concept of the predictive brain is not simply a theory about perception, but is above all a theory about the way people learn. The brain learns something new from every experience we undergo and adjusts its models of the world accordingly, so that it can better anticipate what is likely to happen in that world in future. This means that your brain is constantly changing. Your brain of today is not the same as your brain of yesterday. And as a result of reading what I have just written, your brain will be changing again.

The brain not only learns quickly, but also with great flexibility. This is necessary. There is no clear and fixed link between a sensory experience and whatever in the outside world might have caused that experience. All sensory input is by definition ambiguous, capable of interpretation in different ways.

In short, as far as the brain is concerned there are no certainties in the world. Faced with such uncertainty, flexibility is the only response.

Consider, for example, the following:

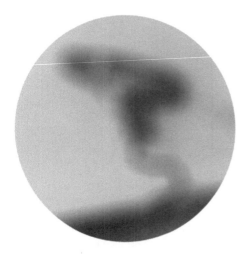

What do you think this is? It is difficult to say, isn't it, because the image is rather vague. All you can do is make a guess.

If I tell you that the object is an electrical device, you can probably make a more educated guess. It could be a drill. But it could also be a hairdryer. Now look at the two images below.

If I now ask you to guess again, I imagine that most of you will now say that the image on the left is likely to be a drill and the image on the right is likely to be a hairdryer. Why? Because your brain is flexibly adjusting its predictions to match the context. In the context of a work bench, there is a greater likelihood that you will find a drill than a hairdryer. And in the bathroom, it is the other way around.

Because there is no fixed one-to-one relationship between a sensory experience and its cause in the outside world, various explanations are always possible. Here is another example of the kind of problem that the brain is constantly facing. Look at the cube below – named after the Swiss crystallographer and geographer Louis Albert Necker, who first developed this optical illusion.

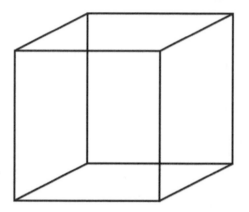

Now look at the next two cubes. How would you describe the position of the ball? At the bottom back left corner? Or at the bottom front left corner? Actually, they are both possible. It all depends on which face of the cube you regard as its front. And this is dependent on whether you look at the cube from the top down or from the bottom up. Adding a little context makes all the difference. Of course, this also influences the size of the ball, which looks further away in one cube than in the other.

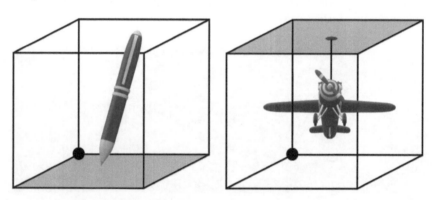

Because the input of the senses is ambiguous and unreliable, nothing in the world is 100% certain, and because the brain therefore also knows that its own model of the world cannot be 100% correct, the brain prefers to work with probabilities. There are always different possible explanations for the origins of our experiences and it would cost the brain too much energy and effort to assess all of these explanations one by one. In a world full of rapidly approaching sabre-toothed tigers, cars and tennis balls, there simply isn't the time. Opting for – or, if you prefer, guessing – the most probable and most credible of the available solutions in the given circumstances is therefore the smartest move.[21] That is the secret to the success of the predictive brain.

Imagine: you are sitting in your car and you hear a fire siren. One possibility is that someone in the neighbourhood has just set off the siren for fun. Hmm. Although that is not impossible, it is not the most likely or most credible scenario. It is not easy to get your hands on that kind of siren and sounding one for 'fun' is not going to make you very popular. In your model of 'why sirens sound' there is currently no place for jokers with a warped sense of humour. No, it is much more likely and much more credible that the siren means that there is a fire engine somewhere nearby. The possibility that the fire engine is heading your way is also not very likely, unless you can smell burning or unless you can see a traffic accident somewhere ahead. Even so, you expect to see a fire engine within the next minute or so, and so you slow down. You still can't see the fire engine, but to better anticipate its possible arrival you pull over, closer to the side of the road. You also turn down the volume of the radio, so that you can concentrate better. While doing this, the sound of the siren also seems to be getting further and further away, until you can no longer hear it anymore. You also notice that none of the other cars are reducing speed. In light of this new information, you adjust your scenario: the sound of the siren was coming from the radio! Your prediction of seeing a fire engine is immediately jettisoned, since the feedback of your senses has confirmed that this prediction was wrong. And when you next hear a siren, whether or not you think it comes from the radio or from a fire engine somewhere in the vicinity will depend on the context (Is the radio turned on? Are other cars slowing down? Can I see smoke?), but in any case your model of 'why sirens sound' will have been adjusted. Let's assume that this incident took place on a Thursday evening, while you were driving home from work. Exactly a week later, the same thing happens again: the sound of a siren blares out from the radio. And again on the Thursday after that. You will eventually conclude that the radio programme that you are listening to with only one ear (after all, you are driving a car) uses a jingle or a sound fragment with a siren. Once you have made this link, you will no longer slow down on subsequent Thursdays when you hear the siren again. The various likely scenarios have been adjusted in your prediction model.

But in other circumstances, the probabilities and, consequently, your brain's predictions could be very different. Let's now imagine that one Thursday you decide to go to work on your bike, rather than in your car. If you now hear a siren on your way home, your brain will place its various prediction options in a different order. Unless you are listening to a radio on your bike, this time your brain will tell you to expect a fire engine.

This story shows how the brain constantly seeks to improve its ability to predict by minimising the number of its predictive errors, and also how it adjusts its predictions to take account of the context.

But this does not mean that the brain is constantly seeking perfection. A model that is 'good enough' to ensure our survival will suffice. This means that the brain does not always immediately embark on a serious revision of its image of the world every time it faces a prediction error. Sometimes these errors are caused by coincidence, chance or sheer bad luck, which means that a revision of its models is not required. Google regularly brightens up its start page with images of important events or persons linked to a particular date, but these chance variations do not make us immediately think that we have landed on a different start page than Google's. It is impossible for the brain to devote attention to every prediction error and to every item of unexpected input, since this would soon result in mental overload. In short, your brain would blow a fuse. For this reason, the brain necessarily needs to make a distinction between prediction errors that can be ignored and prediction errors that need to be taken seriously.

To make this distinction, the brain takes account of the level of 'noise' (interference) and variation to which this sensory input is subjected. Or to put it even more simply: it assesses how much confidence it can have in the certainty of the sensory input it receives.

This time, let's imagine that you are out for a walk on a misty Sunday morning. You hear a dog barking. A few dozen steps later you see a cat sitting at the side of the path. A cat that barks? That is certainly something unexpected! But the chance is small that you will adjust your model of a cat to take account of a new species that barks like a dog, instead of miaowing like other cats. The mist means that the sensory receptors in your retinas are experiencing too much noise and interference to be able to send your brain reliable signals, so that you will regard the unexpected combination of a cat (visual element) and dog (auditive element) as a prediction error that does not need to be taken seriously. In fact, you might even start to doubt your own perception. Was it really a cat you saw? The same applies when there is no mist, but there is a lot of ambient noise around you (passing cars, people who are shouting, fire sirens, etc). You can see the cat clearly and you cannot see a dog anywhere near, but you still think that you hear the cat bark. Once again, there is too much environmental confusion for the brain to rely on the sensory signals which say 'this cat is barking,' so that its cat model will remain unadjusted. But what if there is no visually distracting mist and no aurally distracting noise? What will your brain do then, when you are convinced that the cat you can see is actually barking? In these circumstances, its prediction error will at the very least give the brain pause for some serious thought about the nature of its cat model…

In addition to the amount of noise or interference, the level of variation in the sensory input it receives will also determine how much importance the brain attaches to particular prediction errors. Imagine that one of your colleagues walks into your office on a Monday morning and her hair – which was blond on Friday – is now bright blue. If this is a colleague who makes a habit of regularly changing her hair colour in this dramatic way, you might not even notice the difference. A frequent change of hair colour is part of your brain's model of this particular colleague. In other words, her blue hair is not unexpected and there is no question of a prediction error. Even if you do notice the change, there is still no need to adjust your model. 'Blue this time? Nice....' But if the colleague in question has been blond for the last 20 years, your brain will not be expecting this variation. As a result, you will probably get a bit of shock when she walks in with her new aquamarine perm. 'My God! What have you done to your hair!' This time, your colleague has changed more fundamentally and your brain needs to set to work to adjust its knowledge about her. You have learnt something new that does not match your existing model. In future, your expectations and your predictions about how she will look will need to be different.

Here is another example. Every day, you commute to your work by train. And every day for the past two years, you have sat opposite the same man in the same seats. If one day he is suddenly no longer there, you will notice. Your brain encounters a prediction error. It was not expecting this variation. There are also lots of other people who take the same train every day, but they do not have fixed seats in the same way that you do. Instead, they take different seats, sometimes even in different compartments. If some of these people are not there on any given day, you will not notice that they are missing. In this case, your brain expects variation.

The level of weight[22] that the brain gives to the prediction errors is therefore dependent on the level of uncertainty that the brain expects in the sensory information it receives. If the brain expects a lot of noise/interference and variation, most prediction errors are simply filed away without any further action being taken.

That being said, the likelihood of you noticing a change or something unexpected is not only dependent on the degree of expected certainty and uncertainty about the sensory input. It also depends on the degree of expected certainty in the brain's own models. When confronted with new and unknown situations, the brain will devote considerable attention to prediction errors and feedback from the senses, until it is satisfied that it can have sufficient certainty about its models. Imagine that your colleague with the blue hair-do is actually a new colleague and today is only her second working day in your office. Last Friday, she was blond. Now on Monday, she is blue. Because you do not know the colleague all that well, your brain does not yet really have a good model for her. And that makes you curious: 'Two different hair colours in two days. Will she have a third one tomorrow?' So that you can better predict in future what she might look like, for the next few days you pay close attention to her hair. In this way, you gradually build and amend your model of the colleague. In other words, you learn about her and how she likes to present herself to the world. As soon as you have confidence about your model of the way she looks (and her habit of changing her hair colour regularly), you will notice future colour changes less quickly or perhaps even not at all.

In the final analysis, what it comes down to is this: the importance that your brain attaches to sensory feedback and the resulting prediction errors that this can generate is not fixed, but is highly variable. And to a significant degree, this variability is determined by the context. For example, devoting attention to someone's ever-changing hair colour is of limited importance if what really interests you is the way that person feels. If you want to build up a model about someone's emotional life, visual information about their hair colour is largely irrelevant (unless, of course, the person in question wishes to express her general mood each day with a different colour of hair). In contrast, if recognising different people is your priority, a visual element like a change in the colour of a person's hair can be important.

Here is another example. You are at your friend's house for a cup of coffee and a cake. You have a lot of news to catch up on. Do you want to bet that after a few minutes, perhaps even less, you will no longer hear the cars passing by in the street outside? But if you have ordered a taxi to take you home, you will hear its approach before it stops at the door, even if you are still talking to your friend.

To summarise, then, the brain not only adjusts its predictions to the context, but also adjusts the amount of weight it gives to prediction errors. The predictive brain is therefore a very context-sensitive brain. Jacob Hohwy,[23] an Australian philosopher and author of the book *The predictive mind*, puts it in the following terms: 'Context sensitivity and the minimisation of prediction errors are one and the same thing.'

In a nutshell:

- Our brain has no direct contact with the outside world. It sits trapped within the darkness of the cranial cavity. It cannot see, hear, touch, smell or taste. All it can do is receive and process electromagnetic signals. To know what is happening in the world outside and also in its own body (both of which are necessary for survival), the brain must rely on the signals that it receives from the senses.
- However, the signals received from the senses are anything but reliable. The same signal can have different causes in the outside world. What's more, these signals are received far too slowly for the brain to react to the world with sufficient speed.
- For this reason, the brain does not wait for input from the senses. Perception therefore starts in the brain itself. The brain makes unconscious and superfast predictions about the world. These predictions are based on what the brain already knows about the world, which it stores as different models. These predictions are actually smart guesses about what is most plausible and most likely to happen in any given situation.
- The brain asks for feedback from the senses about the predictions it has made. If this feedback reveals that some of the predictions were wrong, the brain processes this information to reduce the difference between what it expected to happen and what actually happened, either by amending its models or by taking action in the outside world that will generate different sensory impulses that match better with the existing models.
- The functioning of the brain is designed to minimise the number of prediction errors. If it makes fewer errors, the body will be confronted with

fewer unexpected surprises, which in turn means less work for the brain. Even so, the brain does not seek to reduce or eliminate every prediction error. This will depend to a significant degree on the confidence and certainty that the brain has about both the sensory input it receives and the accuracy of its own models.

- Whether it is making predictions or dealing with prediction errors, the brain works in a highly context-sensitive manner.

DID YOU KNOW

Although the theory of the predictive brain is still very recent in scientific terms, having only been developed during the last two decades, the concept of a brain that quickly and unconsciously makes guesses about the outside world is nothing new. Famous philosophers like Francis Bacon (1561-1626), Thomas Hobbes (1588–1679) and Immanuel Kant (1724–1804) all had ideas that pointed in that direction. However, it took a genius to first give those ideas a more concrete shape and form. The genius in question was the German doctor and natural scientist, Hermann von Helmholtz (1821–1894). In his *Handbuch der physiologischen Optik* (Treatise on physiological optics), von Helmholtz argued that the brain made unconscious inferences. He used the example of someone holding a pen in her hand. The pen is in contact with the skin of three fingers. When the woman holds the pen with these three fingers in the same place, this should generate the same tactile stimulus for each of the fingers. But the woman does not think that she is holding three pens. She knows she is only holding a single pen, because she is unconsciously aware – based on her experience of the position of her fingers and her knowledge of her own body – that there is only space for one pen between those three fingers, and not three. In other words, on the basis of our knowledge, which is in turn based on our physical experiences, we draw unconscious and spontaneous conclusions to explain our sensory experiences.

Von Helmholtz also regarded these unconscious conclusions as a possible explanation for illusions. And he quoted an example that squares the circle and brings us neatly back to where we started this chapter: our old friend Copernicus and the illusion of the moving sun. This is the illusion that made it hard for contemporaries to accept Copernicus's revolutionary theories of planetary motion. Although we now know that the sun does not move and the earth does, we still 'see' the sun rise each morning and set each evening. As a result, people in the 16th century did not say 'the horizon is moving,' but rather 'the sun is moving' – because this is what they seemed to see. Von Helmholtz could never have imagined that a century after his death his concept of unconscious inference would form the basis for a new Copernican revolution in brain science.

2   The predictive mind and autism

Many of the insights relating to the predictive mind date from the final decade of the 20th century. However, it took another ten years before researchers used this new perspective on the brain to look at autism in a new light. In fact, the number of researchers investigating autism from this perspective is still relatively small, as is the number of publications on the subject.[24] Even so, a number of matters are starting to become clearer.

The first scientists to suggest that the predictive capacity of an autistic brain might be different from that of a neurotypical brain were Ning Qian and Richard Lipkin, working at Columbia University in New York. In 2011, they wrote an article in which they put forward an explanation for three of the standard observations about how people with autism learn. The first of these observations is that people with autism devote attention to details that other people do not notice. The second is that people with autism find it difficult to generalise what they have learnt and apply it in different contexts. And the third is that people with autism need to learn by rote things that people without autism learn intuitively. In order to better explain these observations, Qian and Lipkin drew parallels with research in the field of artificial intelligence and in particular the mechanisms of machine learning: the various techniques by which computers are able to acquire and use new knowledge and skills. According to Qian and Lipkin, people with autism have a learning style that is perfect for learning telephone numbers, but not for learning categories. Telephone numbers are something that you need to learn by heart, one by one. The relationship between a person and his/her telephone number is both very precise and context-independent: there is no pattern or regularity in the way telephone numbers are allocated to people. When you know the telephone number of your sister and her partner, you cannot use this knowledge to deduce the telephone number of their daughter. All you can do is to memorise each telephone number separately – which means each individual number within that telephone number and all in the right position – and then link it to a particular person. Forgetting one of the individual numbers or positioning it in the wrong place in the sequence means you might end up phoning the local butcher or baker, instead of your mother-in-law. When this happens, you have made a prediction error. In other words, telephone numbers are something

DOI: 10.4324/9781003340447-3

that you have to learn absolutely (although, thankfully, this is something that our smartphone now does for us).

The situation is very different when we need to learn things that are context-dependent, or are less exact, or conform to a certain pattern. Take, for example, the difference between dogs and cats. Initially, a number of characteristics seem to be important – the shape of the nose, ears, head, tail, etc. – but over time you learn to look through the many differences between dogs and cats to discover a kind of pattern in these differences that allows you to distinguish between the two animals generically. Without explicit rules or recognition criteria, you have identified and understood the similarities that dogs have in common (even though the appearance of different species of dog can vary considerably), whilst at the same time understanding that cats and dogs also share a number of similarities (four legs, fur, a tail, etc.). Once you have reached this stage, it is then easy to generalise this knowledge. As a result, you will immediately be able to recognise a species of dog that you have never seen as a dog, and not as a cat. Moreover, when you are deciding whether or not the animal you are looking at is a cat or a dog, you will also use the context, since the pattern of characteristics you were able to establish also contains many contextual elements. For example, your model of a dog will contain many elements that are regularly associated with dogs (a lead, typical dog toys, a dog bench or crate, etc.), even though they are not part of a dog per se.[25] These contextual regularities can even help you to predict the presence of a dog before you actually see one. Or do you expect a goldfish when you see the man in the picture below walking further away?

According to Qian and Lipkin, people with autism learn about the world as though it is a telephone book. They store every experience with precision and memorise every detail, just as though they were learning a telephone number. This perfectly matches a description of the process given by Temple Grandin, a well-known woman with autism. Temple[26] describes her brain as a gigantic collection of concrete perceptual experiences. To develop and understand a concept of orange, she makes a collection of images of all different kinds of orange objects in her head: oranges, pumpkins, carrots, basketballs, etc. In this respect, she compares her mind to an internet search engine like Google, which gathers together images of many different kinds from many different places.[27] Her concept of a dog is therefore a collection of all the images of all the dogs she has ever seen, through which she then mentally flicks at lightning speed in order to be able to recognise a dog as a dog.

Evidence of this kind led Qian and Lipkin to conclude that the models developed by an autistic brain are too detailed, too precise, and too little context-dependent. In other words, they are absolute. This in turn leads to a proliferation of prediction errors. When your model of the bus for which you are waiting includes a very specific make of bus, your brain finds it hard to deal with the situation when a different make of bus actually pulls up at your bus stop. For a brain that sees few patterns and very little regularity, the world can be a very unpredictable place. Qian and Lipkin express it as follows:[28] 'Autistic learning performs poorly when it comes to extracting regularities and is consequently not good at predicting and anticipating. To autistic people a friendly hug might feel like a surprising squeeze and noise from routine events may be largely unexpected and scary.'

Qian and Lipkin published their findings in 2012. A year later, the first explicit plea for the application of the theory of the guessing and predictive mind to autism was made in an article by Liz Pellicano of the University of London and David Burr[29] of the University of Florence. Contrary to what Qian and Lipkin had argued, they now contended that autistic brains have too broad rather than too narrow expectations. In other words, autistic models are insufficiently precise.[30] If you are not able to predict enough, your brain has to attach more weight to sensory input. According to Pellicano and Burr, this explains why people with autism are less susceptible to illusions that occur when people are more inclined to rely on the models in their brain than on what they can see in reality, as is the case with the Hollow Face illusion that we saw earlier in the book. In short, an autistic brain perceives reality more truly than a non-autistic brain. Because the brain of a person with autism attaches less weight to its models, the world is perceived with great accuracy, detail and sharpness. It is almost as if the world becomes too real, a conclusion that Pellicano and Burr incorporated into the title of their article.

The discussion took a further twist another two years later, with the publication of a new article that was the first to describe autism in terms of an impaired ability to predict. The article in question was 'Autism as a disorder of prediction'[31] and was the result of the work of Pawan Sinha and his colleagues at the world-famous MIT (Massachusetts Institute of Technology). The central thrust of their argument was that the predictions in an autistic brain are simply not accurate enough. People with autism fail to see the interconnectedness of events with sufficient clarity, especially in cases where that interconnectedness is not overwhelmingly obvious. When one event follows another in a manner that is more than purely coincidental, a non-autistic brain will automatically adjust its models. For example, if you regularly get stomach cramps after eating mussels, your brain will probably make a connection between these two events. This will help to prepare you for the pain that you can expect the next time you visit your local seafood restaurant – assuming that you still want to eat mussels. According to Sinha and his colleagues, a person with autism would be much less aware (or perhaps even wholly unaware) of this kind of connection, so that he/she would be less able to predict accurately what might happen next time around.

Whereas these early publications all situated the problem for people with autism at the level of making predictions – which were either too precise (Qian and Lipkin), too vague (Pellicano and Burr) or not accurate enough (Sinha and colleagues) – more recent research findings suggest that the real problem lies in a difficulty to deal efficiently with prediction errors. More specifically, an autistic brain finds it difficult to establish the right balance between the weight it gives to its own predictions and the weight it gives to sensory input.

In a response[32] to the article by Pellicano and Burr, Sander Van de Cruys and his colleagues at the Department of Experimental Psychology at the University of Leuven contend that an autistic brain has a constant tendency to take prediction errors too seriously. Small chance variations in events or noise in the information transmitted by the senses are immediately seen as a reason for adjusting existing models.

We have already seen in Chapter 1 how people without autism deal with new, unknown and uncertain situations for which they do not yet have a model. In these circumstances, the brain attaches greater weight to the bottom-up information being received from the senses. It doesn't really have a choice: a model either does not exist or is insufficiently developed, so that little or no top-down activity is possible. Think back to the example of the new colleague with blue hair. However, as soon as we start to see a degree of pattern and regularity in all the different variations with which we are confronted, the balance gradually shifts and the brain gives more weight to its own expectations and predictions. Until, that is, a situation occurs that again demands a greater focus on the input of the senses. Think now of the second colleague, who arrives with blue hair that had been consistently blond for the previous 20 years.

According to Van de Cruys and his colleagues, this flexibility of approach is lacking in an autistic brain. This kind of brain always gives great weight to unexpected variations.[33] As a result, the brain's own models are more or less constantly undergoing revision, based on connections that a non-autistic brain would regard as coincidental and therefore not relevant. This creates a series of models that are increasingly precise, but are also so specific that for all practical purposes they become quite unusable.[34] Think of a model that links the hair of a colleague to specific moments in time (she dyes her hair green every first Wednesday of the month) or to specific moments (had an argument with her husband the night before = purple hair). Models that are so precise not only stand in the way of generalisation, but also inevitably generate lots and lots of prediction errors. Every situation seems new because every situation varies from the brain's very precise model of what should happen. Indeed, Van de Cruys refers to people with autism as 'precise brains in an uncertain world.'[35]

A similar conclusion was reached by Rebecca Lawson[36] at the University College in London. Her research also suggested that the autistic brain finds it difficult to estimate the extent to which it can rely on its own models and the extent to which it should rely on sensory input. When making predictions about their surrounding environment, people with autism have a tendency to regard sensory information as being more informative and more accurate than their own knowledge about the world. In situations where this is advantageous, as is the case with many illusions, this leads to more accurate perception. People with autism are much less susceptible to many kinds of visual and auditory illusions than people without autism. By contrast, in situations where knowledge of the world can help to filter out the ambiguities and uncertainties inherent in sensory input, relying too heavily on sensory information can lead to perceptual confusion, doubt and misunderstanding. Did I really see a cat barking?

Colin Palmer[37] of Monash University in Australia is of much the same mind. In his opinion, autistic perception is directed primarily by sensory data, rather than by prior knowledge and contextual information. When seeking to integrate sensory information and its own models, a person with autism gives too much weight to the signals he/she receives from the senses. It is almost as if the autistic brain does not 'trust' its own models and therefore feels it has no option but to fall back on what the senses are telling it.

'Did I really see a cat barking?'

The theory that the prediction system of an autistic brain is different from that of a non-autistic brain is still very recent. Consequently, it should come as no surprise that there are still minor differences in the views of the different research teams. However, there are two points on which all the researchers agree.

First: both in terms of making predictions about the world and also when dealing with prediction errors, the autistic brain is insufficiently context-sensitive. These are quotes taken from different research publications.

- In comparison with the neurotypical learning style, the autistic learning style is very context-independent.[38]
- In ASD [Austism Spectrum Disorder], the dysfunction of prediction based on context may impair the ability to adapt quickly to an ever changing socio-emotional world.[39]
- In particular, we think autism is associated with an inability to flexibly adjust the degree of precision in a different context.[40]
- Precision-weighting in autism could be aberrant in a number of ways, each resulting in context-insensitive perception and action.[41]
- In particular, autism may relate to finer mechanisms involved in the context-sensitive adjustment of sensory weightings.[42]

Or to put it in slightly different terms: when making predictions about the world, when learning and updating its models of that world, and when dealing with sensory information that deviates from those models, the autistic brain seems as though it is affected by context-blindness. In a world where everything is context-related and therefore relative, an autistic brain attempts to deal absolutely with models and prediction errors.

Because I had previously written in some detail about context-blindness, the results of recent research into the predictive mind and autism did not take me completely by surprise.[43]

> **❝The theory that the prediction system of an autistic brain is different from that of a non-autistic brain is still very recent.❞**

The second point on which the vast majority of researchers agree is that for an autistic brain the world is full of (unpleasant) surprises and prediction errors. Or to use Rebecca Lawson's words:[44] 'In autism, rather than being adaptively surprised when you ought to have been surprised, it's as if there's mild surprise to everything.' Because of their inability to predict what will happen in the real world, Pawa Sinha argues that people with autism live in their own 'magical world,' in which events occur unexpectedly and seemingly without reason. As a result, they overestimate the randomness and capriciousness of the real world and underestimate the hidden laws and patterns it contains.

Being constantly surrounded by this kind of volatile environment must be an overwhelming experience. What's more, for autistic people this is an experience that is repeated day after day. This makes it difficult for them to respond successfully to the challenges they face. A world that is full of unpredictability can be a threatening place and can sometimes induce a state of hyper-alertness. This can be hugely draining on a person's mental energy, which explains why tiredness is one of the most frequent complaints made by people with autism.

The theory of a disruption of the brain's predictive ability in people with autism also goes a long way towards explaining a number of the other social and non-social characteristics of the condition. For example, it seems almost self-evident that people whose brains give too much weight to sensory input are likely to fall easy prey to sensory overload. If you are unable to predict what is likely to happen, the most unpredictable and volatile creature on the planet – man (and woman) – represents a massive source of uncertainty and potential threat, and one that is very difficult to deal with. If you do not have the ability to assess on the basis of context what people are likely to say to you or ask of you, communication becomes a daily nightmare. Even some of the less familiar characteristics of autism – such as motor clumsiness – can be linked to a reduced capacity to predict. Do you remember our story about the tennis ball? Manoeuvring your body in the right way at the right speed to intercept a ball also requires a significant degree of prediction. And what about the love of routines and stereotyped activities that are also frequently associated with autism? In terms of the theory of the predictive mind, it is only logical that people with autism regard such activities as islands of predictability in an ocean of uncertainty, which bring them some much needed mental rest and calm. Routines and repetitive activities are among the few aspects of an autistic person's life that can be kept free of prediction errors. As for their seemingly reluctant approach to change, it is not so much that people with autism are averse to change, but rather that they are unable to predict it. In the following chapters, we will look at some of these themes in more detail.

Is there any scientific support for the assumption that an impairment in the brain's predictive ability lies at the root of many of the characteristics of autism?

Yes, there is. Of course, given the relative newness of the theory only a limited number of experiments have so far been carried out, but studies from around the world are supplying an increasing body of evidence that backs up some of the theory's basic tenets.

For instance, various studies have confirmed that illusions which are made possible by the brain's preference to rely on its own models as the basis for its perception do not have the same effect on people with autism, or at least to a much lesser degree. In this context, the American researcher Carissa Cascio[45] established that it takes two or three times longer before the 'rubber hand' illusion kicks in for children with autism: an average of six minutes instead of the more usual two to three3 minutes. It has also been shown that the 3D model of the world has less influence on the interpretation of visual input in people with autism. As a result, they are less susceptible to the Shepard illusion,[46] whereby the fact that we know that the world has three dimensions makes the table on the left seem longer and narrower than the table on the right, whereas in reality they are identical.[47]

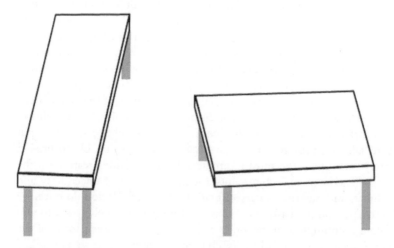

Because they take less account of their internal models of the world, people with autism are sometimes able to perceive the world with greater accuracy than people without autism. On the reverse side of the coin, this also means that they will perceive things less accurately in situations where a model can assist quick and error-free perception. This is often the case when sensory input is vague or ambiguous. Like in the image below.

Do not be worried if you cannot immediately see who or what it is.

This is a so-called Mooney image, named after Craig Mooney, the Canadian researcher who first used this type of image in his laboratory in Toronto (Canada) in the late 1950s. The images are actually reworked photographs in which all the different tints have been reduced to just two colours: black and white. A typical feature of these images is that at first it is very difficult to make sense of them: all that most people can see is a confusing and indefinable mish-mash of black and white smudges. Things only become clear when you get to see the original photo (flick through the next half dozen pages if you want to have a look). This illustrates how the knowledge stored in your brain can often help you to perceive what is really there. And it also proves that meaning is located in the brain itself, and not in the outside world. Without our prior knowledge about the subject of this image, the image would remain totally meaningless.

Studies[48] have concluded that people with autism are also better able to recognise the Mooney image after they have seen the original, in particular for objects, but less for faces. However, the registration of their eye movement has revealed that they need to make a much greater effort than their non–autistic counterparts. Seeing the original helps them to 'guess' better what the image represents the second time around, but they still need to scan the image with their eyes far more than is the case for a person without autism,[49] almost as though it is still the first time that they have seen it. Conclusion: having a mental image, learnt on the basis of experience, does not make perception easier or more efficient for people with autism.

In a similar study carried out at the University of North Carolina in Chapel Hill, Rachel Greene and her colleagues reached similar conclusions. They showed young people, both with and without autism, a series of images. Some of the images were social (for example, a face); some of the images were non-social (for example, a train, a traffic sign, etc.). The young people had previously been instructed that when a red circle was first shown, the majority of the subsequent images would be shown on the left; if a blue square was first shown, the majority of the subsequent images would be shown on the right. The eye movements of the test subjects were then measured when the images were shown. When an image was shown in an unexpected place (for example, on the right after a red circle had first been shown), the non-autistic young people looked far more to the side where the image was supposed to be than the young people with autism. This suggests that the attention of people with autism is much less directed by predictions about the world. The test subjects without autism focused their gaze on the locations where something could be expected and this made the act of perception faster and less tiring. This kind of anticipation was much less evident and much less successful in the subjects with autism. An autistic brain simply has to make do with: 'We will wait and see where something appears and then do whatever is necessary to view it.'

That being said, it is not the case that the attention of people with autism is never directed by expectations. However, they react differently from people without autism when those expectations are not met. In particular, they give far too much weight to exceptions and coincidences.

Imagine that you are asked to identify the heart as quickly as possible in a series of diagrams like the one below:

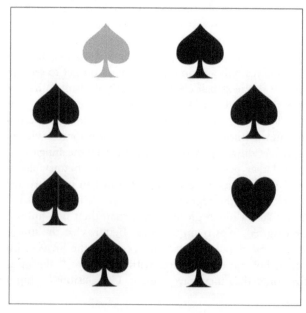

Your target, the heart, is always randomly placed in a different position. Each diagram also contains a 'distractor,' something that tries to attract your attention but that you need to ignore. In the diagram above, the distractor is the gray spade. You will be shown dozens of these diagrams and in 90% of the cases the distractor will be positioned somewhere in the top half, but you're not being told this. Even so, your brain will soon pick up the pattern and will base its further expectations on that pattern: it will expect to see distractors in the top half. This makes it easier to ignore the distractor and to identify the heart quicker and more accurately. Of course, whenever the distractor is placed in the bottom half – one in every ten times – you will make a prediction error. But because the distractors are only infrequently in this position, your brain will conclude that these are only chance deviations from the pattern and will therefore not adjust its expectations. It will continue to assume that the gray spade will continue to be shown somewhere in the top half.

A variant of this experiment was carried out by Fredrik Allenmark[50] at his laboratory in the Department of Psychology at Ludwig Maximilian University in Munich. He used diamonds and circles in red and green instead of hearts and spades, but the basic principles were the same. His findings demonstrated that the test subjects with autism and without autism both identified the pattern of distractors and made use of this pattern to identify the target more efficiently. Nevertheless, there was a difference. The autistic participants needed more time to identify targets that were positioned at locations close to where the distractor had been in the previous diagram, when that distractor had been positioned in a zone where it was not expected. (In my version of the experiment as shown above, this would mean, for example, having the heart in the bottom half of the diagram at roughly the same position where the gray spade had been shown in the previous diagram.) Registration of the eye movements of the test subjects revealed the reason for this discrepancy. People with autism reacted more slowly to this kind of 'trick' diagram, not because they were slow to identify the target – in this respect, they were just as fast as people without autism – but because they then went in search of 'another target' in the area of the diagram where they had been expecting it, before eventually returning their attention to the actual target. It was almost as if they had first regarded the target as the distractor, because it was located in roughly the same place as the distractor in the previous diagram.

In other words, it seemed as though the prediction error caused by the unexpected position of the distractor in the previous diagram resulted in an updating of the expectation pattern in people with autism. Their brain had effectively concluded: 'Aha – so now I can expect a distractor in the bottom half as well!' Having noticed the target in the bottom half in the next diagram, they wanted to make sure it that wasn't a distractor, and so checked in the top half as well. This was not the case with the non-autistic test subjects. They regarded the prediction error as something purely coincidental and therefore irrelevant. As a result, their pattern of expectation remained unaltered. To make this easier to understand, I have tried to express it visually in the diagrams below, using my 'hearts and spades' example. The first diagram shows how the non–autistic brain learns; the second diagram shows how the autistic brain learns:

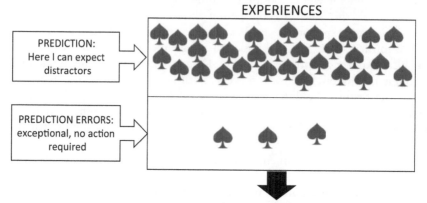

WHAT I HAVE LEARNED:
Where can I expect the distractors?
In the top half!

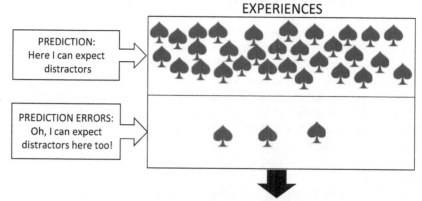

WHAT I HAVE LEARNED:
Where can I expect the distractors?
Everywhere!

Autistic brains overreact to prediction errors in contexts in which it is better to ignore them. Whereas other brains react to such errors along the lines of 'So what? That kind of thing happens from time to time, but we don't need to worry about it,' the reaction of an autistic brain is more panicked: 'O my God! A change! I had better do something about it. It might be important!'

That the reactions of people with autism to unexpected events differ from the reactions of people without autism was also made clear in another of the experiments carried out by Rebecca Lawson in her laboratory in London.[51] She let her test subjects listen to a high tone or a low tone. After listening to the tone, they saw either a house or a face projected on a screen in front of them. The participants were also given two buttons to use: one for the house and one for the face. They were asked to press the corresponding button for the image they saw on the screen as quickly as possible. At the start of the experiment, the high tone was followed in almost every case by the picture of a house. After a while, the brain begins to recognise this as a pattern: high tone = house. This allows the brain to start predicting what it will see, based on the tone it hears. When this happens, the pressing of the correct button gets quicker. Once this stage of predictability had been reached, the link between the tone and the image was changed. For the next phase, the house image nearly always followed a low tone. The first few times that this happens, nothing changes as far as the test subjects without autism are concerned. They regard the change as nothing more than chance variations, just like the distractor spades in the bottom half of the Allenmark experiment. But when the house image starts to follow the low tone more consistently, the reaction speed of these non-autistic test subjects starts to slow. It slows even more when a further change is made, so that there is no longer any clear link between tone and image (the house image now follows the low tone in 50% of cases and the high tone in the other 50% of cases). In other words, they are no longer able to predict what is going to happen! And the test subjects with autism? Their reaction speed remained the same throughout the experiment, in both the predictable and unpredictable phases. Dr Lawson also measured the size of the pupils in her test subjects' eyes. When you are surprised, the pupils get bigger. These measurements showed that people with autism were 'mildly surprised' for the entire duration of the experiment. This meant that, in comparison with the test subjects without autism, they were too little surprised when the predictable pattern of high tone = house was broken and too much surprised when a clear pattern between sound and image was established.

In addition to reaction speed and the size of eye pupils, there are other reactions that can be measured with an electro-encephalogram (EEG) to show how the brain is surprised by prediction errors.[52] Researchers[53] have demonstrated that there is much greater activity in the brains of people with autism when unexpected events occur. The autistic brain responds powerfully to these events and the prediction errors they create. It is as though it takes these errors too seriously, even when such seriousness is wholly unnecessary because the error is based on something coincidental or exceptional. People without autism classify these happenings as 'nothing to worry about' and therefore ignore them.

People with autism see them as a cause for concern and action, and therefore adjust their internal models accordingly.

If you now return to page 39, you will see that the Mooney image depicted a koala.

All the matters mentioned above in relation to the brain's predictions and its reaction to prediction errors happen unconsciously in a fraction of a second, thousands and thousands of times each day. But would the same conclusions be reached if a person with autism was asked to make predictions at a conscious level? This was a topic that arose several times in my book *Autism as context blindness* and the conclusions of the relevant experiments in this field show that while people with autism perform less well in situations where context needs to be engaged unconsciously, this difference in performance with non–autistic people disappears completely when conscious thought is involved. Dealing unconsciously, intuitively and context-sensitively with predictions and eventual prediction errors is not something that the autistic brain does well. But as soon as the context button in the conscious brain is pushed, the situation improves dramatically.

An example? Researchers[54] at the University of Exeter (UK) asked a group of test subjects to pick up cylinders of different sizes. Sensors in the cylinders measured how tightly they were gripped and how much force was used to shift them.

It is reasonable to assume that large cylinders will weigh more than smaller cylinders, and therefore require a firmer grip and the use of more force. Before they were allowed to pick up the cylinders, the test subjects were first asked to say how much they thought they weighed. The measurements later revealed that for all the test subjects – those with and without autism – the estimated weight corresponded to the amount of grip and force applied. In other words, when people with autism 'know' that something is heavy, it is this expectation that determines their motor response. As soon as reflection and conscious thought come into play, people with autism can make predictions as effectively as anyone else.

In a nutshell:

- The predictive capacity of an autistic brain differs from that of a non-autistic brain.
- The process of predicting the world and dealing with prediction errors is much less context-sensitive in people with autism than in people without autism.
- The models used by the autistic brain to predict the world are absolute and therefore insufficiently contextual.
- The autistic brain takes prediction errors seriously, even when there is no need to do so. Unexpected deviations from what is predicted that are coincidental and exceptional, so that they can usually be ignored by people without autism, are seen by people with autism as a reason for adjusting the model and therefore the future predictions they will make based on that model.
- It seems that in certain situations, particularly when uncertainty is a factor, people with autism trust their brains less than they trust the input they are receiving from their senses. An autistic brain regards sensory input as being more informationally correct than the models of the world that the brain has at its disposal. Every prediction error allows the brain to learn more about the world. However, an autistic brain processes such errors in absolute terms, rather than seeing them as being relative. All deviations from what is expected are regarded as being important, at all times and in all places.

This continuous attributing of too much weight to prediction errors ensures that the predictive models in an autistic brain become so specific that they are actually useless for attempting to predict the world. As a result, the number of prediction errors systematically increases, creating a vicious circle of hypervigilance for a world full of volatility and unpredictability.

The next chapters explore what the consequences are of all of these for the well-known difficulties in autism: sensory issues, social interaction and communication and coping with changes.

DID YOU KNOW?

The idea that people with autism are absolute thinkers in a relative world may seem like something new, but in fact this hypothesis in embryonic form can be seen at various stages throughout the history of the condition. For example, I recently discovered (almost by chance) that Leo Kanner also thought in terms of absolute thinking. Of course, he did not use the same terminology, nor did he place the idea within the recent conceptual framework of the predictive mind. Instead, he approached it from the perspective of what he called the 'insistence on sameness' in children with autism. In a little-known article, published in 1951 under the title 'The conception of wholes and parts in early infantile autism,' Kanner cited a number of telling examples of how children with autism became upset by miniscule changes, which meant nothing to other children. In terms of the recent model, we would now say that the children in question were attaching too much weight to prediction errors that they should have ignored, because they were no more than the consequence of natural variations in the world. In his article, Kanner quoted the mother of Joseph C.: 'When I have read him a story in a certain tone of voice, my husband has to read the next story in exactly the same tone of voice, otherwise Joseph becomes agitated.' About autistic children in general, Kanner wrote: 'When a child is observed over a longer period, it becomes clear that, unless he is completely alone, the large part of his activities is devoted to the serious, dutiful and priestly maintenance of sameness, of absolute identity.'

3 The predictive brain and sensory processing in autism

Elaine is very scared of noises. In fact, she is scared of everything that happens around her. She is so scared of the vacuum cleaner that she won't even dare to go near the cupboard where it is kept. Whenever the vacuum cleaner is used, she runs and hides in the garage, covering her ears with her hands.

When Richard comes into a room, he turns the lights constantly on and off.

Donald likes to throw things on the ground and is pleased by the sound it makes. He also has a mania for spinning toys and he continually sings the same three-note tune.

Herbert jumps for joy whenever someone lights a match, but he is frightened of running water.

Charles can play with spinning jars and lids for hours. He is fascinated by the light reflections they make.

Frederick does not want me to touch him or even put my arm around his shoulders. But he likes to come and touch me.

Frederick and Alfred are scared of mechanical noises, such as escalators and vacuum cleaners.

It was originally thought that Richard, Barbara, Herbert, Virginia and Elaine were deaf, but that turned out not to be the case.

These are extracts from an article published in 1943 by Leo Kanner, one of the first people to describe autism. Kanner was a cardiologist by training, but was also a talented all-round doctor who eventually converted himself into the world's first child psychiatrist. His article detailed his study of 11 young children with unusual behaviours. Even after more than 75 years, his descriptions are still instantly recognisable and testify to his remarkable observational powers. He accurately identified and recorded the children's sensory 'oddities' and concluded that while on the one hand they had a dislike or even a fear of all kinds of sensory stimuli (especially noise, but in some cases also food), on the other hand they also went in search of stimuli or even produced them themselves. He thought that such oddities were a

DOI: 10.4324/9781003340447-4

consequence of the children's desire for what he called 'aloneness' and 'sameness.' Sounds, light and touch were intrusions into their safe autistic world. Some children tried to shut themselves off from these intruders, which explains why almost half of them were initially thought to be deaf. Others responded to the intruders with anxiety and stress.

Many of the children also resorted to forms of behaviour that resulted in the same repetitive sensory experience, such as the spinning of objects or the making of monotonous noises (humming, short tunes, repeated words and sounds), since this allowed them to create an environment that was less subject to variation and change.

Leo Kanner knew what he had seen and recorded it faithfully. But for the interpretation of what he saw, he was reliant on the insights into psychology and psychiatry that were current in his day. Even so, some of the explanations he offered were fairly close to the mark, but the discovery of the predictive brain at the start of the 21st century means that we now have a much better understanding of why these sensory 'oddities' occur.

Although articles have been published regularly since 1943 about sensory problems in relation to autism, for a long time these problems remained under the radar for the wider community.[55] Until 2005, there were fewer than 20 publications per year on this aspect of autism, which was less than 2.5% of the total number of publications. Scientists focused primarily on the characteristics of autism that affected the people around the autistic person in a negative way, such as strange, unexpected or socially inappropriate behaviour, communication problems, repetitive and stereotypical behaviour, and – last but not least – resistance to change. This situation only began to improve when people with autism also started to write books and articles about their own autism and how they experience the world. This made clear, perhaps for the very first time, that for them the sensory environment can sometimes be a living hell. Autistic authors wrote about the challenges they faced with noise, light, smells, touch, the flavour and texture of food, clothing, sudden movement, etc. In other words, things that were troublesome for them, rather than for the people around them. Professionals and researchers began to realise that they had overlooked a crucial aspect of autism, or at the very least had not given it the attention it deserved. The tide began to turn.

At the time of writing, the pendulum has swung completely in the opposite direction. Above all on social media and in popular literature on autism, there is a risk that autism will be reduced to nothing more than hypersensitivity or sensory overload. The other characteristics of autism (such as social and communication difficulties) are being increasingly pushed into the background.

In almost every autism awareness campaign we are overwhelmed by an avalanche of images and sounds that are intended to convince us that the world for people with autism is a ceaseless sensory inferno. Autism experience sessions – which are designed to allow non-autistic people to experience what autism is like – also focus almost to the point of exclusion on activities where the participants are subjected to a non-stop sensory bombardment of (unpleasant) sound, light, touch and taste.

> *Above all on social media and in popular literature on autism, there is a risk that autism will be reduced to nothing more than hypersensitivity or sensory overload.*

The result of these trends is not only that the other important behavioural characteristics of autism are being neglected, but also that two other crucial factors in the sensory story are similarly being pushed increasingly to the side lines: namely; the failure or inability to react to stimuli (hyporeactivity) and the search for or the self-stimulation of certain sensory experiences, generally referred to as sensory seeking behaviours. Of course, it is not easy to deal easily with these two aspects (particularly hyporeactivity) in information campaigns. Organising an experience session in which the participants experience nothing is unlikely to attract much interest, just as images of people with autism failing to react to stimuli hardly makes great viewing on YouTube...

For much the same reason, it is also understandable that people with autism testify primarily about sensory overload. This is what they consciously experience and it makes life hard for them. In contrast, they are hardly aware (or not aware at all) of being hyporeactive and they do not experience it as being difficult. At least, not directly.

That being said, the indirect consequences can sometimes be serious. Not reacting or reacting insufficiently to pain can mean that serious illnesses and diseases can sometimes go unnoticed. Or that physical injuries result. A woman with autism once told me: 'When I cook, I occasionally burn myself, because my brain does not react or reacts too slowly to heat and pain.' Likewise, a man with autism once explained to me how he used to get headaches and start to feel unwell at the start of almost every evening. It later transpired that he regularly forgot to eat during the day, because his brain failed to detect any feelings of hunger. A similar failure to detect bladder and intestinal signals can lead to serious toileting issues. Studies have already revealed that this kind of non-stimulation or hyporeactivity can occur in respect of various senses and sensations: smell, touch, taste, temperature, pressure, pain and signals transmitted by the digestive system.

To summarise, then, there are three aspects that characterise the sensory profile of autism: reacting too strongly to stimuli; not reacting or not reacting strongly enough to stimuli; and self-stimulation or sensory seeking behaviours. Every person with autism displays this profile in their own unique way but in the majority of cases all three aspects are present. This explains why the most widely used diagnostic manual in the world, the DSM-5, now lists all three in its diagnostic criteria for autism.

If you read these criteria carefully, you will note something unusual. Instead of the terminology that you hear almost everywhere else when autism is mentioned (hyper- and hyposensitivity), the terms hyperreactivity and hyporeactivity are used. There is a good reason for this: namely, that there is insufficient evidence (in fact, there is no evidence at all) for the existence of hyper- and hyposensitivity in autism.

Is there really a difference, then, between sensitivity on the one hand and reactivity on the other hand? Yes, there is. And that distinction is important, not in the least because of what it implies in terms of how we can help people with autism deal with the unpleasant and sometimes frightening effects of sensory experiences.

Sensitivity relates to physiological threshold values: what is the threshold beneath which a certain stimulus – for example, a sound wave – can no longer be perceived? How 'quiet' does a sound need to be before people are no longer capable of hearing it? Or, alternatively, how much salt do you need to put in a glass of water before someone can identify a salty taste? Psychophysics is the field of science that investigates such matters. In this discipline, researchers measure threshold values either through the monitoring and recording of reaction ('Put your hand up if you hear the noise') or through the registration of brain activity in the zone that is responsible for detecting the stimulus in question, such as the visual cortex for light and the auditory cortex for sound. It is possible to speak of hypersensitivity when someone's threshold level is lower than the threshold level of an average person. This might mean, for example, that a hypersensitive person hears sounds that the majority of other people cannot hear. In contrast, hyposensitivity takes matters to the opposite extreme. This is something that a growing number of people experience as they get older. For instance, sounds now need to be louder before they can hear them. That is why the rest of us often raise our voices when speaking to the elderly, many of whom necessarily wear a hearing aid for the same reason.

Reactivity, as the word itself suggests, relates to the reactions of a person to a stimulus. A reaction can be behavioural (like putting your hands over your ears if you hear a loud noise) and/or emotional (experiencing anxiety, stress, dislike, etc.). Research into reactivity attempts to chart these responses primarily by means of interviews and questionnaires,[56] although the measuring of brain activity – this time in the limbic system, the zone of the brain that deals with emotional experiences rather than sensory experiences – also provides valuable information.

Sensitivity and reactivity are not completely unrelated phenomena. True, if a certain stimulus is not detected by the brain, there is unlikely to be much in the way of a behavioural or emotional response. Even so, we can still assume that there is a direct connection between the two. For example, it is possible for someone to hyperreact to a stimulus because his or her brain is oversensitive (hypersensitive) for that particular stimulus. But the same excessive reaction can also occur when that brain picks up the stimulus at the same level as other brains, so that there is no question of hypersensitivity. This explains why a child that is not hypersensitive for noise sometimes also covers its ears. Or why someone spits out a piece of salted chocolate, not because they are hypersensitive for salt, but simply because they do not like the taste of salt, and certainly not in chocolate (which is something that my brain finds hard to understand, but that, I suppose, is beside the point...). For an outsider, the behaviour seems to be the same, but the underlying cause is different. This means that it is not possible to draw definite conclusions about hyper- or hypo-sensitivity in autism on the basis of what we see. Which in turn means that sensory questionnaires to determine the level of sensitivity to stimuli in people with autism are largely a waste of time.

Researcher Samantha Schulz,[57] working at the University of Western Ontario in the Canadian city of London, wanted to know if there was a con-nection between the sensory sensitivity of people with autism and the lim-ited interests and repetitive behaviour that these people sometimes display. It is no coincidence that in the diagnostic criteria for autism Kanner's 'sensory oddities' have been categorised within this second group of autistic charac-teristics, because sensory problems could indeed be one possible underlying cause of these behavioural characteristics (I will tell you why shortly). To investigate this possibility, Schulz focused on visual perception. To measure people's visual sensitivity she made use of the techniques of psychophysics, which involved her setting her test subjects[58] a visual detection task, whereby increasingly blurred diagonal lines needed to be identified in a field of white and grey spots. The test subjects were also asked to fill in two questionnaires. The first was a list of questions about their sensory perception. The second was a list of questions about their tendency towards repetitive behaviour. Schulz found no connection whatsoever between performance in the visual detection task and the results of the sensory questionnaire. In this way, she was able to provide proof for the contention that sensitivity and reactivity are two differ-ent phenomena and that sensory questionnaires tell us nothing about a person's sensitivity to stimuli.

Schulz did, however, find a connection between both the visual detec-tion task and the sensory questionnaire on the one hand and the scores for the repetitive behaviour questionnaire on the other hand. Schulz suspects that this connection has something to do with increased irritability of the brain – another matter that we will be looking at later on.

Because the stimuli about which people with autism complain most fre-quently are auditory stimuli, these are also the stimuli that have been most investigated in recent years. The results of the first studies all seemed to point in the same direction: namely, that the people in question were oversensitive for noise. But these studies all made use of questionnaires and interviews (pri-marily with parents) and therefore provided no real evidence to back up the oversensitivity claim.

For this reason, Jay Lucker[59] of Howard University in Washington DC decided to take a different approach. He conducted a series of hearing tests among children both with and without autism, but who were all regarded as being 'hypersensitive for noise.' On the basis of his tests, Lucker determined their threshold values and sensitivities for certain sounds. He concluded that all

200 children in his study had normal hearing and were not in any way over-sensitive for noise. This included the children with autism. Having reached this conclusion, he wanted to know why these so called 'noise hypersensitive' children nevertheless found it difficult to cope with certain noises – because this was, indeed, effectively so – and whether there was any difference in this respect between his test subjects with and without autism. During the first hearing test, the children had only had to listen to relatively soft sounds. After this initial test, Lucker told the children that they would now be asked to complete a second test, which would be different from the first one. Once again, he asked the children to raise their hand as soon as they could hear the sound. The first sound had a strength of 80 dB (decibel), which is equivalent to someone shouting directly into your ear. Understandably, the children all reacted with surprise and shock, because they had not been expecting something so loud. However, these behavioural reactions disappeared as soon as they had heard the sound three or four times. In other words, their brains had adjusted their pattern of expectation. Once these behavioural reactions had ceased, Lucker systematically increased the level of sound until a child had shown three negative behavioural reactions in succession, which was taken as an indication that the child could not bear to hear the sound. Some of the reactions were quite forceful, even dramatic: pulling off the headphones, screaming, shouting, even falling backwards off their chair. Nevertheless, the results that Lucker was able to collate were striking: 86% of these supposedly 'noise hypersensitive' children were able to tolerate noises of up to 110 dB, which is the level of sound produced by a chain saw or a rock concert! In other words, noise that can actually lead to hearing damage if you are exposed to it for more than five minutes! And while it was true that more of the children with autism were among the group of test subjects who were not able to tolerate such extreme noise, this distinction disappeared for sounds of up to 90 dB, which is still more than averagely loud (shouting people, passing lorries, high-speed food mixers, etc.). What did Lucker make of all this? His first conclusion was that the number of children with autism who are not able to tolerate loud noises is much lower than generally assumed (and that Lucker himself had expected). His second conclusion was that the cause for negative reactions to sound that are reported in some children with autism must not be sought in their auditory system, but must be the result of other factors, which Lucker believed were more likely to be found in their emotional system. This presumption has since been confirmed by other studies.

One such study was carried out by researchers at the Leo Kanner House[60] in the Netherlands. They were curious about the connection between sensitivity for and reactivity to noise in adults with autism. They let their test subjects listen to two different sounds. One was just a neutral tone; the other was the siren of an ambulance. The tone was used to establish the test subjects' threshold values and measurements were also taken to monitor how quickly they became accustomed to the noise. The test subjects were also fitted with a finger sensor that recorded their skin conductance, which was used to quantify the amount of agitation or stress they were feeling when listening to the sounds. Afterwards, all the participants were asked to describe how pleasant or otherwise they found the noises and how calm they felt when listening to them. They were further requested to fill in a standard questionnaire about their sensory experiences during the test.

> **'The number of children with autism who are not able to tolerate loud noises is much lower than generally assumed.'**

The researchers discovered no difference between the threshold values of the test subjects with and without autism. People with autism did not generally have lower levels and there was no evidence to show that they had greater hypersensitivity to noise. Similarly, there was no difference in both groups' ability to become accustomed to the tone: people with autism got used to the tone no slower than their counterparts without autism. But perhaps the most striking conclusion was that there was no connection between sensitivity (the threshold values and the process of accustomization) and reactivity. Even though they had the same threshold values and the same level of accustomization, the test subjects with autism reported in the questionnaire that they had experienced many more sensory problems during the tests. They found the noises in the experiment less pleasant and more stressful than the non-autistic participants, which was also confirmed by the results of the finger sensors. In short, the Dutch researchers confirmed what Lucker had supposed: autistic brains are not more sensitive to noise, but react more forcefully and more emotionally to it.

Given these findings, you might be forgiven for asking whether or not the supposedly sensory problems in autism are actually sensory at all. Moreover, you would not be the first person to pose precisely that same question. At the 2016 meeting of INSAR, the International Society for Autism Research, Marla Zinni and her colleagues had these same words (more or less) printed in big, bold letters on their conference poster: 'Are sensory problems in autism really sensory?' On the basis of their research, carried out at their laboratory in San Diego (California), they also provided the answer: a resounding 'No!'

Their test subjects included people with autism who had reported clear sensory issues. They took part in three experiments that again required them to listen to sounds. The researchers monitored the reactions in their behaviour, the auditory cortex and their heart rate, not only to the sounds, but also to changes in the volume level and to the addition of repeated background noises. The reactions in the brains of people with autism were the same as in the brains of people without autism: their brains did not react more forcefully or more passively to differing volumes of sound. When the volume was increased, the level of brain activity increased correspondingly, but this was also the case with the non-autistic test subjects. When two sounds were played close together, the reactions in both groups were less pronounced for the second tone than for the first.

Where a difference was noted was in the level of agitation caused by the different sounds. This was clearly discernible in the heart rate. When the sound was continuous, the heart rate of the test subjects with autism was higher than the rate of the test subjects without autism. When a background noise was added and repeated, people without autism were able (as they had been instructed) to ignore the noise after just a few minutes, whereas the people with autism continued to react to it. There was something that made it difficult for them to become accustomed to the secondary noise and this something – as was evident from the heart rate measurements – was connected in some way with their arousal/stress and their attention.

Similar scientific studies that investigated senses other than hearing also reached broadly the same conclusion; namely, that the sensory problems of people with autism do not have their origin in stimuli and the senses. In other words, the sensory problems of autism are indeed – as Marla Zinna claimed – *not* sensory, although they are experienced as such. You can compare this – at least up to a point – with the way that I experience the working of my brain as a stimulus-response process, even though I know that this is not the case.

At Vanderbilt University in Nashville, Carissa Cascio has spent more than two decades studying the sense of touch. In particular, she was interested in the brain reactions of people with autism to different forms of tactile input. With this in mind, she conducted an experiment that involved people with and without autism being asked to put their hand into three non-transparent bags, which contained a piece of plastic mesh, a piece of jute fabric and a soft make-up brush. Throughout the experiment, the heads of her test subjects were enclosed in an fMRI scanner, so that Cascio could see which parts of the brain responded to the different tactile sensations. Afterwards, she also asked all the participants to describe how rough and how pleasant they had found the three different textures. The research team knew from other studies that in general people prefer soft and smooth surfaces – in this case, the make-up brush – to hard and rough ones – in this case, the plastic mesh. The piece of jute was somewhere in between and therefore served as a neutral element. Although the reactions in the parts of the brain that are responsible for touch were broadly the same for people with and without autism, people with autism assessed the experience with both the 'unpleasant' plastic and the 'pleasant' make-up brush in more extreme terms than the non-autistic test subjects. The brain scans also revealed that in comparison with their non-autistic counterparts the limbic systems of the people with autism reacted less strongly to the pleasant and neutral stimuli and much more strongly to the unpleasant stimulus given by the plastic mesh. Consequently, this is yet another example of how the emotional brain of people with autism reacts differently from people without autism, even though the sensory brain of both groups responds in exactly the same way.

This reinforces the fundamental conclusion that the sensory issues so often reported by people with autism – and in particular the difficulties they experience with stimuli – are not rooted in the stimuli themselves and the manner in which they find their way into the parts of the brain that are responsible for their processing, but are caused by the brain's emotional response to those stimuli. But why should this be so? Why does the autistic brain respond more forcefully to stimuli, even though it is not more sensitive to them?

The theory of the predictive brain offers us an explanation.

From various studies, but also from the stories told by people with autism themselves, we know that people with autism find it difficult to adjust to or get used to stimuli of different kinds. In the first instance, this is related to predictability. When a certain stimulus repeatedly occurs, the brain includes it in its future predictions of what will happen. In short, it will expect the same stimulus next time around. When the stimulus does indeed reoccur, there is no question of a prediction error being made. The brain has got it right! As a result, the brain thereafter loses track of this stimulus; it becomes no longer aware of it. This explains, for example, why you do not continually feel your clothes on your skin. When do you become aware of your clothes? When the feedback from your senses no longer agrees with the prediction made by the brain. When something happens that you do not expect and/or does not feel familiar. Like the time when the tailor who shortened my new pair of trousers forgot to remove one of the pins from the seam he had stitched. A sharp stab of pain in my ankle was not part of my brain's tactile pattern of expectation for trousers, and so I let out a yelp of surprise.

When people with autism are less able to habituate to (or cope with) certain stimuli, unpredictability must play an important role. Or as Sander Van de Cruys[61] and his colleagues put it: 'Unpredictability is at the core of the sensory overload in people with autism.'

Why does the autistic brain respond more forcefully to stimuli, even though it is not more sensitive to them?

Have you ever tried to tickle yourself? You probably didn't succeed. Why? Because the process of self-tickling does not involve a prediction error![62] When you try to tickle yourself, your brain immediately predicts that tactile input can be expected. As a result, predicted sensation = actual sensation. There is no difference and therefore no surprise. When, however, other people tickle you, the brain is less able to predict accurately the sensations that are likely to result, so that there is much more room for prediction errors to occur. In this case, the surprise leads to the reaction with which we are all familiar when someone is tickled: laughter and merriment. Put simply, sensory stimulation that we create ourselves leads to less brain activity, because that stimulation is more predictable than stimuli generated by our environment.

This leads on to an interesting question: in view of the fact that people with autism have brains that predict less effectively, does this mean that they are able to tickle themselves more successfully than people without autism?

To date, this is not a subject that has been investigated scientifically (more's the pity!), but there is at least one other study which has shown that, in contrast to non-autistic brains, there is no difference in autistic brains between the brain activity resulting from self-created stimuli and stimuli emanating from the environment.

Prediction errors can be identified by the strength of the electrical activity they generate within the brain. This is known as brain potential and can be measured using an electro-encephalograph (EEG). When we hear a noise, a small positive peak appears on the EEG after 50 milliseconds, followed by a negative peak after 100 milliseconds. This potential is known as the N100. The size of the N100 peak is dependent on the unexpected nature of the sound: the more the sound was unexpected, the bigger the surprise and the bigger the peak. This means that sounds you produce yourself generally have a lower peak than sounds produced by your environment. Researchers at the University of Tilburg[63] in the Netherlands conducted an experiment in which they asked people both with and without autism to listen to certain sounds. In the first test, a sound came immediately after the participants had clicked on a mouse. In the second test, there was no mouse and the sounds came automatically. For the test subjects without autism, the N100 peak was much smaller for the sounds that were predictable (the sounds following the mouse) than for the sounds that were not predictable (the sounds generated automatically). In contrast, the N100 peak for the test subjects with autism was equally high for both the predictable and the unpredictable sounds. Notwithstanding their use of the mouse, it seemed as though their brains were unable to anticipate the imminent arrival of a sound, which therefore came as a surprise and caused them to react more forcibly than their non-autistic counterparts.

'Why are we unable to tickle ourselves? Because no prediction error is involved!'

The conclusion is once again clear: the fact that many people with autism have difficulty in dealing with stimuli like light and sound is caused to a significant degree by the unpredictability of these stimuli for the brain. Or as Temple Grandin expressed it in her book *The Autistic Brain*:[64] 'I am sensitive to noises. Loud noises. Sudden noises. Worst of all: loud and sudden noises *I don't expect.*'

In March 2019, I gave a lecture on sensory issues in autism in Birmingham at the 10th Autism Conference for Professionals, organised by the National Autistic Society. Afterwards, a fierce discussion broke out on Twitter with and between people with autism. Although some of them found it difficult to link their sensory problems to the idea of unpredictability, many others gave examples that seemed to underline the role that predictability plays in these matters:

> 'I can get overstimulated when two people are talking at the same time, but feel fine at a concert with 20,000 others. I think that familiarity with the noise and the expectation of it are more important than how loud it is.'

> 'For me, it is all about unpredictability: it is the things I can't predict that cause me problems. When someone drops a spoon in the kitchen, I jump out of my skin, but not when I do it myself (which happens often, because I am the original Mr. Clumsy!)'

Someone else immediately said the same thing: 'Using the vacuum cleaner myself is not a problem. But if someone else uses it...'

'For me, it is not so simple as being just a matter of loud noises. I am starting to discover that my sensory problems are context-specific. I have no problem with a racing car revving up its engine just a few metres away, but I can't deal with a room full of people.'

And what applies for noise, also applies for pressure and touch:

A noisy and bustling group of people in a crowded store: no way! An overfull mosh-pit at a concert: no problem!'

(For the uninitiated, a moshpit is a group of people who jump, bounce and knock into each other at the front of a hard rock or heavy metal concert. Speaking personally, it gives me a headache just to look at the photos!)

As we saw earlier, predictability is more than just a question of being consciously aware of what is going to happen. That certainly plays a role, but when we move on to talk about prediction errors, we are dealing primarily with matters that take place under the radar of our awareness: namely, the thousands and thousands of unconscious, super-fast predictions that the brain makes every day. Try this mini-experiment: put two bowls of water in front of you, one of them lukewarm and the other ice-cold. Put your hand in the cold bowl for a minute, and then transfer it to the lukewarm bowl. Even though you know that the water in this second bowl is lukewarm, it will feel hot. This is probably a very common experience of people with autism: (unpleasant) surprise despite conscious knowledge. The test subjects with autism in the Tilburg study 'knew'[65] just as well as the people without autism that a sound would follow once they clicked on the mouse, but when the sound actually came it still seemed as though their brain was not expecting it.

In this Tilburg study, the sounds that followed the mouse click were identical to the sounds in the parallel test without the mouse. In other words, it was the (un)predictability of the stimulus that determined the brain's reaction, and not the stimulus itself. Our sensory responses are not dictated by stimuli, but by our expectations or predictions. The brain does not process stimuli; it processes prediction errors.

Perception is therefore a matter of aligning predictions with sensory data. That being the case, the brain should react more strongly also when a stimulus is expected, but nothing happens. The following image gives a summary of the different possibilities for the perception of sound:

expectation ➡	event ➡	prediction error
🔊	🔊	✗
🔊	🔇	✓
🔇	🔇	✗
🔇	🔊	✓

As you can see, a prediction error also occurs when you were expecting a sound, but none came (the second row in the image). Unexpected silences can be just as surprising as unexpected noises. As already mentioned, people with autism often complain about the effect that noise can have on them. But if the problem with the processing of stimuli is above all connected with unpredictability and prediction errors, should it not also be the case that people with autism should react more forcefully to unexpected silence?

This was something that the researchers in Tilburg[66] set out to test. They repeatedly showed a series of short films to a group of young adults, some with autism and some without. In the films, there was always someone clapping and in 90% of cases there was both sound and image. When the hands of the clapper(s) came together in the film, the test subjects all heard a clapping sound. However, in the remaining 10% of cases the clapping sound was missing. The 'soundless' films were intermixed randomly with the ordinary films, so that the sequence was unpredictable. The measuring of the test subjects' N100 potential revealed that youngsters with autism reacted more forcefully to the omission of the clapping sound than the non-autistic participants. Although the silences were just as unpredictable for the young adults without autism, at a certain point their brain had developed an expectation that from time to time an unexpected silence would occur, instead of the expected sound of hands clapping. This was not the case for the youngsters with autism: for them, the occasional and random silences continued to come as a surprise, provoking a strong mental reaction. It was as though their brain was not capable of regarding these chance variations as noise/interference, so that they took them more seriously than was necessary.

'The strength of the brain's reaction to sensory stimulation is dependent on the importance the brain attaches to the difference between what it had predicted and the sensory signals it receives.'

Once again, this study showed clearly that people with autism find it harder to habituate than other people, both to stimuli and to their absence. As a result, an autistic brain continues to be surprised when that is no longer the case with a non-autistic brain.

Sometimes you hear people with autism being offered advice along the lines that they should be exposed more frequently to sounds that cause them problems, on the assumption that this will help them to become more accustomed to the sound in question. Unfortunately, it is not quite that simple. This is also logical: the problem is not linked to the stimulus itself, but the prediction error it causes. If we want to help people with autism with their sensory problems, we need to do something about the prediction errors. How? I will tell you later.

As we saw in the previous chapter, an autistic brain lacks the necessary context-sensitivity to deal with prediction errors. The strength of the brain's reaction to sensory stimulation is dependent on the importance the brain attaches to the difference between what it had predicted and the sensory signals it receives. And that importance is dependent on the context.[67] When the brain regards prediction errors that are unimportant in their context as something to which attention nonetheless needs to be devoted, this is when sensory overload occurs.[68]

Given this conclusion, repeating a stimulus will only lead to less strong reactions in contexts in which the brain expects repetition. If, in contrast, the brain is expecting variation and change, such repetition will lead to prediction errors and surprise. When you are used to having a different person sit opposite you on the train each day, you will be surprised when it is suddenly the same person on two successive days.

Imagine that I show you several series of two cards. During the first session, I always first show you a card with an image of a bicycle. In 75% of cases, the second card I show is also a bicycle. In the other 25% of cases – one in every four – the second card is not a bicycle, but a lion. During the second session, I do something different. The first card I show you is now a tortoise. In 75% of cases, the second card is a car. In the remaining 25%, the second card is a second tortoise. The diagram below will make this clear:[69]

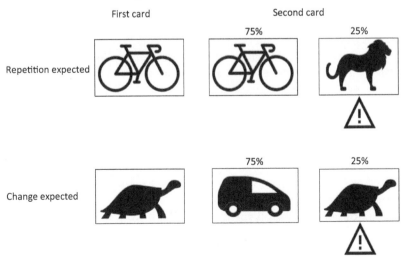

In the first session, your brain will expect repetition. As a result, the lion is an unexpected change. But in the second session, after a short time your brain will expect to see something other than a tortoise. As a result, when you do see one, it is an unexpected repetition. The exclamation marks in the diagram therefore represent prediction errors.

This was the basis of an experiment carried out by Christian Utzerath[70] and his colleagues at Radboud University in Nijmegen (the Netherlands). The test subjects included young people both with and without autism and the reactions of their brains to the different cards and images were measured with an fMRI scanner.

Research has consistently demonstrated that when a certain stimulus is repeated frequently, the brain's reaction to it gradually diminishes. This is the case both for people with autism and people without autism. What the theory of the predictive brain further predicts is that expected events cause less brain activity than unexpected events. That was indeed the case among the young people without autism in the Nijmegen experiment, both for the expected repetitions and the expected changes. However, the brain activity of the young people with autism did not decrease. Quite the reverse. In this respect, the Nijmegen results are reminiscent of the conclusions that Rebecca Lawson reached in her laboratory in London: autistic brains continue to be surprised, even when it is not (or no longer) necessary.

As part of her doctoral studies, Judith Goris[71] conducted a similar study that made use of sounds rather than images. She asked a group of test subjects with and without autism to listen to 100 short sound fragments of five identical tones. Occasionally, however, the fifth tone was different. Hearing a different tone in a series of identical tones naturally provoked a prediction error, which could be monitored in the brain by measuring the electrical potential that is automatically and unconsciously generated when a change occurs in a repetitive pattern of sound.[72] The extent to which your brain is surprised in these circumstances depends on the context. If the deviant tone only occurs infrequently, the brain will react more strongly to it than when the deviant tone is offered with greater regularity, because the deviation is then more in line with what the brain is expecting. This difference between more and less expected deviations is something that Judith Goris and her colleagues saw clearly in the test subjects without autism. For the test subjects with autism, that difference was smaller. Once again, their brain did not adjust its reactions to unexpected stimuli to match the context. Moreover, it is worth noting that we are dealing here with reactions that occur unconsciously, because the brain scans revealed that people with autism were also aware that the sound of the tone could occasionally vary.

It seems that the autistic brain, particularly at the unconscious level, responds with too little context-sensitivity to possible changes and deviations from what it expects. As a result, it is too little surprised when it should be surprised (hyporeactive) and, above all, too much surprised when an exception is in the line of what can be expected (hyperreactive). This exception can either be a stimulus or the absence of a stimulus. Or an unexpected repetition or an unexpected change. I know that this sounds complicated, but at least it makes clear that the sensory issues in autism are not as straightforward and simple as they are sometimes depicted.

In essence, the inability to flexibly align sensory expectations with sensory input is the main reason why it is harder for people with autism to habituate to stimuli and why many people with autism are troubled by sensory overload: their brain is in a constant state of hyperalertness, because it takes the unpredictability of the world too seriously. As a result, it systematically reacts too strongly to prediction errors. Chance exceptions and differences that are not contextually relevant are exaggerated and give rise to unnecessary updating of the brain's own models of the world. This, in turn, results in models that are too specific for most situations, so that the number of prediction errors increases still further, leading to ever-greater levels of overstimulation. The diagram below illustrates this vicious circle to which people with autism are subject each and every day.

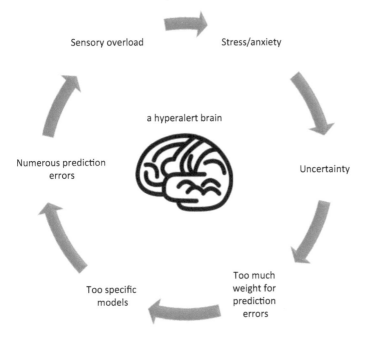

In unpredictable situations, anxiety, stress and uncertainty are key elements in the resulting sensory overload.[73] If we wish to help people with autism to alleviate these symptoms, it is necessary in the first instance to concentrate not on the stimuli themselves, but on the hyperreactivity they cause inside the brain. And in view of the fact that sensory hyperractivity does not manifest itself in the sensory areas of the brain but in its limbic system, this is where we must primarily focus our attention.

Unfortunately, the current approach to dealing with sensory overload is focused first and foremost (almost to the point of exclusion) on the removal and reduction of stimuli. 'Reduce sensory input' is the new buzz phrase in the world of autism. And autism- or sensory-friendly equals stimulus free or low-stimulus. What people with autism supposedly need is quiet, dimmed lights and as few people as possible around them. Supermarkets now offer 'autism-friendly' shopping hours, when the muzak is turned off, the lights are turned down and cashiers are instructed not to talk to their customers. Low-stimulation fun fairs. Sensory-friendly classrooms. Low sensory parties. Contrary to what you might think, I am not against reducing sensory input. On the contrary, given the hectic world in which we live, those few moments of the day when we are not bombarded with sensory input are a blessing. Many people do enjoy peace and quiet, subdued lighting, soft textures and a general lack of hustle and bustle. It is not only people with autism who occasionally need a sensory cease-fire. 'Low-stimulation' is something that we can all use from time to time. But there is also a reverse side to this coin, of which we need to be aware: autism-friendly does not necessarily and automatically mean 'low-stimulation.' An adult with autism once replied to one of my tweets on this subject in the following terms:

> I'm not a big fan of these autism-friendly shopping hours. Okay, they turn down the lights and soften the music, but all this means is that I can now hear the footsteps of the other shoppers and the buzzing of the freezers. I think I preferred the music; at least it was relaxing!

❛"Reduce sensory input" is the new buzz phrase in the world of autism.❜

The following is currently the procedure most commonly used to deal with sensory overload:

Eliminate stimulus ⟩ Reduce stimulus ⟩ Control stimulus ⟩ Cope with stress

First try to eliminate the stimulus. If that fails, try to reduce it. If that also fails, try to give the person with autism some control over the stimulus. If you are still getting nowhere, teach the person how to deal with the stress caused by the stimulus.

Sadly, this procedure seldom brings much relief, because it is based on the computer metaphor of 'input–processing–output,' which we now know is not how the brain works. The brain does not process stimuli; it predicts them. At the same time, it also works hard to minimise the number of prediction errors it makes, because this creates mental calm and tranquillity. What's more, the brain does both of these things with a great awareness of context.

Based on the theory of the predictive brain, we need to develop an alternative and very different strategy for dealing with sensory problems, particularly hyperreactivity.

⁶It is not only people with autism who occasionally need a sensory cease-fire.⁹

To begin with, we need to avoid the assumption that 'low-stimulus or stimulus free' is automatically 'autism-friendly.' Anna Remington of the Centre for Research in Autism and Education (CRAE) in London recently came to the conclusion that turning classrooms into places of low-stimulation is not necessarily what children with autism need, if they are expected to perform to the best of their ability at school.[74] Contrary to general expectations, it seems that children with autism are perfectly capable of paying attention, even when things are going on in the background and even if this background is irrelevant. Remington believes that reducing sensory input might actually have a negative effect, because children with autism have a larger perceptual capacity and therefore need input to remain focused.

Eliminating or reducing stimuli and creating low-stimulation environments may seem like obvious solutions to help people who have difficulties dealing with the sensory environment, but it is not the best strategy. As we have already mentioned, the stimuli themselves are not the real issue. The sensory problems in autism have nothing to do with oversensitivity to stimuli and are therefore not really sensory at all. Autistic brains are not – repeat *not* – more sensitive to light, sound, touch, etc.

The second thing we need to remember is that over time reducing the number of stimuli to which a person with autism is exposed can actually lead to an increase in the experience of sensory overload. If someone is being troubled by a particular stimulus, reducing its frequency can bring immediate relief in the shape of greater calm inside that person's head, but in the long run this reduction makes the brain even more sensitive to that stimulus. Why? Because it adjusts its model of the world accordingly.

An example? Noise-cancelling headphones are a great solution for people who are troubled by particular sounds. They are no longer plagued by prediction errors, because they are no longer subjected to unexpected sounds. But if you wear the headphones too often and for too long, your brain will eventually 'learn' that the world is a quiet place and will then adjust its model of the world to reflect this new 'knowledge.' This means that when in future you are once again exposed to noise (which is inevitable at some point), even if it is only relatively mild noise, your brain will be shocked by what is now a disproportionately large prediction error and you will become overstimulated as a result.

Every creature on earth gets a brain that is adapted to its environment. For instance, the deeper a species of marine life lives in the ocean, the fewer its number of photoreceptors, the cells in the retina that respond to light. What's more, this adaptive process happens quickly, perhaps not so much at the level of the development of the sensory organs, but certainly in terms of constructing new models in the brain. Do you remember the 'rubber hand' illusion, where it took only a few minutes for the brain to add a new limb to its model of your body? This illustrates once again that while eliminating stimuli might have a short-term calming effect, in the long term it can have even more troublesome and painful consequences, because the brain constructs a new model of the world that is even more at variance with your true environment. In short, it creates a false world inside your head that is less noisy, less bright, less crowded, etc. than the real world can ever be. This explains why sensory deprivation – cutting off a person's access to all sensory information – is regarded as a form of torture. Prisoners are sometimes confined for days, or even weeks or months, in a sound-proofed cell, where everything is either pitch dark or blindingly white, so that there are no shadows. They are fed on food without taste and in some cases may even be physically restrained, to deprive them of movement and touch. After a time, the effects are terrible: in addition to anxiety, hallucinations and bizarre psychotic thoughts, once their senses are restored, they experience the world as being terrifyingly fierce and intense. Even dimmed light seems unbearably strong and whispering can sound like someone screaming in your ear. Their brain can scarcely tolerate sensory input of any kind and every stimulus is a source of pain, pain and more pain.

> **'Autistic brains are not – repeat not – more sensitive to light, sound, touch, etc.'**

So unless you can guarantee that you are going to spend the rest of your life in a super-quiet environment, wearing noise-cancelling headphones for most of the time is not a good idea. And the same applies to constantly wearing a pair of sunglasses, which is something that I now see with growing frequency among people with autism.

More realistically, if we want to help people to alleviate their sensory difficulties, it is not a bad idea to look over the wall and see how the world beyond autism seeks to deal with sensory problems.

At least 3% of the population suffer from hyperacusis. This means that they are oversensitive for sound. Sound that for other people seems to be 'normal' is troublesome, unbearable or even painful for people with hyperacusis. Those affected by this condition are subject to the same vicious circle that we saw in the case of hyperalertness for stimuli in people with autism. Because most sounds lead to an unpleasant experience, the brain becomes more alert than ever for these sounds. As a result, it gives more weight to sensory signals transmitted by the auditory system. This inevitably results in more prediction errors, so that a kind of unconscious reflex is created, a stress reaction in the limbic region of the brain. This stress is almost continuous in people with hyperacusis, whereas for other people this is only experienced when an unexpected and loud noise is triggered in their immediate surroundings, such as the setting off of a fire alarm.

Given this knowledge, hyperacusis experts know that they need to focus their attention on the limbic system, if they wish to relieve the discomfort of their patients. For this reason, the advice offered to these patients does not include suggestions that they should continually wear ear protectors or that they should try to avoid the noises and sounds that trouble them, since this has been proven to make things worse rather than better. Instead, the recommended course of treatment involves relaxation and cognitive behavioural therapy. The aim is to reduce the level of the sufferers' anxiety by teaching them how to think differently about sound. One of the techniques used is acoustic therapy, during which the patient is exposed to 'noise.' Not just any noise, but the kind of noise that might be produced by a radio that is not properly tuned in.[75] Noise of a similar kind is also used in the treatment of tinnitus, a condition in which people hear whistling, buzzing, hissing, etc. without any exterior sound actually entering their ears. To ease this condition, tinnitus sufferers are often advised to turn on an air conditioner, ventilator or diffuser in the room where they are sitting, working, sleeping, etc., since this helps to mask the sound in their ears.

At first glance, this kind of treatment seems strange. Why would you recommend sound to people who are already being seriously troubled by... sound? And why the kind of 'white noise' that most people find irritating rather than pleasant or helpful? Once again, the theory of the predictive brain offers an explanation.[76] White noise is a sound that is repetitive and to which (in contrast to words and music) it is difficult to attach meaning. When you listen to this kind of noise, after a time its monotonous and predictable nature means that the brain no longer makes prediction errors. And this helps to create mental calm. There is predictability and certainty, as a result of which the brain starts to give less weight to sensory information, since a brain that is certain requires no feedback from the senses. In turn, it also devotes less and less attention to auditory signals in general. However, there is a second and equally important reason for this. Because white noise has little or no meaning, the brain learns that it can be ignored, because it has nothing to communicate and is therefore seldom relevant. It therefore updates its models to take account of this fact, leading to a reduced focus on sound.

Because perception is a construction of the brain, we therefore need to concentrate our efforts to find a solution for sensory problems on the brain itself and not on external stimuli. This is perhaps even more the case with conditions such as tinnitus, which takes place exclusively within the brain. In fact, tinnitus can be compared with what is often referred to as phantom pain, in which there is no sensory input but a very clear and frequently extreme form of sensory perception.

Before we look more closely at this, it is worth noting in general that the world of autism can learn much from recent evolutions in the field of pain relief, since the discomfort experienced by people with autism as a result of sound, light, touching or pressure is every bit as unpleasant as pain itself.

Pain, like every other form of perception, is something that happens inside the brain. Chris Frith would say that pain is an illusion. Anil Seth would say that it is a hallucination. In the old computer model of the brain, pain was seen as the experience of damage or dysfunction somewhere within the body. This damage was located by the body's pain receptors and the necessary pain signals were transmitted to the brain. Of course, we all know that when our body is damaged a pain experience is likely to follow, but the classic 'input–processing–output' model has never been able to explain three associated pain phenomena: phantom pain, the fact that pain is highly context-sensitive, and the reason why placebos work.[77] Yet as soon as we start to look at pain as something that takes place entirely within the brain and is closely connected with predictions and expectation, the explanations for each of these phenomena suddenly becomes logical. It needs to be remembered that what we perceive is not the world but rather our best guess of what the world is like and how we can best respond to it. And this applies equally to your own body. In essence, the brain asks itself: 'Is this body going to be okay for a while or not, and what must I do to anticipate what might happen to it and in it?'

It is the conscious and, above all, unconscious ideas that we have about our body (in particular, should we expect pain and, if so, how much?) that determine our experience of pain. This becomes very clear when you examine the following stories of two building workers, who in their different ways had a very close encounter with a nail (of the spiked variety, not the finger variety!).[78] In 1995, a man was rushed from a building site to the A&E department of the Royal Infirmary in the English city of Leicester. He had jumped off a piece of scaffolding and his right foot landed on a 15-centimetre-long nail that was sticking out of the ground. The force generated by the jump drove the nail through the sole of the man's boot and out through the toe cap. Not surprisingly, he screamed with pain and every attempt to remove the nail simply made him scream even louder. Once he was at the local hospital, a large dose of painkiller finally made it possible to extract the nail and take off his boot. And what did the administering doctor find? The nail had not gone through his foot at all, but had passed neatly between his toes! The extreme pain that the man had experienced was the pain that his brain had expected to experience, given the circumstances.

Ten years later, another building worker, Patrick Lawler, made it into the American press with his own equally remarkable story. After a busy day at work, during which he had used a nail gun for a couple of hours, Patrick arrived home with what he thought was toothache and slightly blurred vision. Thinking nothing of it, he went back to work the next morning. After six days, however, the toothache was still there and painkillers were no longer doing their job. Reluctantly, he decided to make an appointment with his local dentist. The dentist could not immediately see anything wrong with any of his teeth and so decided to take an x-ray. When he looked at the result, he could hardly believe what he saw. Neither could Patrick: there was a three-inch nail inside his head! By accident, the nail gun must have backfired, sending a second nail upwards instead of downwards and through the roof of Patrick's open mouth, before lodging in his brain, just a centimetre from his right eye. Patrick had not been aware of any of this and his brain, confronted with the body's signal of slight pain and fuzzy vision, had 'guessed' that the cause must be toothache...

Do you need any further proof? Pain, like every other form of bodily and sensory perception, is primarily the product of the brain.

Researchers[79] discovered as long ago as the 1990s that you can induce a feeling of pain simply by giving people information. Two electrodes were placed on the heads of a group of very brave test subjects. The electrodes were attached to a stimulator, which, the participants were told, would pass mild electric currents through their brains. They were assured that these currents were harmless, but that they might cause a temporary headache. In reality, the stimulator did nothing, other than produce a humming noise when it was supposed to be transmitting the electricity. The stimulator was also fitted with a turnable dial that the test subjects could see. The researchers pretended to activate the stimulator and gradually turned the dial higher and higher. Each time they turned the dial, the humming noise got louder and louder. The test subjects were asked to indicate if and how much pain they were feeling each time the dial was turned up another notch. More than half said that they experienced pain at some point during the experiment, even though nothing physically had been done to them.

These and other similar studies, which demonstrate that pain is a construction of the brain, prompted the Australian neuroscientist Lorimer Moseley to dispense with the classic approach to the reduction of pain. He developed a form of pain relief 2.0, which is based entirely on the principles of the predictive brain. In his TED talk,[80] Moseley explained that pain signals are not a bottom-up phenomenon, but a top-down one. In other words, they are not sent from the body to the brain, but from the brain (where they originate) to the body. This means that if you can induce pain simply by giving information, you can also reduce or eliminate it by giving information; in particular, information that will ensure that the (unconscious) predictions made by your brain expect less pain.

Moseley had already seen how many patients suffering from painful arthritis in the knee felt less pain after they had undergone exploratory keyhole surgery, even though this surgery had done nothing to physically improve their situation. With this in mind, Moseley decided to conduct a more formal experiment,[81] in which patients would undergo either a genuine exploratory operation (arthroscopy) or a 'placebo' operation: an incision would be made in the knee but no actual surgery or clinical examination would be carried out. And what Moseley expected to happen, happened: the patients who had undergone the placebo operation reported the same level of improvement as the patients who had undergone an arthroscopy. What's more, they not only reported less pain, but also an improvement in knee function.

This experiment reflects how the theory of the predictive brain has caused scientists and doctors to take a completely new look at the efficacy of placebo effects. In the past, it was often thought that placebos could only work their effect on naive and gullible people, people who could be 'tricked' by a 'fake' course of treatment. But since it became clear that the experience of bodily sensations, including pain, is largely a mental construction based on what the brain expects to happen, the use of placebos has been given a more valued and respected position in the treatment of many (primarily chronic) conditions.[82] The idea that you are being treated changes the pattern of expectation and prediction in your brain: 'my pain will diminish and my body will get better!' And the more fully the case doctor can reinforce this expectation, the greater the effect of the placebo will become, because the brain will give more weight to its own internal model than to the input it receives from the senses. In essence, this means that doctors need to lay on the enthusiasm with a trowel, without straying into the realms of fantasy: an upbeat 'This is a new, expensive and super-powerful painkiller' will have more effect than a dry 'Some people experience less pain if they take this pill.' Other factors such as the size and colour of the pill also play a role.

Moseley wants to take things another step further. The experience of pain is the result of the careful weighing and assessment of internal predictions against signals received from the body. This assessment process is unconscious and lightning-fast. But if it were possible to change those unconscious predictions by changing the brain's own mental model of the body (in a manner comparable with the rubber-hand illusion), might this have an effect on how we experience pain? This is what Moseley wanted to find out and so he devised another new experiment to seek the answer. This time he asked patients with painful complaints in the wrist, hand or fingers to carry out a series of movements, such as twisting their wrist, spreading their fingers, etc. While they were doing this, the patients were also asked to look at the affected wrist, hand or fingers. Moseley's idea was to try and manipulate this visual input. He did this by introducing a pair of binoculars into the experiment. Although all the patients continued to complain of pain after completing the requested hand, wrist or finger movements, they complained of more pain when they viewed that movement through the binoculars: the hand seemed bigger than it really was, and so the pain felt bigger as well. But when they turned the binoculars around, the opposite effect was also apparent: the hand now seemed smaller and the pain less! But that was not all: in addition to a reduced feeling of pain, there was also a reduction in the swelling of the hand. The 'mental shrinking' of the problem not only had an effect on the brain's perception of pain, but also on the physical reactions of the body.[83]

At the University of Washington in Seattle (USA), the brain is the main focus for the treatment of serious burn injuries, injuries that are particularly painful. Professors Hoffman and Patterson discovered that patients who played a virtual reality game during their treatment – a game in which they threw snowballs at snowmen and penguins – had less pain than they usually had when receiving classic treatment.[84] The patients were distracted by the Snow World game and, as a result, became more relaxed. And a brain that is more relaxed attaches less weight to sensory input. However, there is also a second reason why Snow World had a beneficial effect. By playing a game that takes place in a cold environment, even if that environment is virtual, the brain expects to feel less warmth/heat and this plays a role in its perception of the pain associated with the burn injuries.

The treatment of tinnitus, hyperacusis and pain are all based on the same three brain-related pillars:

- They focus on the brain's expectations – its own top-down feedforward – and not on sensory stimuli.
- They try to reduce the weight attached to sensory information in the brain's balancing act between expected and effective input.
- They focus on stress and uncertainty, and therefore primarily target the limbic system and not the sensory system.

In fact, what they attempt to do is to break the vicious circle that we saw on page 61 and turn it into a virtuous circle:

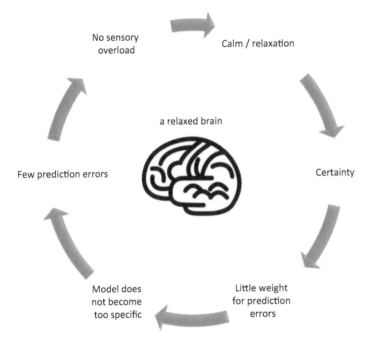

What can we learn from this to assist us in our efforts to deal with sensory problems – especially sensory overload – in autism?

In the first instance, it underlines the need for a radical change of course, above all in our long-term strategy. When someone goes into mental meltdown under the pressure of a sudden tsunami of impulses and sensations, it obviously makes sense to adopt an immediate low-stimulation and low-arousal approach. But effective long-term help requires something more than the elimination or reduction of stimuli, because in the final analysis it is impossible to create a world without such stimuli. Even if you could, this would not be in the best interests of people with autism. Because in a world without stimuli, the brain can learn nothing and could never become more resilient.

However, we can make the brain more resilient when dealing with the sensory environment by attempting to influence its predictions and models and by tackling the problem of stress. This would convert our strategy into the following sequence:

Because the brain does not process stimuli but instead processes prediction errors, this is where we first need to concentrate our attention. This means that we need to find a way to externally reduce both the number of these prediction errors and the weight of the importance that the brain attaches to them. So how exactly can we do this in concrete terms?

> **❛We can help the autistic brain to experience less trouble from variations in sensory input if we can make those variations predictable and explicable, so that the brain no longer needs to devote unnecessary attention to them.❜**

In the first instance, we can reduce the number of prediction errors by pressing the context button. From the experiments involving people with autism that we described earlier in this and the previous chapter, it is clear that an autistic brain deals with prediction errors in absolute terms. It does not adjust the level of importance it attaches to sensory information to reflect the nature of the context. This means that if we wish to reduce sensory overload, we must first help people with autism to better clarify contexts, particularly sensory contexts. Offering predictability to people with autism is usually limited to telling them what will happen, when, where and with whom. Think, for example, of the classic day planners and day schedules that are often used to help people to deal with the course of events. However, tools such as these seldom or never offer predictability in sensory matters. Matters such as:

'The class next door will soon be celebrating someone's birthday, so we might hear people laughing and singing.'

'New shoes can feel a bit tight in the beginning, but that will soon wear off once the leather becomes more supple.'

'We are sitting right above the company restaurant, so there is a good chance that you might start to smell the aroma of food from ten o'clock onwards.'

'We will soon be taking a bus to the museum and, in view of the time of day, it might be quite crowded.'

But also:

> 'Today, the pupils in the class next door are visiting a factory. So it will be quieter than normal.'

These examples make clear that offering predictability does not mean attempting to predict exactly which sensory impressions people with autism are likely to receive. That is not possible, nor is it the main reason for pressing the context button. The purpose behind hitting the button is to make unconscious expectations in the brain more context-sensitive and to ensure that possible variations in the context do not lead to major prediction errors that can result in the brain's models becoming too precise. Just like the day planners and agendas, the aim is to provide predictability about possible variations. Do you also note down in your planner or diary the things that happen every day, like getting up, having your breakfast, getting dressed, etc? Of course not! Nor is that necessary for people with autism. However, we can help the autistic brain to experience less trouble from variations in sensory input if we can make those variations predictable and explicable, so that the brain no longer needs to devote unnecessary attention to them. By contrast, in contexts where variation is expected, you need to do the opposite: namely, provide predictability about the fact that nothing will change ('Today's playlist will be the same as yesterday's.').

Pressing the context button also means that you need to provide as much clarity as you can about the context of stimuli. Stimuli cause stress in people with autism, because they are unable to give them a proper place in their mental models. And it is not just unpredictable stimuli that can lead to uncertainty and stress; unclear, vague and ambiguous stimuli can also have the same troubling effect.

> Edward does voluntary work for a non-profit organisation, where he helps out in the garden. He is often troubled by the barking of a dog in one of the neighbouring gardens. Dogs cannot tell the time and therefore bark at irregular moments throughout the day. As a result, the barking is highly unpredictable and this causes Edward stress. Because of the high wall separating the two properties, he cannot see the dog. This makes everything even more unpredictable. It also means that he cannot know why the dog is barking. Edward's autism coach takes him to the second floor of the organisation's building. From there, he can see the dog in the neighbour's garden. In other words, he now has a visual image of what is causing the barking. He can also see that the dog is kept in a cage, so that it forms no threat to Edward and cannot hurt him. The autism coach, who also has a dog of his own, explains to Edward why dogs bark. It does not always mean that they are angry or are planning to attack someone. This, the coach adds, is the basis for the well-known saying: 'A dog's bark is worse than its bite.' He then goes on to further explain to Edward that the dog might be barking because it can hear him working in the garden and wants

to warn its owner. That is what guard dogs are supposed to do. They are not used to hearing noise in the next garden and so they bark to signal that someone is there. This explanation about why dogs bark and the fact that Edward has now been able to see the situation for himself makes Edward feel more relaxed. He still does not like dogs, but at least he is now less troubled by the barking of the neighbour's dog when he is working.

Making the sensory environment predictable and understandable needs to be done in the right way and in the right context. It is not a good idea to make someone aware in advance of stimuli for which he or she is afraid or finds horrible. In these circumstances, the context is not always relevant or beneficial. If you are informed that you will be receiving electric shocks in the next few minutes, this does not do much to improve your peace of mind. Similarly, if you think that peas are revolting, knowing that pea soup is on this evening's menu will not make you thrill with anticipation. For stimuli of this kind that already have a strong negative image in the brain, it is better to concentrate on stress management rather than on prediction and explanation (see below).

When we talk about the predictive brain, we are talking primarily about the unconscious brain. Pressing the context button and offering people with autism predictability and explanation, as we have just described above, focuses on the conscious brain. Yet even if the conscious brain has information about the sensory environment, this does not mean that the unconscious brain can no longer be surprised. The participants with autism in the experiments outlined earlier in this chapter were usually aware in advance of the unexpected noises and images that formed part of those experiments, but this did not stop their brains from reacting with surprise. In other words, knowing what is going to happen does not always prevent prediction errors from being made, with sensory overload as a possible result. The slower and more difficult process of habituation that we see in people with autism is primarily concerned with this unconscious side of the brain. It will require the creativity of researchers and scientists like Moseley, Hoffman and Patterson to develop strategies that will make it possible to change sensory expectations and predictions at this unconscious level.

In response to one of my tweets about the predictive brain and sensory problems in autism, a certain Samantha replied:

> Knowing that music will be playing in the fitness centre is not enough for me. The music continues to overwhelm me. But at one point they played *Irreplaceable* by Beyoncé and that was fine, because I know that song so well and am able to predict every sentence of the lyrics.

This shows that in addition to predictability, familiarity and preference also play a role. And these factors are anchored in our unconscious brain.

One of the things that we can learn from Moseley's experiments is the importance of hopeful expectations. It is our expectations of pain that determine our perception of pain. If we are expecting pain, we feel pain and often feel it even stronger. And as with other forms of stimulation, such as noise, the resulting hyperactivity mainly takes place in the brain's limbic system; in other words, in our emotional brain. The American Gil Sharvit and his Swiss colleagues Vuilleumier and Corradi-Dell'Acqua[85] have made a close study of the part of the limbic system that is responsible for processing pain: the Island of Reil, better known as the insula. They discovered that it is not only the specific expectation of pain that strengthens the actual pain experience, but also the more general expectation that something will be pleasant or unpleasant. This should not perhaps come as a surprise, if one realises that the insula, in addition to pain, is also involved in the response to various other less pleasing events and stimuli, such as the things that revolt and disgust us. This means that the predictions that are generated by the insula[86] are probably not pain-specific: in other words, 'this will cause me pain' leads to the same prediction as 'this will not be pleasant.' If we turn this around to view it from the perspective of positive expectations, this might mean that the placebo effect does not necessarily need to be limited to the creation of the expectation of less pain or no pain. Consequently, it may be possible to generate a positive general expectation in the emotional brain ('it will be good,' 'it is going to be okay,' etc.), which in turn will lead to less strongly negative sensory experiences. At the same time, the connection between optimism and the perception of pain, particularly at the unconscious level, has been repeatedly shown in other studies.[87] That being said, if we want optimistic and positive expectations to have a beneficial effect on pain perception, it is important that they are sufficiently credible and realistic,[88] in a manner similar to treatment with placebos. A simplistic and exaggerated 'hip-hip hooray!' will have no impact on our unconscious predictions. At the same time, it must be remembered that no real research has so far been carried out into the effect of optimistic expectations on sensory overload in people with autism, but there is nothing to suggest that the effects we can see in the field of pain perception would not remain valid in other areas of sensory perception. The most difficult part of the challenge will be to convert the unconscious brain to greater optimism. Many people with autism will simply not believe you if you confine your mental support to bland statements like 'It will be alright' or 'You might even find it pleasant.' What you need to do is to create a context in which a person with autism is relaxed, has confidence and experiences a feeling of control (see further). It is only in such a context that there is any possibility of increasing the level of unconscious optimism.

> **‘What you need to do is to create a context in which a person with autism is relaxed, has confidence and experiences a feeling of control.’**

Various studies have demonstrated that autistic brains are also capable of becoming accustomed to sensory stimuli, although this takes longer. If you want to teach someone with autism how to get used to a particular stimulus

– in other words, if you want to update the brain's model, so that the stimulus comes as less of a surprise when it occurs – it is necessary to be patient and to take one (small) step at a time.

As a child, Temple Grandin hated balloons, because of their propensity to explode suddenly and unpredictably. Looking back on those childhood years, she now knows what she – or her parents – could have done to help her to deal with the problem more effectively: 'If I had been given the chance to pop some balloons for myself – first a partially inflated one that wouldn't have made much noise, then a slightly bigger one, and so on – I probably would have been able to put up with having balloons around me.'

Viewed from the perspective of the theory of the predictive brain, these small steps are logical. By starting with a part-filled balloon that bursts with only a mild 'pop,' you help a child with autism to tolerate that particular noise and make it 'manageable.' This success reduces the level of fear for the future. Reduced fear means less stress and more confidence, so that the brain attaches less weight to sensory information. Smaller prediction errors are eliminated and the vicious circle is broken. However, the most important element in Temple's story is the fact that she wanted to be able to burst the balloon herself. Stimuli that you generate yourself always result in fewer (or no) prediction errors. Just as crucially, generating your own stimuli gives a feeling of control. And as we shall see in the pages ahead, control is a key player in the battle against sensory overload.

> *Autistic brains are also capable of becoming accustomed to sensory stimuli, although this takes longer.*

This immediately explains why self-stimulation or 'stimming' so frequently occurs in autism. Stimming is an action or movement that is repeated time after time for the specific purpose of generating a particular kind of sensory perception. Common acts of stimming include rocking the body back and forth, twirling or flapping the hands in front of the eyes, chewing gum, humming the same tune over and over, and spinning coins, lid, tops, etc. Whereas in the past there was a tendency to persuade people with autism to 'unlearn' this kind of behaviour, we now know that this is not a good idea, because the actions in question all serve a functional purpose. In a world full of prediction errors, they provide a few moments of predictive certainty. They create mental calm in brains that are otherwise seldom calm. For this reason, stimming should be accepted as an aspect of stress management in autism, provided it does no damage or harm.

Hyperreactivity in autism largely takes place in the limbic system. For this reason, it is also the logical place to focus our attention if we wish to ameliorate sensory problems. Uncertainty, anxiety and stress cause sensory overload. As a parent, you probably have days, especially busy days and days when everything is going wrong, when it seems that your kids are making much more noise than usual. This, too, is a form of sensory overload – and you don't need to have autism to experience it.

> *'Uncertainty, anxiety and stress cause sensory overload – and you don't need to have autism to experience it.'*

In any attempt to prevent sensory hyperreactivity, the reduction of stress must be at the top of the list of priorities. How exactly can you do this? I could write (another) book on just that subject alone, so there is no space to go into detail here. Suffice it to say that instead of attempting to reduce stress in people with autism, it is probably wiser to try a different and more positive strategy; namely, an approach that seeks instead to increase the feelings of happiness and pleasure they experience. Once again, there are many different ways to do this, but making a connection with their interests and preferences is always a good starting point. When you read the responses of people with autism to my lecture in Birmingham, did anything strike you as unusual about what they said? If you can't remember, go back a few pages and read them again. Do you see it now? Apart from the common link with unpredictability, most of them had no problem with noise, pressure and touch in situations in which they had voluntarily chosen to place themselves, in order to pursue their own interests and preferences. No one – and certainly no one with autism – would go to a concert of 20,000 people unless he/she loves music and is a fan of the bands who are playing. And it is no surprise that the man who was comfortable with the noise of a revving engine is also a big Formula 1 fan. Activities that reflect our interests and preferences are activities that we seek to perform on a regular basis. As a result, we become more familiar with them, and this makes them more predictable. Viewed from the perspective of the predictive brain, increasing levels of predictability and certainty inside a person's head and connecting with that person's interests are two sides of the same coin. You have probably never thought of it in these terms, but offering activities that match the interests of a person with autism will also make that person's brain less reactive for sound, light, touch, etc.

Another way to make someone feel good is to let them do something that allows them to experience a state of flow. Flow is a concept first developed by the American psychologist with a real tongue-twister of a name, Mihaly Csikszentmihaly, and it plays an important role in the school of positive psychology. You are in flow when you become so engrossed in what you are doing that you lose track of time and just about everything else. An activity needs to satisfy a number of requirements before it is capable of generating flow. It must be enjoyable; you must have chosen it yourself; it must have a clear purpose or objective; it must demand concentration and be challenging, but not to the extent that you will find it hard to complete successfully. Flow activities are an ideal way to distract someone from a sensory experience that is unpleasant and overwhelming. This explains why the Snow World virtual reality game was able to have such a positive effect on the perception of pain in patients suffering from burn injuries. Hoffman and Patterson previously tried to create a positive pain effect by asking the patients to view a series of relaxing and pleasant images, but without success. In this context, passive relaxation does not work. In contrast, Snow World is an active form of relaxation that also satisfies many of the flow criteria. As a result, it succeeded where the images failed: the patients became so wrapped up in the game that the pain of their treatment was pushed into the background. It may sound strange, but the evidence is there to support it: flow activities have a place in any plan to deal with sensory overload and discomfort in people with autism.

Of course, a world wholly without unpredictable stimuli is an illusion. It does not and cannot exist. And if there is one thing worse than an unpredictable stimulus, it is an unpredictable and uncontrollable stimulus.

In the spring of 1969, four children were playing outside an apartment block in the Bronx, one of the districts in New York. Suddenly, a shot rang out and one of the children fell dead, while the other three ran for their lives. The gunman, who was a night worker, later explained to the police that he had been driven mad by the noise the children were making, which prevented him from getting to sleep. This tragic incident inspired two psychologists, David Glass and Jerome Singer, to investigate the phenomenon of urban stress, which is the stress caused when too many people live too close together in big cities. One of the crucial factors in causing this stress is noise. Glass and Singer conducted a number of experiments and came to the disturbing conclusion that people can indeed be driven mad – or at least to the point of anger – by noise that is both unpredictable and uncontrollable.

They subjected their test subjects to an unpredictable noise with an intensity of 108 dB, which is very – even unpleasantly – loud. Half of the test subjects had a button that they could press to stop the horrible noise. Glass and Singer[89] asked them to do this as little as possible, but they at least had the option when the noise became unbearable. The other half of the test subjects had no such escape button. This meant that the group with the button had a degree of control over the situation. The group without the button had no control. Afterwards, the participants in the first group – very few of whom actually used the escape button – reported that they had experienced the noise as being much less irritating than the participants in the second group. The degree of control had a clear influence on the level of perception.

❛People with autism who are hyperreactive for noise, light, touch and pressure do not need 'low-stimulation' environments but rather the possibility to control the stimuli within their environment.❜

In this experiment, the first group of participants had actual physical control – a button – over their sensory environment. But in a later experiment Glass and Singer[90] discovered that this control does not need to be physical: an illusion of control can also have a positive effect on perception. This time, they subjected their test subjects to electric shocks while they were trying to solve a number of puzzles. They were told that if they failed to solve a puzzle, they would be given a shock. But each time they solved a puzzle successfully, the following electric shock would not be given. Half of the test subjects were given easy puzzles to solve; the other half were given puzzles that were more or less unsolvable. In reality, all of the test subjects were given the same number of shocks, whether they solved the puzzles or not. But the group with the easy puzzles felt that they had been able to influence the number of shocks (even though they hadn't) and this illusion of control meant that they experienced measurably lower levels of stress than the group with the hard puzzles. In another similar experiment[91] a group of student volunteers agreed (goodness knows why!) to allow themselves to be subjected to ten unpleasant electric shocks, each lasting six seconds. In the first part of the experiment, they were asked to press a button as soon as they felt each shock. In the second part of the experiment, half of them were told that if they now pressed the button quickly enough, the length of the shock would be reduced by 50% to just three seconds. The other half were told that the shocks in the second part would now only last for three seconds. In other words, everyone received shocks of the same duration, but half of the group thought that they had been able to reduce this duration by their own actions, as a result of which they again experienced significantly less measurable stress (based on their skin conductance).

These experiments show that if we wish to reduce the sensory discomfort of people with autism, it is first necessary to give them, wherever possible, some degree of control over their sensory environment. And where it is not possible, we must do everything we can to at least give them the maximum feeling of control. (And no, I am not saying that we must consciously 'trick' people with autism, as was the case with many of the experiments carried out in the 1970s.) The importance of this control was made evident by the work of two researchers at the University of Glasgow.[92] They organised sessions in which six adults with autism were questioned in detail about their sensory experiences. This brought a number of issues to the surface and one of the most prominent was the question of control. According to the participants, it was the presence or absence of control that determined whether or not stimuli were experienced as being positive or negative. One woman expressed it in the following terms: 'When I am unexpectedly touched or when I have no control over the situation – for example, because the other person is bigger and stronger than I am – I experience this touching as being more upsetting than when I do have some control.' Someone else commented that although he obviously did not have total control over the environment in his place of work, he at least felt less stress and performed better when he could put on his headphones and listen to his favourite music, which was something his employer had been happy to allow. An autistic brain does not want or need a world without prediction errors. It wants a world where it can control those errors and, if it so chooses, reduce them in number.

In short, people with autism who are hyperreactive for noise, light, touch and pressure do not need 'low-stimulation' environments but rather the possibility to control the stimuli within their environment.

Some time ago, I and a number of colleagues were contacted by a museum in the Belgian city of Ghent: the House of Alijn. This is a kind of folklore museum, which shows people what life was like in the Flanders of the 20th century. Using all your senses, you can experience an old-style wedding ceremony and reception, see how people used to celebrate Christmas and New Year, where they went and what they did for their holidays, and how they spent their free time. The museum wanted to take the opportunity presented by a series of planned renovation works to make their displays more autism-friendly. They were aware of the sensory problems that people with autism often face and were concerned that the essence of their museum – experiences that are based to a large degree on the senses – might actually be autism-unfriendly. For example, the display that shows how people used to eat breakfast has a strong aroma of coffee; the wedding celebration has a selection of songs that married couples used for the opening dance at their evening reception; etc. If all this was removed, the heart and soul of the museum would also be removed. But unless something could be done, the museum would also continue to be unwelcoming to autistic visitors. The solution was to give people with autism control over their own sensory experiences. In the breakfast room there is now a diffuser that only emits an aroma of coffee if you hold your nose close to it and squeeze. Similarly, you only get to hear music at the wedding party when you press a special button. Because other people can also press those buttons, visitors with autism are provided on request with a bag that contains, amongst other things, noise-cancelling headphones and other tools and materials that can help to make the museum visit more predictable.

There are many different ways to give people control in situations, and this applies equally to people with autism and other intellectual disabilities. If, for example, someone is no longer capable of washing himself, as a carer you can let him choose with which foot you begin. Or you can let him smell the different kinds of shower gel and let him decide which one he wants you to use. Choices can also be offered about which clothes to wear and with what textures. If there are things that the people in question can still do – like combing or brushing their own hair – let them do it. Every action that they can do for themselves provides them with predictable sensory feedback. And no prediction errors mean no stress...

To summarise: dealing with hyperreactivity in autism is first and foremost a matter of providing people with a good feeling, predictability and a sense of control.

In 2016, I had the honour of speaking at the very first conference held by AsIAm, an Irish autism organisation led by my good friend, Adam Harris. Adam has also been diagnosed with autism, so it was hardly surprising that he and his team did everything possible to make the conference as autism-friendly as possible. One of the many innovations in that respect was the introduction of the 'flapplause,' a form of applause that originated in deaf culture and involves waving or flapping – as opposed to clapping – your hands. It is a demonstration of appreciation that is quiet and therefore seemed appropriate for a conference where many of the people present would be hypersensitive for noise. Personally, I was not convinced. There might be no noise but two hundred people all flapping their hands certainly creates a huge amount of potentially challenging input for people with visual oversensitivity! Then there was also the question of predictability. When Adam announced the flapplause, the man sitting next to me immediately tut-tutted his disapproval. When I asked why he, as a person with autism, was not happy with the idea of silent applause, he answered: 'I like normal applause. It is what I expect at performances and conferences…' During lunch time, there was a quiet room available for the delegates with autism. Because there were people there that I knew, I popped inside as well and after a few minutes began to conduct an informal survey of the opinions of people with autism about clapping or not clapping.

The results (albeit limited) revealed that few people with autism have a problem with traditional hand clapping. As for those that did have a problem, it was not the noise itself that was the key factor. Wholly in keeping with the theory of the predictive brain, their main complaint was the sheer unpredictability of the applause: it could break out at any moment. For most, applause at the end of a lecture was acceptable, but they had more difficulty with spontaneous applause half way through, if, for example, the speaker had said something special or amusing. What's more, they never knew how long the applause would last. Ten seconds? Fifteen seconds? Longer? And would everyone remain seated or would some people stand up?

Armed with this information, I decided to conduct my own experiment, designed to make applause more autism-friendly, but without the need to stop traditional hand clapping. My solution was as follows:

- With a little humour and a few jokes, I made sure that the atmosphere was light and relaxed before the moment came for people to applaud. In this way, I focused on the limbic system of the people in my audience.
- I told them that I was testing out an experiment and that I was the only person who could fail, adding that I had sufficient trust in the resilience of the people with autism in the auditorium to feel confident that they would survive my experimental venture. In this way, I tried to create greater self-confidence and optimism at the unconscious level.
- I made the applause predictable, by saying exactly when it would begin and exactly how long it would last; namely, six seconds. A time line on the final slide of my PowerPoint presentation made this very clear visually. In this way, I gave the people with autism in the audience the necessary degree of predictability, so that they would know what to expect, in the hope that this would minimise their prediction errors.
- I told them that everyone who so wished was free to use the ear-plugs that were in the tote bag that we had all received at the start of the conference.

Putting fingers in ears was also okay (but preferably their own fingers in their own ears!), and I visualised this with some amusing pictures on my slides, again with the intention of creating a good feeling.

If all else failed, I said that anyone who wanted to leave the auditorium before the applause started was free to do so, in this way effectively giving them control over the applause.

Although there were plenty of people in the auditorium with autism, no one opted to leave. But that is more or less what I had expected. The vast majority were curious to witness the outcome of the experiment and all eyes were focused on me as the moment for the applause approached (creating my own Snow World-like diversion). When the applause started, most people burst into laughter as well and had to restrain themselves from applauding a second time (which I had forbidden, so as not to breach the agreed terms of predictability that I had previously offered). All-in-all, the experiment was a great success and since then Adam and his team have always made use of autism-friendly applause instead of flapplause at subsequent conferences. There was, however, at least one person with autism in the auditorium that day who had a minor criticism of the way things had gone. Afterwards, he approached me and said in a loud voice that the applause had lasted 5.85 seconds and not the six seconds that I had promised! He had measured it on his iPhone...

Almost this entire chapter has been about hyperreactivity. There are two reasons for this. The first is that being overstimulated is something that people with autism complain about much more frequently than hyporeactivity. The second is that even today the factors that cause hyporeactivity are still not fully understood.

One of the most noticeable things in the personal accounts of people with autism is the fact that their hyperreactivity is primarily concerned with the senses that are focused on the outside world: seeing, hearing, feeling, touching. These are the exteroceptive senses and the process of detecting and interpreting external stimuli is known as exteroception. The process of detecting and interpreting signals transmitted from inside the body – signals such as hunger, thirst, mood, pressure, pain, temperature etc. – is known as interoception and in general it is this internal process that is most frequently mentioned in connection with the hyporeactivity seen in people with autism. For example, some people with autism find it difficult to recognise when they feel pain or are hungry or thirsty. Others do not know whether they should put on an extra pullover or not, because they do not know whether they feel hot or cold.

Like exteroception, interoception is also a predictive activity. In order to guarantee our survival, our brain must make sure that we have everything we need to function effectively.[93] And it seeks to do this proactively, rather than waiting for problems to arise and then correcting them. As a result, the brain attempts to predict what kinds of problems the body might face, so that it can take corrective measures in good time. For example, it makes sense not to wait until we are totally dehydrated before drinking something. In other words, thirst is not a reaction to a shortage of water in the body, but is a prediction: 'If I do not drink something now, I will soon be dehydrated.' It takes at least five minutes for the water you drink to find its way into your bloodstream. But the feeling of thirst disappears the moment you stop drinking. And if we were only to stop drinking at the moment when the water we need reaches our cells, we would quite literally drown ourselves! Fortunately, as soon as we drink, the possibility of a prediction error is eliminated: the brain now predicts that our water management system is once again fully operational and therefore orders the body to stop drinking. This ability to predict what Lisa Feldman Barrett[94] has called the 'body budget' is something that often works less well in people with autism. An autistic brain seems to be less able to anticipate possible shortages or surpluses in its management of the body's resources.

One of the explanations that has been put forward to account for this is the idea that hyporeactivity for bodily signals is a consequence of hyperreactivity for signals from the external world. A brain that is hyperalert for prediction errors in the sensory external world has no spare capacity for making predictions and dealing with prediction errors in the interior world. Because of the many sensory threats that exist in the outside world, interoception is simply not at the top of the brain's 'to do' list. The uncertain and stressed autistic brain is so strongly focused on what is happening outside the body that it hardly has any time, energy and space to monitor what is happening inside the body. As a result, its predictions about what might happen to the body and the problems it might face are not updated. This creates a new kind of vicious circle, but one that now moves in the opposite direction. Because these unamended predictions are now insufficiently precise, many of the unexpected interior signals it now receives are dismissed by the brain as noise or interference, and are therefore not taken seriously. This means that the predictions again remain unaltered and that gradually fewer and fewer prediction errors are registered. Over time, the brain therefore becomes less and less aware of what is happening in the body.

> '*The uncertain and stressed autistic brain is so strongly focused on the outside world that it hardly has any spare capacity for monitoring the condition of the body.*'

When it is dealing with signals from the external world, an autistic brain seems to consistently attach greater weight to those signals than to its own predictions, largely because it takes too little account of context when setting the balance between the two. A similar process probably takes place with regard to internal signals and predictions, but in this case that balance falls in favour of the brain's own predictions about the body, rather than trusting the signals that the body is sending it. To add to the complications, people with autism also find it difficult to adjust the balance between their attention for the external world and their attention for the interior landscape to take account of the prevailing context.[95]

This, at least, is the theory. At the moment, there is not much hard evidence to back it up. Until now, scientists have devoted much more attention to hyperreactivity than to hyporeactivity. That being said, the research carried out by Sarah Garfinkel and her British colleagues[96] seems to support the hypothesis. She wanted to find out (via a questionnaire) how competent people with autism regard themselves when it comes to detecting the signals of their own body and then compared these results with the results of a test designed to establish their actual level of competence. The test in question was a classic test in which the participants were asked to count the number of their own heart beats and then say whether or not this rate was synchronous with a series of noises they were asked to listen to. What did the results show? People with autism consistently gave themselves a better score for interoception on paper than they were able to achieve in practice: the majority found it hard to keep track of their heart rate accurately.[97] It therefore seems that in general people with autism overestimate their ability to pick up the signals of their own body. This is perhaps a slightly surprising conclusion, given the large numbers of accounts about people with autism in relation to their own hyporeactivity for such signals.

However, there is a possible explanation for this discrepancy. As we saw earlier with hyperreactivity, questionnaires often tell a different story from what is actually going on inside the brain – and that is probably what was happening in Garfinkel's hyporeactivity experiment as well. To answer a questionnaire, you need to think consciously about your responses. This involves a number of different factors, including self-knowledge, past experiences, properly understanding the question, etc. Bearing in mind that many people with autism describe themselves as being oversensitive, is it not plausible in a questionnaire about their sensitivity to their body's own reactions that they also regard themselves as being more sensitive than is actually the case?

Another possible explanation relates to the link between stress/anxiety and the ability to recognise your own bodily signals and emotions. Sarah Garfinkel concluded that the people with autism who showed the largest discrepancy between their estimated and actual interoceptive accuracy were also the people who were clearly the most anxious during the experiment. In cases of depression and anxiety, a person's inability to look deep inside himself or herself, notwithstanding an increased level of attention for the body's own signals and emotions, has long been known. Although she found no evidence for self-overestimation, Eleanor Palser and her colleagues at the University College in London also concluded in a study involving children with autism that there was a connection between stress and the level of discrepancy between estimated and actual levels of interoception.

At the present time, it is not clear whether anxiety is the cause or the consequence of not being able to accurately detect the body's signals. But one thing is clear; namely, that stress is once again a factor in the overall mix that need to be considered. If it is indeed the case that people with autism can sometimes devote too little attention to what is going on inside the body because their brain is devoting too much attention to what is happening in the outside world, any reduction in the level of stress relating to the outside world should therefore put them in greater contact with their own selves. Shouldn't it? Be that as it may, it still seems well worth the effort to help people with autism to better detect and read their body's own signals, if for no other reason than it forms the basis for the ability to read other people's internal signals, which is generally referred to as Theory of Mind.[98]

Of course, even if a person with autism is able to pick up bodily signals, it needs to be remembered that there is no guarantee that these signals will be correctly interpreted. As with signals received through the senses from the outside world, signals received from the body's internal sensors can also have a number of different causes. For example, an increased heart rate can indicate stress or fear, but it can also be the result of sexual excitement. Two minutes of skipping will likewise increase your heart rate. Once again, the brain needs to predict what a specific internal signal might mean, dependent on the context, and, subsequently, what action, if any, needs to be taken in response. If you are skipping and an increased heart rate results, your brain can predict that this increase is not caused by sexual excitement but by physical exertion, so that it does not need to add skipping ropes to its mental model of the things that turn you on. At the same time, it also predicts that it might be a good idea to take a short breather.

> ❛As with senses in the outside world, we can also help people with autism to find their way through their internal world by providing them with predictability, by offering greater clarification, and by pressing the context button.❜

When you are not able to place the signals coming from your body in their proper context, this can result in both hyporeactivity and hyperreactivity. In one of her many books, Donna Williams[99] speaks of 'under-firings' and 'over-firings.' Her brain failed to pick up signals that were important, such as hunger, when it was occupied with processing other matters. These were the under-firings. Her brain was also capable of reacting in an exaggerated manner: she could experience a small dip in her mood as a serious depression and a mild preference for someone as a full-blown passion. These were the over-firings. Worst of all were what she referred to as 'mis-firings': when her brain interpreted the body's signals incorrectly in the given context. She gave the following example:

> Mis-firings are where the brain gets the message mixed up. This may happen because the brain hasn't processed the context of the emotion that has been felt so that it doesn't distinguish between different emotions properly. If I felt deep emotion for someone I was seeing, my body might respond with an increased heart rate, deeper breathing, etc. If, however, my brain

had stored the formula that 'increased heart rate + deep breathing, etc. = terror', and that 'terror is to be responded to by actions of avoidance', then my brain might drive me to instinctively, but mistakenly, respond as though I am in danger and may give all the messages to body parts, eyes, face and voice to avoid the source of the feelings or to run or even attack. Imagine what it is like seeing someone you are really glad to see and who you are affected by and secure with, but you are driven to look away from them or run away from them, busy yourself with every other distraction, be overly formal or push them away from you....

Donna's brain made a fixed connection between a bodily signal and an explanation for what had caused that signal: namely, fast heart rate and deep breathing *always* = terror. When seeking to construct emotional meaning, her brain always fell back on this kind of absolute interpretation.

In view of the fact that the theory of the predictive brain is also (and perhaps above all) a theory that explains how we learn about the world and ourselves, hyporeactivity for the body's internal signals and an inability to place those signals in their proper context inevitably leads to an atypical image of that body and – if we can believe the claims of one of the theory's founding fathers, Karl Friston[100] – an atypical image of self. It further explains – and the story of Donna Williams is a good example – why the emotional reactions of people with autism are sometimes different from the reactions of people without autism. Bodily signals, like the signals from the outside world we receive via the senses, are highly ambiguous. What we call emotions are actually the explanations created by the brain to understand the cause of the body's various signals, based on the context and the expectations that we attach to that context.[101] Consider, for example, an increase in your heart rate. This is a deviation from your normal heart rate. In other words, a prediction error. Because you have just heard that you have won the jackpot on EuroMillions, your brain will explain this error as a consequence of your happiness and excitement at receiving this fantastic news and *not* as a consequence of your being afraid of something, which is another possible explanation for a faster beating heart. In reality, however, your heart rate does not increase because you are happy or excited. It is receiving the news that makes your heart beat faster and, once that is registered in the brain, it is this that leads to the feeling of happiness and excitement, because that is what it predicts you should feel in this particular context. This means that emotions, like the perception of colours we discussed earlier in the book, are figments of the brain's own imagination. Or to express it in slightly different terms: emotions are the brain's predictions about how we should best react in any given set of circumstances. However, brains that tend to think in absolute terms and are insufficiently context-sensitive will give a different explanation to the same bodily phenomena, resulting in a very different emotional experience. For the outside world, this can sometimes come across as indifference ('He's a cold fish') or affectation ('She's a drama queen'). In reality, this has nothing to do with emotional oversensitivity or undersensitivity, but is the product of a brain that interprets signals from the body absolutely and is unable to place those signals in context.

As with senses in the outside world, we can also help people with autism to find their way through their internal world by providing them with predictability, by offering greater clarification, and by pressing the context button. In 2019, Kelly Mahler – an occupational therapist and a good friend of mine from Pennsylvania – developed a teaching programme designed to allow children to learn about their own body and how to regulate it for themselves. A first study[102] suggests that the programme, known as the Interoception Curriculum, is achieving positive results.

That being said, it is not always necessary to organise courses to give people with autism a helping hand in this respect. When you see that someone with autism is finding it difficult to interpret the signals of his/her own body and to place those signals in their proper context, you can help them quickly and easily with 'à la carte' explanations that will allow the context button to be pressed.

> David, a young man with autism, is following a Monday to Friday course. For the first two days in a row, he has complained that by the end of the morning it is all getting a bit too much for him. As a result, he experiences a mental dip and feels a bit 'down.' This gives him an unpleasant sensation and his heart starts to beat faster. At the same time, he feels mentally sluggish and finds it hard to concentrate. However, he cannot explain why this should be the case. In the circumstances, we decide to let him go to his room. In the afternoon, however, we see a completely different person: a mischievous and excitable David, who takes part in all the activities with great enthusiasm. His 'mini-depression' seems to have disappeared like snow melting in the sun. One of my colleagues who has diabetes suggests that the problem might be that David is hungry or experiencing a small hypoglycaemic dip. On the third day, David makes the same complaint. This time, we decide to give him an energy bar. After a quarter of an hour, he informs us that he is starting to feel better. Until recently, David was undergoing psychiatric therapy. In the group sessions, he had learnt that mental problems such as depression can often lead to physical problems and that consequently, if you are not feeling well, this might be the result of a psychological cause. Because David, as a person with autism, thinks in absolute rather than contextual terms, he had 'learnt' that 'physical signals of discomfort = psychological origin.' We explain to him that what he is feeling in his body in the context of 'late morning' simply indicates that he is hungry and has a low blood sugar level. This is what we mean by 'pushing the context button': if people cannot assess the context for themselves, help them to assess it. For the remaining days of the course, each morning at around 11 o'clock David asks without fail for his 'energy bar against depression.'

Because the ability to guess accurately about the meaning of your own bodily signals is the cornerstone of emotional intelligence, dealing with this aspect is an important challenge for everyone who is involved with children, young people and adults with autism. It is vital to clarify and explain the context of the signals that their body is sending them. Teach them how to press the context button, not only for the outside world but also for their own inner world. The better they are able to make predictions about what is going on inside their own selves, the better they will be able to predict what is going on inside others. This will be the subject of the next chapter.

In a nutshell:

- There is a difference between sensitivity (the threshold value for stimuli) and reactivity (the strength of the reaction to stimuli).
- An autistic brain is neither more nor less sensitive to stimuli than a non-autistic brain, but reacts to those stimuli more strongly. Strictly speaking, the sensory peculiarities in autism are not really sensory at all, because they take place in the limbic system of the emotional brain.
- An autistic brain is insufficiently able to place unexpected sensory input in the right context. Instead, it will deal in absolute terms with any prediction errors. As a result, people with autism sometimes react too strongly (hyperreactivity), but sometimes also too feebly (hyporeactivity) to sensory input.
- Low-stimulus is not the same as autism-friendly. The avoidance of stimuli in the long term can actually make hyperreactivity worse. The correct exposure to stimuli is what needs to be sought.
- The sensory overload that people with autism often experience is the result of a vicious circle in which their brain finds itself and in which uncertainty and its related stress play a key role.
- The way to approach hyperreactivity is to try and break this vicious circle. This requires a focus not on the stimuli, but on the brain itself. The aim is to reduce the number of prediction errors by making the stimuli more predictable. This requires us to press the context button, so that the brain can correctly assess the weight and importance of unexpected sensory information. Above all, it is necessary to try and provide greater certainty and calm in the mind of the person with autism. This can be achieved through targeted distraction (via flow activities), by giving them a good feeling about themselves, and by increasing their optimism and self-confidence when dealing with stimuli. This offers greater benefits over time than the superficial treatment of symptoms through the reduction or removal of stimuli.
- It is not necessary to turn the environment of the person with autism into a low-stimulus environment. It is much more important to give people with autism control over their own sensory environment.
- Self-stimulation or stimming is functional: it is the brain's reaction to sensory overload. As long as self-stimulation does not cause any harm to the

person with autism or the environment, there is no reason to try and reduce or eliminate this practice. On the contrary, it is important to give it a place in the sensory strategy for the person concerned.

- In general, the autistic brain reacts weakly (hyporeactivity) to the signals of its own body (interoception). The autistic brain finds it difficult to detect these signals and correctly interpret their context. There is a possible connection here with stress and anxiety, and a problem with finding the right balance between attention for the exterior world and the person's interior world. Reducing stress and helping people with autism to learn how to read the signals of their own body and to know when to press the context button are all recommended techniques for dealing with this situation.

DID YOU KNOW?

In April 1968, a colloquium on autism was organised at the University of Indiana in Indianapolis. These were the early days of organised meetings to discuss the subject. The American Autism Association had only been founded two years previously and two of its leading scientists – psychologist Eric Schopler and psychiatrist Robert Reichler – were invited to give lectures at the colloquium. Four years later, they set up the widely praised TEACCH programme at the University of North Carolina. In their lectures, Schopler and Reichler both spoke at length about hyperreactivity and hyporeactivity in children with autism. In particular, they focused on the difficulty that these children have to monitor, organise and integrate sensory input, which involves both high and low thresholds for sensory information. Even so, it was destined to take another half century before sensory behavioural characteristics were included in the official criteria for autism. This is amazing, if one considers that as long ago as 1965 Eric Schopler wrote: 'A view of autism that is currently gaining ground is to characterise it as a cognitive disorder in which there is an inability to relate sensory experiences to memory.' In other words, decades before the emergence of the theory of the predictive brain, Schopler was effectively describing the nature of perception in the concept of predictive coding; namely, the alignment of internal models with sensory data. As such, he was one of the first people to suggest that the explanation for autism must be sought in the brain. Eric Schopler died in 2006, at the age of 79 years.

4 The predictive brain and navigating in social traffic

As we have seen, the brain is capable of predicting the flight of a tennis ball travelling at 250 kilometres per hour. But if you think that this is one of the more remarkable achievements of the predictive brain, it is nothing in comparison with what the brain needs to predict simply to allow us to react quickly and appropriately to the everyday behaviour of the people around us. The complexity of human behaviour is gigantic when placed alongside the behaviour of your average tennis ball. For instance, a tennis ball cannot decide half way through its trajectory to suddenly change course and do something new, just for the hell of it. Equally, a tennis ball cannot take pity on you as a new and inexperienced tennis player by slowing down the speed of its approach. And in contrast to a tennis player, a tennis ball cannot have an off-day, simply because it doesn't feel in the right mood. Whether it likes it or not, a tennis ball is always subject to the same laws of physics. Okay, human beings are also subject to those same laws (if you don't believe me, try floating on thin air!), but the laws that determine human behaviour are much more complex and much less absolute. And it is this fact that makes people like you and me the most capricious stimuli on the planet. And to deal with these fickle, volatile and erratic creatures, it has been necessary for the brain in the course of its evolution to develop its predictive powers to unprecedented new levels.

To predict the behaviour of a tennis ball, it is sufficient to apply a number of natural laws and formulas, such as the law of gravitational acceleration. This is the rate of acceleration achieved by an object in free fall when dropped from a height. Expressed in figures, it amounts to 9.81 metres per second squared. The flight that a tennis ball follows can also be expressed as a formula (albeit a relatively complex one, so I won't bother you with the details), which, like the rate of gravitational acceleration, is absolute. Whether I hit the tennis ball or my 80-year-old neighbour hits it, the formula always remains the same. Moreover, it makes no difference whether the tennis ball is yellow or green. Or whether the ball is hit in your local park or in a Grand Slam final at Wimbledon. If Nadal is in a good mood, it makes no difference. If Nadal is in a bad mood, it makes no difference. The influence of gravity on every ball that Nadal hits in whatever mood will always remain constant. For this reason, the world of physics is often referred to as an example of a closed system. Closed systems are highly predictable, because they are regulated by fixed, universal and clearly defined laws and rules: if you perform operation B on input

DOI: 10.4324/9781003340447-5

A, you will always get output C. In concrete terms, this means that if you have a tennis ball in your hand (input A) and allow it to drop (operation B), the law of gravity will ensure that it always moves downwards and never upwards. This result (output C) will be the same, always and everywhere (unless you play your tennis in outer space).

By contrast, the social world is an open system.[103] Of course, open systems also have their own laws, but they are seldom fixed and straightforward. This means that the outcomes in an open system are far less predictable, because the system is 'open' to all kinds of different influences and variations. Social situations are invariably open-ended, because interpretations, intentions and a thousand and one other contextual factors all play a role.

> *For a brain that has a tendency to think absolutely, predicting the outcome in an open system is a serious challenge. Predicting the behaviour of people is not a matter of calculation on the basis of (fixed) formulas and laws. It is a matter of context-sensitive guessing.*

For instance, we are inclined to think spontaneously that if someone gets a present, he or she will be happy. But that is not always the case. The 'system' of presents is an open system, because – in contrast to physical laws – the operation of giving a present can (in theory) have an infinite number of different outputs. This is a consequence of the fact that open systems are far more subject to contextual influences. Applied to social situations, this means that the output or outcome – a person's reaction – is dependent on countless different elements in the context. In the case of getting a present, these elements might include: What is the present? What did the receiver expect to get? Who is giving the present? Why was the present given? Does the receiver already have the present...? This is only a very small selection of the many possible factors that can help to determine the receiver's reaction.

Open systems are therefore more complex and less predictable than closed systems. To understand and predict the outcome in an open system demands much greater feeling for the context. For a brain that has a tendency to think absolutely, predicting the outcome in an open system is a serious challenge. Predicting the behaviour of people is not a matter of calculation on the basis of (fixed) formulas and laws. It is a matter of context-sensitive guessing.

Various studies have shown that people with autism can make very good predictions when the output can be assessed deterministically; in other words, when there are fixed laws and rules that can be used to help make the predictions. Autistic brains like closed systems and perform well within them. However, as soon as the system becomes open, an autistic brain starts to struggle and finds it much, much harder to predict outputs accurately. This inevitably means that attempting to predict human behaviour can often be a nightmare for people with autism.

A group of French researchers[104] showed children and adolescents a series of short films in which a number of familiar and less familiar activities were demonstrated. Examples of the familiar activities included eating a sandwich, getting dressed and reading a book. Examples of activities that were less familiar to children and adolescents included shaving, ironing and starting a car. Immediately before the final step of the activity in question, the film was stopped. The children and adolescents were then shown four different photographs, each showing an option of what might happen next, one of which logically followed on from what they had just seen and could therefore be regarded as the 'expected' option (for example, pulling on a t-shirt in the 'getting dressed' film), while the other three options were much less likely (for example, putting the t-shirt on top of your head).

The purpose of this experiment was to see whether children and adolescents with autism would be able to predict the following step in the behaviour of the people they saw in the different films. The results showed that the children and adolescents with autism more frequently chose a photograph of an action that was unlikely in the given context than their non-autistic counterparts. In fact, they also performed less well than children and adolescents with an intellectual disability. And in contrast to the children and adolescents without autism, they did not perform better with the familiar activities than with the less familiar activities. This all underlines that predicting what a person will do next on the basis of what you have just seen is difficult for an autistic brain. And the greater the number of contextual elements involved, the more difficult it becomes.

Judith Pijnacker and her colleagues at Radboud University[105] in the Netherlands asked a group of people with and without autism to predict a person's behaviour. The adults with autism were able to make predictions every bit as good as the adults without autism when the behaviour could be predicted on the basis of classic 'if-then' logic, as in the following example:

> If Marie has an exam, she studies in the library.
> Marie has an exam tomorrow.
> Will she study in the library?

To reach the correct answer to this question requires nothing more than the application of classic logical reasoning – and this kind of reasoning is non-contextual. If Marie has an exam, she will study in the library. Full stop. End of story. Adults with autism had no problem dealing with this kind of question.

It was different, however, when the situations were less obviously straightforward:

> If Marie has an exam, she studies in the library.
> If the library is open, she studies in the library.
> Marie has an exam tomorrow.
> Will she study in the library?

The answer to this question is no longer a simple 'yes.' It depends on whether or not the library is open. The answer is therefore influenced by the context. The adults with autism had far more difficulty with this kind of question.

This experiment is therefore confirmation that the greater the role played by context in predicting human behaviour, the harder people with autism will find it to predict that behaviour accurately. Imagine that Marie only studies in the library when things are too busy at home and a difficult subject requires her to concentrate more fully. In this scenario, there are immediately more contextual factors that need to be taken into account – and this is where the autistic brain starts to struggle.

> *The greater the role played by context in predicting human behaviour, the harder people with autism will find it to predict that behaviour accurately.*

In an effort to find out what makes it so difficult for people with autism to understand and predict behaviour, the Argentinian researchers Sandra Baez and Agustin Ibanez[106] compiled a battery of tests to investigate the different aspects of social and emotional intelligence. One test measured emotional intelligence, while others measured empathy, prior knowledge of social norms, the ability to make moral judgements, and the ability to recognise social blunders.

Fifteen adults with autism and fifteen adults without autism completed all the tests. For some tests, both groups performed equally well, but in others the performance of the group without autism was better. So what were the main similarities and differences?

The tests where the results were broadly comparable for both groups were the tests where the social situation was clearly described and where the right response could be found by making use of abstract and general rules. This was the case, for example, in the test where it was necessary to decide if a certain act of behaviour was morally correct and also in the test to establish the level of knowledge of current social norms. If you know the rule, such as 'theft is wrong,' then as soon as an act of theft occurs you know that this act is wrong. People with autism can reach this kind of conclusion just as well as anyone else.

However, people with autism were less successful when it came to tests where, if you wanted to understand a social situation correctly, it was necessary to quickly, unconsciously and automatically use a number of contextual cues. One example of this was the so-called 'faux-pas' test. A faux-pas (a French term meaning 'wrong step') is a social blunder, of the kind committed by John in the following example.

> John is visiting his girlfriend, Susan. Because it is John's birthday, Susan has baked him an apple cake. She says: 'I have made a cake especially for you. It is on the table in the kitchen.' To which John replies: 'It smells delicious and I love cakes – except apple cake, of course, which I hate....'

There is no general rule to say when something is a faux-pas or not. This means that it is not possible to say: 'It is socially inappropriate not to like apple cake.' In fact, it is not really possible to say that there is any such thing as socially inappropriate behaviour. What is appropriate in one context is often not appropriate in a different context. This means that determining what is socially appropriate behaviour requires a fast and unconsciously context-sensitive brain – and that is precisely what people with autism do not have.

Chris Frith and his wife Uta, both of whom are highly respected neuroscientists, have spent decades conducting research into the social brain. They have come to the conclusion that two different kinds of processes take place inside our heads.[107]

First, there are implicit processes. These are fast processes that take place automatically and unconsciously. As a result, our conscious brain has no control over these processes. Second, there are explicit processes. These are processes of which the brain is aware and over which it does have a level of control. As a result, they demand a degree of mental effort and take longer to perform.

This can be simplified in the following terms: on the one hand, there is social intuition (unconscious sensing); on the other hand, there is social reasoning (conscious thought). These processes are separate from each other and can sometimes even work against each other. For example, people who record a low score when completing a questionnaire about racial prejudice, and are therefore not racist at a conscious level, can nevertheless react negatively to photographs of coloured people that they are shown for such a short period of time that they cannot perceive them consciously. Similarly, some people who are shown an awareness video about autism consciously adopt a more positive approach to people with autism, whereas tests show that at the unconscious level they continue to associate autism with its less attractive characteristics.[108]

Further proof of these conclusions was provided by perhaps the most well-known test for assessing empathy (Theory of Mind): the Sally–Anne test. This test measures whether someone is capable of recognising a false belief in someone else. The test tells the story of Sally, who hides her marble in a basket and then goes away. While she is gone, another girl – Anne – takes the marble out of the basket and puts it into a box. Where will Sally look for her marble when she comes back into the room? Children of five years of age watching this test usually succeed in giving the right answer: Sally will look in the basket. They can also tell you why: because Sally did not see that the marble has been moved and so wrongly thinks that it is still where she left it. In other words, five-year-old children are aware of what Sally knows and what she does not know. But that is not the case for three-year-old children: they answer that Sally will look in the box. But at the same time when answering… they look at the basket. Their unconscious brain predicts Sally's behaviour correctly, while their conscious brain gets things wrong. This is not uncommon, even in later life: our unconscious brain often knows things that our conscious brain does not. In this respect, our unconscious brain is much smarter than our reason, our conscious thought.

Much research has been conducted into Theory of Mind in people with autism. Gifted people with autism often do remarkably well in Theory of Mind tests, even the more advanced ones. But as Baez and Ibanez discovered, this excellent performance relates primarily to tests that target explicit and conscious processes in the brain. When social reality can be predicted by conscious, logical reasoning and by the application of general rules and laws, people with autism are no different from people without autism. But in comparison with the non-autistic brain, the autistic brain is less good when it comes to fast, unconscious and contextually determined predictions. And it is this latter kind of prediction that we need to navigate smoothly and flexibly through the social world. It is simply not practicable to constantly stop and spend time thinking rationally about the inner life of others. In day-to-day existence, there simply isn't time. What was valid in our tennis ball example, is also valid for the behaviour of others. If our brain would only start to act after it has received all the input it needs from the senses, we would never be able to respond quickly enough to what other people are doing and saying, just as we would never be able to hit the tennis ball before it had already passed us. In other words, we do not first need to observe the behaviour of others in order to know and decide how we should react. Instead, we must predict that behaviour, so that we can respond in time and (hopefully) in an efficient and appropriate manner. In short, perceiving what others do is essentially a predictive activity: we predict what other people are going to do, when, where, how and for how long.

At the most basic level, this means, for example, that we will predict the movements of those around us. If we failed to do this, we would be constantly bumping into each other. Literally.

People with autism do not have a problem perceiving body movement.[109] They are also more than capable of differentiating different forms of this movement, such as fighting, dancing, etc.[110] So far, so good. But can they also predict body movements?

Several studies suggest that the prediction of movement per se is not really a problem for people with autism. Researchers at the University of Oxford[111] let children with autism watch a film in which a car was driving along a path. At a certain moment, the car disappeared behind a wall of a given length and was hidden from view. The children were asked to predict when the car would come to the end of the wall by pressing a button. The children with autism performed just as well as their non-autistic counterparts.

In this experiment, context does not play a role in the predictive process. All that is required is to mentally extend the existing progress of the car. The speed and the direction are both absolute. They do not change and are therefore not context-dependent. For absolute thinkers, like children with autism, this was a piece of cake.

But the same cannot be said of human movement. The speed, direction and manner in which people move are all dependent on the context. There is nothing absolute about these factors; they are all highly variable. And this is what causes problems for the autistic brain – as was discovered by Lucia Amoruso and her colleagues at the University of Udine in Italy.[112]

Amoruso let a group of children watch a number of short films in which two children were sitting at a table. Between them was an apple on a plate. The child on the left moved its hand in the direction of the apple. When the apple was on a green plate, in nine out of ten cases the movement with the hand gripped the fruit from the side, in a manner suggesting that the child wanted to eat it. When the apple was on a black plate, in nine out of ten cases the movement with the hand gripped the apple from above, in a manner suggesting that the child wanted to give it to the other child.[113]

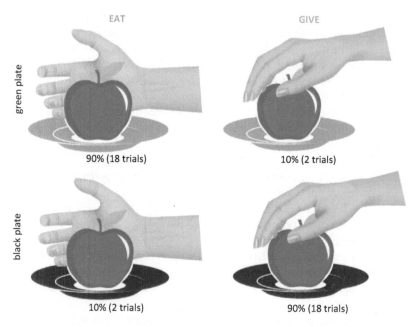

The children were able to identify the patterns quite quickly. After viewing just a few of the films, all the children, both with and without autism, could tell whether the child wanted to take or give the apple.

In a second series of films, the children were shown broadly the same scenario, but this time with a glass on a placemat of differing colours between the two children. If the glass was on a white mat, in six out of ten cases the child took the glass as though it wanted to drink from it. If the glass was on a blue mat, in six out of ten cases the child took the glass as though the child wanted to give it to the other child.

After this learning phase of the experiment, the children were shown the same films again, but this time for a much shorter duration: each film was stopped when the moving hand was still some way away from the apple or glass. The children were then asked to say what the child in the film was going to do: give or take? Because the hand was still some distance away from the object, the test children could no longer see the hand grip (from the side or from above) of the child in the film. As a result, they had to make a prediction based on what they had learnt about the contextual influences: the colour of the plate and the mat. Children without autism were better able to do this for the plate than the mat. And that is logical: the connection with the context was stronger in the case of the plate/apple (90%) than in the case of the mat/glass (60%). However, for the children with autism there was no such difference. Their brain had not learnt how to use the context to predict the movement of the hand. In other words, the children with autism were able to perceive things correctly – as in the first series of films in which there was a difference in the grip for giving and taking – but they were unable to predict those two actions on the basis of context. One other conclusion of this experiment is worth noting: the questioning of the children about their decisions made clear that none of them – with or without autism – was aware of the contextual cues (the colour of the plate and the placemat), which again proves that context works unconsciously.

In this study the children were shown the films a number of times. Of course, it helps to predict someone's behaviour if you see the same action repeated on several occasions. But this does not mean that it is essential: it is still possible to predict behaviour without having first seen it on multiple occasions. We do this by making use of context and what we expect to see happen in that context. When you see Robert in the kitchen with an egg in his hand and a hot pan on the stove, you can predict that Robert will crack the egg into the pan. If Robert is sitting at a table with a painting set in front of him and an egg in his hand, you can predict that he is not going to break the egg, but rather paint it for Easter. What's more, you can predict this behaviour when you have never seen Robert with an egg in his hand before.

What is the hand going to do with the cup?

In the situation on the left, 'pick it up and drink' seems the most likely option. The situation on the right is more suggestive of 'pick it up and clear it away.'

Lucia Amoruso[114] let people watch a series of films in which they could see a hand moving towards a cup. Sometimes the position of the hand was in agreement with an action that you could reasonably expect in that context, such as a certain kind of grip that suggested 'eating and/or drinking' in a context that contained a full cup of coffee and a plate of biscuits, or a different kind of grip that suggested 'clearing up' in a context that contained an empty cup and plate. In some of the films, the grip did not match the expectations for the context. For example, the 'clearing up' grip from above might be combined with the full cup and plate or the 'drinking' grip with the empty cup and plate. Of course, the films of this latter kind generated plenty of prediction errors, and these could be monitored in the test subjects' brains. Amoruso and her colleagues concluded that the brains of people with a high score in a questionnaire for the characteristics of autism reacted differently to the films with the 'unexpected' hand position than the brains of people with a low score in the questionnaire. What was the difference? They seemed less surprised. This proves once again that in people with autism there is only limited context-sensitivity for the prediction of behaviour.

When we predict someone's behaviour, we base our conclusions on two sources:

- The behaviour that we have seen just previously in the person.
- The behaviour that we expect in the prevailing context, given the behaviour that we have just seen.

The French cognitive psychologist Valerian Chambon[115] discovered that people with autism make less use of their expectations and more use of what they see, especially in relation to social behaviour. It is not the case that people with autism are not capable per se of identifying the intentions of others, but when social behaviour is involved they find it harder to make accurate predictions when the amount of available information is limited. This is in keeping with what we saw earlier in connection with predictive capacity in autism: an autistic brain seems to give greater weight to sensory information than to its own models and expectations. When assessing what other people are going to do, it is almost as if the autistic brain adopts the principle of 'first see, then believe.' People with autism need more information before they can predict the behaviour of others, especially in social contexts.

So far, we have only discussed the prediction of behaviour on the basis of non-social contextual elements, such as the colour of a plate or the fullness/emptiness of a cup. But in the social world the social context also inevitably plays an important role: what one person does has a consequence for the reaction that we can expect from another person. The human brain must not only be capable of predicting individual reactions, but also various interactions.

'When assessing what other people are going to do, it is almost as if the autistic brain adopts the principle of "first see, then believe."'

To ascertain whether an autistic brain can do this as well as a non-autistic brain, a European research group[116] made use of so-called point light displays, a technique that has been applied since the 1970s for the study of the perception of human movement. Instead of showing test subjects a moving body, they are only shown the movements of a number of orientation points in the body, usually the joints, in the form of points of white light against a dark background. The images below[117] make this clear: participants in this kind of experiment are shown films similar to the image on the right, where the actual person can no longer be seen.

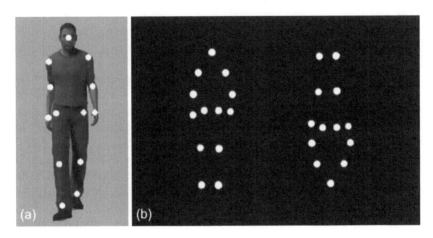

In the European study, the test subjects were asked to view short films containing the point light displays of two people: person A and person B. In some of the films there was a suggestion of communication. For example, a movement in which it seemed that person A was saying something to person B and pointing to the ground, as though asking person B to pick something up. Or a movement in which A seemed to be saying 'stop' to B. In other films there was no suggestion of communication. Instead, the two 'people' performed individual actions, such as jumping, drinking or sneezing. The test subjects were asked to describe the different actions in the film and to say whether there had been any communication between A and B. The results of the people with autism were every bit as good as the results of the people without autism. This again confirms that people with autism are capable of correctly identifying human behaviour and human interaction, and that their ability to perceive social behaviour is intact.

Yet, although they were capable of recognising the communicative behaviour of person A, people with autism were not able to use that behaviour to predict what person B would do in response. The test subjects were twice shown a set of short film fragments with two point light displays. In some of these films, B was also present alongside A. In others, there was just a succession of randomly moving white dots next to A. After viewing the fragments for the second time, the test subjects were asked to say whether or not they had seen B. Once again, there were films with and without communication. In the films with communication, the behaviour of B can be predicted on the basis of the communicative action of A. If A looks downwards, you can expect B to make a movement towards the ground. This in turn makes it easier to decide whether or not you have seen the movement of a person (B) or just a collection of randomly moving dots. However, when A displays no communicative behaviour, it becomes harder to distinguish between B and the random dots. These effects were very clear in the participants without autism: they used A's communicative behaviour to predict what would happen, so that they were also better able to recognise B. The participants with autism found it much harder to recognise B. It appeared that their brain did not make use of the behaviour of A to form an expectation of what would follow.

Conclusion: people with autism are capable of recognising and describing (social) behaviour when they see it, but their brain does not use this information to predict what will follow on from that behaviour.

We have already mentioned several times that the predictive processes of the brain are fast and largely unconscious. And it is no different with the predictive processes and abilities of our social brain. Unfortunately, it is precisely in this aspect of unconscious predicting that the autistic brain does not perform well. This has been demonstrated by, amongst other things, research focusing on shared attention.

Shared attention is when two people both focus their attention on the same object, person or event. When you are sitting in a pub with a friend and he says 'Look who's coming in now!', you turn towards the door and follow the line of his gaze: that is an example of shared attention. Knowing what someone else is looking at is one of the foundations of empathy. Moreover, it has been known for some time that shared attention develops very slowly or occasionally not at all in children with autism. In fact, it is one of the earliest indications for a diagnosis of the condition. For this reason, researchers are particularly interested in how this process of shared attention actually works.

> *'The predictive processes of the brain are fast and largely unconscious. And it is no different with the predictive processes and abilities of our social brain.'*

A research team at Kyoto University[118] in Japan created a computer version of shared attention. Young people with and without autism were shown a simplified drawing of a neutral face on a screen. The eyes of the face were able to look both left and right. The direction of the face's gaze matched the position where a ball would appear on the following screen.[119] If the face looked to the left, the ball on the following screen would also be on the left (and vice versa, if the face looked to the right). In other words, the direction in which the face was looking predicted where something would soon be seen. When they were shown each new screen, the young people were asked to indicate as quickly as possible whether or not the ball would appear on the left or the right on the following screen. This was relatively easy for all the participants: both groups (with and without autism) used the direction of gaze to successfully predict what would happen. Next, the researchers shortened the length of time that the young people could see the face. In fact, the time was now so short that the young people said that they could no longer see a face at all! Consciously, this was true, but during that split-second an image of the face had nevertheless been projected onto their retinas. The researchers were curious to see whether in these circumstances the young people would still be able to predict the direction in which the ball would subsequently appear. The results showed that the young people without autism could still do this fairly well. Although they had not been able to perceive a direction of gaze at the conscious level, their unconscious brain had picked up the information and used it to make an accurate prediction. But that was not the case with the young people with autism.

This Japanese research demonstrated that people with autism do not have a problem with consciously shared attention, but that they do have a problem with unconsciously shared attention. This same conclusion has also been reached by Chris and Uta Frith, who believe that unconsciously shared attention is just one of the many rapid and implicit processes that do not function properly in an autistic brain. This explains why people with autism sometimes perform well in many different kinds of Theory of Mind tests, but still find it difficult to faultlessly predict the behaviour of others in 'real' life, the life beyond the research laboratory. Or why children and adolescents with autism are able to easily answer all different kinds of questions about social behaviour in a coaching session, but are hopelessly lost outside the meeting room, in what for them is an unpredictable social jungle. Notwithstanding their conscious knowledge of the social world, their brain does not succeed in predicting that world quickly and unconsciously.

Another of the most important contextual elements that the brain uses to predict the behaviour of another person is what it knows or thinks it knows about what that person wants. Our own behaviour is always conditioned by what we want. There is always an intention behind everything we do. It is this intention that motivates us to formulate our behaviour in a particular way. It sets us in motion – quite literally. And what applies to us also applies to other people.

You want proof? Meet Floris the tortoise. Floris loves lettuce. He just can't get enough of the stuff and wants to eat as much of it as he can as quickly as possible. So...

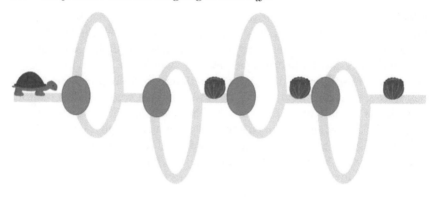

... what route will Floris take to get to the lettuce?

This was the task that Tobias Schuwerk and his colleagues at Ludwig Maximilian University in Munich[120] gave to groups of children and adults, both with and without autism. They were shown a film in which Floris was making his way towards three delicious heads of lettuce. Each time Floris came to a junction, he disappeared briefly from view behind a shaded ellipse. Schuwerk and his colleagues followed the eye movements of their test subjects. They were interested to see if the participants in the various groups could predict from which side of the ellipse Floris would emerge. Already at the first junction, it was apparent that as soon as Floris disappeared from view the test subjects without autism immediately focused their gaze on just one of the two possible exits. In short, they made a prediction. The children and adults with autism were much less inclined to do the same. Instead, it seemed as though they were waiting for Floris to reappear and only then turned their gaze in his direction.

If you know that Floris loves lettuce and has a raging hunger, you might reasonably expect that he will take the shortest route to his favourite food. Curiously enough, however, there was no clear preference for this shorter route among the test subjects, both with and without autism, at least not at the first junction. This suggests that people without autism do not necessarily make much use of their 'conscious' knowledge to predict what someone is going to do. On the face of it, this is strange: it means that we do not always predict the behaviour of others on the basis of what seems to be the most efficient likelihood. Perhaps this is because we know intuitively that people do not always act in the most logical and efficient way. On the contrary, we know that they are highly unpredictable. People are not tennis balls: they can choose what they want to do and where they want to go, and they do so in a manner that is not subject to laws, logic and efficiency.

Floris, of course, was not a person but a tortoise, and so he always followed the shortest and most logical route. At the second junction, this also became more evident to the test subjects without autism and there was now a greater difference between the focus of their gaze and the gaze of the test subjects with autism. From this point onwards, the non-autistic children and adults began to look more consistently at the exit on the short side of the ellipse *before* Floris emerged. This shows that we learn to predict the future behaviour of others on the basis of patterns that we perceive (largely) unconsciously in their present behaviour. Perhaps this is not so surprising: the spontaneous, unconscious and implicit prediction of other people's actions is much faster and much easier than consciously trying to assess what they might or might not do.[121] Do you remember the Sally–Anne test? Even children as young as three years of age were unconsciously aware of where Sally would look for her marble, but gave the wrong answer when asked to express 'consciously' what she would do.

The children and adolescents with autism in Schuwerk's experiment looked far less at the shortest route than their non-autistic counterparts. The fact that Floris took this route on the first few occasions did not help them to establish a pattern that would allow them to predict his future behaviour.

However, this leads on to a follow-up question: did they learn nothing from their experience of Floris's behaviour or was that experience simply too short to effectively identify the necessary pattern? This latter eventuality was certainly possible, since all the participants had only seen Floris make his choice four times. As a result, Tobias Schuwerk and his team were not able to offer any conclusive answer.

This answer was subsequently provided not by a tortoise, but by a pig. This was the animal used by Kerstin Ganglmayer,[122] a colleague of Tobias, in a later experiment. She asked groups of children, adolescents and adults, both with and without autism, to watch a series of ten films that showed a pig making its way towards its destination (a house or a wood). Like Floris, the pig was confronted en route with a junction in its path. The destination was the same in each of the ten films, but sometimes this destination was at the top of the screen, which meant that the pig had to take the left-hand turn, and sometimes the destination was at the bottom of the screen, which meant that the pig had to take the right-hand turn. Again like Floris, the pig disappeared from view as it reached the junction and, as previously, the eye movement of the test subjects was monitored: would they be able to anticipate where the pig would appear? On the basis of what they could see, would they be able to deduce the pig's destination and then, on the basis of that deduction, be able to predict whether the pig would turn left or right?

After just three showings of the film, the children, adolescents and adults without autism were able to predict which turning the pig would take. The test subjects with autism could eventually do that as well, but it took more than three showings of the film before they understood the pattern. Ganglmayer and her team therefore concluded that people with autism are certainly capable of learning what other people want and then predicting their behaviour on this basis, but it is a process that takes more time and requires more repetition than in non-autistic people.

Another of Tobias Schuwerk's[123] experiments in his Munich laboratory demonstrated that this kind of learning is an unconscious process, which has nothing to do with consciously reflecting on what might be going on inside other people's minds. His study revealed that people with autism score reasonably well in tests that measure explicit Theory of Mind (finding out what others think, feel and want through conscious thought), but that their brain needs more repetition and more time before it can implicitly predict (without conscious thought) what others are thinking, feeling and wanting. This supports the conclusion reached by, amongst others, Sandra Baez and Agustin Ibanez, which we discussed earlier. It also confirms what Chris and Uta Frith thought more than a decade ago: people with autism do not learn quickly and spontaneously to understand what motivates other people. And if the necessary time and repetition are not available or not possible, there remains only one other alternative: to compensate for the lack of high-speed intuition with the use of intellect and conscious thought to assess the behaviour of others. Yet when all is said and done, and not-withstanding a perfectly intact ability to discover the mental condition of other people, people with autism still find it difficult to predict quickly and accurately what those other people are going to do. And that makes it difficult for them to react to those people swiftly and fluently.[124]

'Unconscious prediction: that is the real problem in autism.'

This also explains why so-called Theory of Mind training seldom has any real effect on the social functioning of people with autism.[125] Theory of Mind training only trains the conscious, explicit social brain. It is based on a series of tasks that require children and adolescents to reflect on what someone might be thinking, feeling or expecting. Of course, it is not a bad thing – quite the reverse, in fact – if people of all ages with autism learn about the inner life of others and how this directs their behaviour, but 'knowing' and 'knowledge' are not the problem. Unconscious prediction: that is the real problem in autism. And as I already explained at length in my book *Autism as context blindness*, the crux of the matter is not the ability of a person with autism to learn what other people think, feel, expect and want, but the difficulty to use that knowledge flexibly in the function of the context.

Moreover, the brain not only uses context to guess what others are going to do or say, but also to assess their likely emotional reaction. In this respect, Theory of Mind is in essence a predictive activity.[126]

Even today, many people think that we recognise emotions in others by looking at the expression on their face. However, this is a misconception based on the now outdated computer metaphor for the brain's functioning.

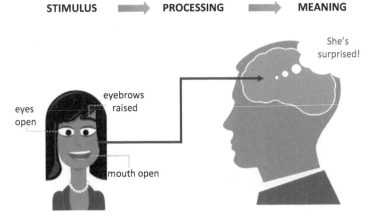

That is not how it works. The brain is not the passive recipient of the emotions and feelings expressed by others. Instead, the brain predicts the emotions of others. And – as you might be able to predict for yourselves by now – context plays an important role.

Contrary to what many people think, most facial expressions – if not all of them – are ambiguous. Most of us are convinced that we can quickly and accurately read emotions from the faces of others. However, when researchers made photographs of people's facial expressions for the first time at the start of the 20th century, they were amazed at the level of disagreement among their test subjects about the emotions that these photos depicted. For many of the photos, the test subjects often suggested very different emotions. It became clear that facial expressions were not as obvious as had previously been assumed, but were actually capable of multiple interpretations. However, these varying interpretations quickly became uniform as soon as contextual information was given to the test subjects. Unfortunately, these early research results relating to emotional perception have been overshadowed for many years by the work of the psychologist Paul Ekman. Ekman is something of a scientific celebrity and *TIME Magazine* included him in its list of the 100 most influential people. After a series of exotic journeys, including time spent with indigenous peoples in New Guinea who had never previously had contact with the outside world, he concluded that the facial expressions for seven basic emotions are universal. No matter where you are on the planet, people will always display the same facial expressions for the emotions of fear, anger, disgust, joy, sadness, surprise and contempt. Or that, at least, was his opinion Ekman took photographs to prove his point and even today they are still used worldwide in psychological research. As a result, most people still think that you can read a person's emotions simply by looking at their face.

However, that is simply not true. The only thing that you can read from a person's face is whether or not they are feeling good or not good, and also the extent to which they are feeling emotional. And that's all. Nothing more. Facial expressions are, by their very nature, ambiguous.[127]

This is Judith. What do you think she is feeling?

James Carroll and James Russell[128] of the University of British Columbia in Canada used a photo similar to the one above in an experiment. Almost 90% of the first group of test subjects who were shown the photo thought that Judith was frightened. A second group of test subjects were then shown the same photo, but only after Carroll and Russell had first told the following story:

> Judith wants to treat her sister to a meal at the most exclusive and most expensive restaurant in town. She makes the necessary reservation months in advance. When the big day finally arrives and she enters the restaurant with her sister, the maître d'hôtel tells them that their table will not be ready for another 45 minutes. They wait in the reception area and time passes, but after an hour they have still not been given a table. Judith has another word with the maître d'hôtel and he says that he will see what he can do. Ten minutes later, a well-known local celebrity arrives at the restaurant with his girlfriend. He is immediately shown inside and led to a table. Judith now goes to talk to the maître d'hôtel again. He informs her that all the tables are now in use and it will be at least another hour before one becomes free.

Having heard this story, 60% of the test subjects now thought that Judith looked angry, rather than scared. Their interpretation of the facial expression was clearly influenced by the context.

Carroll and Russell were able to demonstrate the same effect with 21 other stories and different emotions: in each case, the majority of the test subjects opted for the emotion that seemed to best match the context of the situation. In this way, now more than 25 years ago, Carroll and Russell laid the foundations for a new way of looking at emotional recognition: context determines how we assess the emotions we can see in a person's face. The situation, what is happening to someone, what other people are doing and saying, body language, voice intonation and volume, cultural background and even words all influence the process of recognising emotions. Gender can also play a role in determining how easily we can identify some emotions; for example, people generally recognise anger more quickly in a man than in a woman. Why? Because in our model of the world anger is more generally associated with men than women. We expect men to be angry rather than sad, which in turn is an emotion that is easier to recognise in women.

We urgently need to discard the current way of thinking about emotional recognition. In fact, what we refer to as emotional recognition is not recognition at all. On the basis of context, we make a prediction about how someone might be feeling. Emotional recognition is therefore emotional prediction. Half way through Judith's story, you can already predict that Judith is more likely to be angry than afraid. But you will not be aware of that prediction.

If we use the face at all during this process, it is purely to check whether or not our prediction is accurate. Or to express it in slightly different terms: we do not read emotions *from* someone's face; we project emotions *onto* someone's face. It works like this:

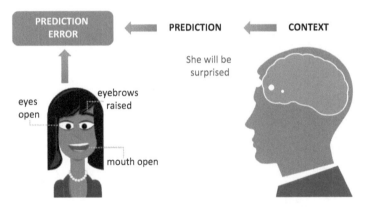

Contextual sensitivity works just as quickly, unconsciously and automatically to predict emotions as it does to predict movement and behaviour. This influence of context starts at a very early stage of the brain's processing of information, long before we are aware of the emotion that we are attempting to perceive.[129] In relation to facial expression, context therefore acts at the most basic and preconscious levels of attention and perception. Moreover, there is a clear correlation between the extent to which we (are able to) use context and the speed and accuracy with which we can perceive mental states such as emotions.[130] We recognise an emotion more quickly and with greater precision when a facial expression occurs in a context that also suggests that same emotion than when the emotion occurs in a neutral context or a context that suggests a different emotion.[131] In this way, for example, people more readily recognise fear in a frightening context than in a joyful context. You will find it harder to recognise that someone is afraid at a New Year's Eve party than in a hostage situation – unless, of course, something goes badly wrong with the midnight fireworks display...

> *What we refer to as emotional recognition is not recognition at all. On the basis of context, we make a prediction about how someone might be feeling. Emotional recognition is therefore emotional prediction.*

When the context and the facial expression contradict each other, the brain needs more time and energy to construct its prediction of the emotion. Once again, we can talk here of a prediction error. But what will weigh more heavily in the final and unconscious decision that the brain takes: the context or the facial expression? Like in the following instance:[132]

Is this young woman feeling happy or sad?

The Dutch researchers Righart and De Gelder used a series of photographs in which the facial expression was sometimes congruent with the emotion that you could expect to see in the depicted situation and sometimes incongruent, as in the case of the young lady above. As the researchers had expected, people needed slightly more time to identify the emotion when there was a conflict between the facial expression and the emotional charge of the situation. More surprising was the fact that in most cases they identified the emotion that you could expect in the given context and *not* the emotion that the facial expression itself seemed to suggest. In concrete terms, this means that when you show someone the above photo for just a short time – which replicates the dynamic of real life, since people are not photos and they move and change at high speed – he or she will probably say that the woman in question is happy, because that is what you normally expect when you get lots of Christmas presents. This sounds hardly credible, but its truth has been proven in numerous studies. When information is unclear or confused – in short, when a prediction error occurs – the brain will give more weight to what it knows about the expected emotions in the given context than to the sensory information transmitted by the facial expression. Conclusion: context is more important than facial expression for recognising emotions.

Dina Tell and Denise Davidson[133] of Loyola University in Chicago were curious to know whether this would also apply to children with autism. Their experiment revealed that when the context and the facial expression were in agreement, children with autism were generally able to identify emotions with as much accuracy as children without autism. This was also the case when the facial expression in the photo was blanked out, but only in instances where the situation was very clear and prototypical, such as a child whose toy was broken. In less clear situations, they found it more difficult to identify what the child was feeling based purely on the context. These latter findings supported the conclusion of a French research study[134] carried out a number of years previously, when children with autism had also found it hard to identify emotions when the faces of the figures in the photos they were shown were covered with an ellipse. However, what most surprised Tell and Davidson about their own results was the difference between the responses of children with and without autism to photographs in which the facial expression did not match the context. When shown an image similar to the one above, almost all the children without autism said that the young woman with the Christmas presents was happy. In contrast, seven out of ten of the children with autism said that she was sad. Whereas the children without autism were able to deduce from the context the expected emotion, the children with autism were not able to make that same deduction and instead had to rely on the woman's facial expression to recognise her emotion.[135] It is possible that this might be a consequence of the emotional recognition training that many children with autism receive. As part of this training, they are shown photographs of facial expressions and are asked to identify them as angry, frightened, happy, sad, etc. It is unfortunate that this practice is still widespread in the world of autism (and beyond), since more than a decade has now passed since brain scientists confirmed beyond doubt that we deduce and predict emotions on the basis of context and not on the basis of facial expression. Another possible (or contributory) reason to explain the 'preference' of children with autism for expression above context is the same phenomenon that we saw earlier in the book with regard to their processing of sensory information: they have a tendency to give more weight to the information that they receive through the senses (in this case, the visual signals from the face) than to the things that you would usually expect to see in the given context. This is then further reinforced by the absolute nature of their thinking: a sad face is a sad face is a sad face... End of story. As an interesting aside, it is perhaps also worth noting that some of the children without autism commented on the contradictory content of some of the photographs.

> '*The theory of the predictive brain teaches us that it is high time to change course with regard to the various interventions that are intended to make children, adolescents and adults with autism more socially competent.*'

The theory of the predictive brain teaches us that it is high time to change course with regard to the various interventions that are intended to make children, adolescents and adults with autism more socially competent. Showing children and young people with autism photographs and drawings of facial expressions is perhaps useful to help them to learn the words for the different emotions, in a manner similar to what we also do to teach them words for animals, objects, etc., but we must avoid making the mistake of thinking that this also teaches them how to recognise emotions. Children who can name the emotions they see in photos and drawings are not necessarily – repeat *not* – capable of recognising those emotions in real life.

An American research team[136] recorded the eye movements of children both with and without autism when asked to view facial expressions in four different forms: photographs of just a face, short films of just a face, photographs of a face in a context and short films of a face in a context. The eye movements of the children with autism only differed significantly from the eye movements of the non-autistic children when they were watching the moving images of facial expressions in a context, which was also the form of viewing that most closely corresponds to real life. As far as emotional recognition in the photographs and films of an isolated face were concerned, both groups of children scored equally well. The children with autism again did slightly (but not significantly) less well than their non-autistic counterparts when attempting to recognise emotions in still photos of contextual scenes. Other studies[137] have since confirmed these findings: the naming of isolated facial expressions presents no problems to people with autism. What does present a problem is the identification and prediction of facial expressions in a context.

If we want to strengthen the skills of people with autism when it comes to the recognition of emotions, we need to move away from straightforward images of facial expressions and turn instead towards facial expressions placed in contexts and scenes that evoke specific emotions. Once again: we need to press the context button!

Teaching emotion recognition

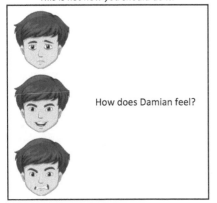

This is not how you should do it:

How does Damian feel?

It is better to do it this way:

This is Damian. He is getting a present.

How will Damian feel?

Scientific evidence already exists to confirm the value and effectiveness of this approach. When the context is activated, children, adolescents and adults with autism are all much better able to recognise and predict emotions.[138] Moreover, this also applies to emotions other than the basic emotions, such as fear, anger, happiness and sadness.

And it doesn't stop there. Context not only allows people with autism to predict how other people are feeling, but also makes it possible for them to predict what other people want and are going to do. The experiments of Tobias Schuwerk and his colleagues – the ones with the tortoise and the pig – make clear that we can help people with autism to better predict the behaviour of others, provided we keep on repeatedly hitting the context button and allow them sufficient time to discover the recognisable patterns in the context.

Other research has demonstrated that people with autism are more than capable of learning 'if…then' rules, but with the caveat that they have a tendency to apply these rules absolutely, rather than to contextualise them spontaneously. For this reason, social skills training must focus far more heavily on the contextualisation of such skills than is currently the case. Most training of this kind takes a specific skill as the starting point: starting a conversation, asking for information, dealing with criticism, standing up for yourself, making friends, etc. Unfortunately, the training has little or no real effect on improving the social competence of people with autism in real life. But that is only logical: situations in real life involve contexts that are completely different from training situations. In fact, it is not going too far to compare current social skills training with learning to cook in a child's play kitchen with a set of plastic pots, pans and ingredients: it just isn't true to life. To make matters worse, you often see that a different skill is on the programme for each new session, and this while scientific studies have again clearly shown that repetition and longer training periods are necessary to achieve the best results. The crux of the problem is, of course, that social skills training almost exclusively addresses the conscious brain, whereas navigating your way through the complex social world is largely a matter of fast, intuitive and unconscious predictions. This makes it all the more surprising that so little attention is paid in the training to the contextual variations in social behaviour. Engaging in conversation at a funeral is not the same as engaging in conversation at a party (or at least it shouldn't be). Similarly, how you stand up for yourself at work is not the same as standing up for yourself when you are amongst friends. These are the kinds of variations that cause problems for people with autism. At King's College in London, Eva Loth[139] showed children with and without autism a photograph of Toku, a young boy with Asiatic features and clothing. She told her test subjects that the boy had never before been in the United Kingdom and knew very little about life there. If he asked, what would they tell him about Christmas and eating at a restaurant in the United Kingdom, two events that should be familiar to every British child? The research team regularly stimulated the children to flesh out their descriptions, with questions like 'What decorations do people hang in their homes?' or 'When people have finished eating, what do they normally do?' The children with autism could describe the various aspects of Christmas and dining out just as well as the children without autism. Even so, there was a significant difference between the two groups. Whereas the children without autism used words like 'sometimes' and 'if' when describing (social) behaviour, that was not the case with the children with autism. For example, the non-autistic children would say things like 'Sometimes in the restaurant we have a dessert,' if there was something on the menu they liked. The comments of the children with autism were far more absolute: 'When we eat at a restaurant, we finish with dessert.' Their scenarios had far less variation, much less feeling for nuance.

> **‘***Social skills training almost exclusively addresses the conscious brain, whereas navigating your way through the complex social world is largely a matter of fast, intuitive and unconscious predictions.***’**

If we want to increase the effect of social skills training, we need to devote much greater attention to context. Clarifying contexts, exploring them repeatedly and helping people with autism to discover what is socially relevant in those contexts and what is not: this is the way forward. In other words, clarifying the things that they are not able to spontaneously recognise for themselves. So instead of 'how to start a conversation,' we need to begin with the different contexts in which a conversation can take place: a funeral, a party, a family gathering, a hospital visit, etc. Carol Gray, who over the years has become a good friend of mine, realised as a teacher more than 30 years ago that classic social skills training was not helping her autistic pupils. As a true autodidact, she understood that what those pupils really needed was explanation about the nature of the different social situations in which they would find themselves:

what do other people do in this or that situation and how should they, as people with autism, react? To meet this need, Gray developed Social Stories®, a powerful learning tool to help children, adolescents and even adults to find their way in what for them is a highly unpredictable social world. When I first met Carol several years ago, we immediately began a lively discussion about the importance of context in Social Stories®, a discussion accompanied by a bottle of Carol's favourite wine, Pinot Gris. We soon found common ground in our desire to make interventions designed to improve the social competence of people with autism more context-sensitive. In this respect, her Social Stories® do not tell people of whatever age with autism how they should behave. They simply clarify contexts.

The social world is an open system. In our efforts to predict the behaviour of others, there are no fixed and absolute rules. Temple Grandin, a well-known engineer with autism, has wrestled from an early age with the complexities of social relationships. As a result, she has learnt a lot about the problem. In 2005, she wrote (with Sean Barron) a book of tips designed to help others with autism deal with the social difficulties they face. The book was entitled *The unwritten rules of social relationship*[140] and according to Temple rule number 1 is this: rules are not absolute; they are dependent on the situation and the person.

People with autism are capable of learning social rules. They can also cope with 'if...then' reasoning. The studies that I have described in this chapter show that people with autism, at least at the conscious level and providing they are given sufficient time, are equally able to use context to predict the behaviour and emotions of others. At the same time, recent research[141] has also demonstrated that when people with autism do master social rules and contextual indicators, they have a tendency to apply them absolutely. Getting a present = always being happy. Losing your job = always being sad. Being insulted = always being angry. The problem, of course, is that context is seldom absolute.

> *'The social world is an open system. In our efforts to predict the behaviour of others, there are no fixed and absolute rules.'*

For this reason, it is important in social skills training and Theory of Mind training to place greater emphasis on variations in contexts. There is certainly no harm in first teaching a child that whoever is given a present will be happy, by using the drawing of Frank that we saw a few pages ago. But having done that, so that the child can now predict a 'happy' feeling when he sees one, we then need to move on to introduce some common variations. This means that we no longer use Frank alone, but also Simone, Adil, Louis and Rosa. Children, adolescents and adults. After this, we can also introduce a variation in the presents, as well adding a number of contextual variations: who is giving the present, what does the recipient hope/expect to receive, etc.? Eventually, the person with autism will have a set of situations with relevant contextual variants at his/her disposal that will allow him/her to determine what someone might be feeling when that someone is given a present. However, it is important to understand that this set will not be developed and activated spontaneously. Eva Loth[142] discovered that people with autism do not look at contextually relevant elements in scenes in a spontaneous manner. Analysis of their initial eye movements revealed that they find it difficult to make a distinction between what is important in the scene, and should therefore attract their attention, and what is not important. This is broadly in keeping with what we saw earlier in the book: the visual behaviour of people with autism is less context-driven than the vision of people without autism. After the test subjects had watched Loth's experimental scene, she asked them to name as many of the things they had seen as they could remember. The participants with autism remembered all kinds of different things, almost randomly, as if all these elements had entered their brain unfiltered. The participants without autism tended to remember primarily the things that were important to the context of the scene.

When we are making social scripts for children and adolescents with autism, it is therefore best to start as early as possible with contextual variations, to prevent the learners from applying the lessons of the script in an absolute way. We can do this by using sentences that begin with words like 'when…,' 'if…,' or 'in case….' Below you can find an example of a contextualised social learning story for a young boy with autism who found it difficult to deal with the unpredictability of the time when his mother would come and collect him from school:

Contextualized scripts

Mummy picks me up from school at 3.30.
I wait for mummy on the playground, by the gate.

If there is lots of traffic, mummy might be late.

If mummy has not arrived by 3.40, I go back inside and wait in the reception area. I can play with my Game Boy until mummy comes and finds me there.

The story as I have told it so far in this chapter may create in some of my readers the impression that people in general have almost clairvoyant-like powers that allow them to always predict accurately what other people in any given context will feel, think, say and do. Of course, that is not the case. If it were so, other people would never be able to surprise us. They would never be able to disappoint, move or deceive us – nor we them. No, when we talk about predicting the behaviour and feelings of others, this is with the same degree of certainty (or lack of it) that we have already seen earlier in the book for other kinds of predictions, such as those relating to sensory input. In both cases, the process remains a game of chance, a calculation of probabilities. On the basis of the behaviour we have just seen in others, allied to what we know about human behaviour in the context in question, we will (gu)es(s)timate what someone will think, feel and do. As a result, we expect a certain (re-)action from the other person. Sometimes our predictions will be right. Sometimes they will be wrong. In this latter eventuality, we will be confronted with a prediction error.

When faced with a prediction error, the brain needs to make a choice: does it ignore the error or is the error important enough to take corrective action, so that the same error is not repeated in the future? The brain does not like prediction errors and the mental doubt and confusion they cause. As is also the case with sensory stimuli, these errors challenge the brain to make a distinction between noise and normal variation on the one hand and important deviations from the norm on the other hand. In other words, a distinction between unexpected events that are random and incidental, and unexpected events that must mobilise us either to adjust our expectations or else to take action in the real world to adjust reality. Or put even more simply: we either update our empathy or ensure that people display the behaviour we expect of them.

Imagine the following situation. You know that your colleague Eddy, who sits next to you in the office, is a positive person. Always in a good mood. Always ready for a laugh and a joke. One day, he arrives at the office later than usual. He slumps down in his chair and sighs deeply. You say 'good morning' to him, but he fails to answer, which is not like him at all. Instead, he lets out another deep sigh, followed by a heart-felt 'Shit!' This is not the behaviour that you were expecting from him. However, you know that Eddy has a young baby, who often keeps him and his wife awake. You also noticed that he was late this morning. Perhaps he overslept after a restless night? Or got caught in traffic? At this stage, the chance that you will completely revise your ideas about Eddy is minimal. You will not assume that he has undergone a total change of personality in the last 24 hours, so that your good-natured friend has suddenly become a morose, impolite and unfriendly man. Even positive-thinkers like Eddy can have an off-day, so that they are less full of beans and optimism than normal. In short, we accept a degree of variation in people's behaviour. After all, we are not machines who always show the same reactions. As a result, you do not attach too much importance to Eddy's unexpected behaviour. You just put it down to 'a bad night with baby' and get ready to carry on with the rest of the day. But not before you say something amusing, in the hope that this might be enough to bring a smile to Eddy's lips and so further minimise the importance of your prediction error.

If, however, this unexpected behaviour in Eddy becomes more frequent, even when you know that the baby is now sleeping better, you might start to think about changing your pattern of expectations and predictions about him. And when your manager asks how things are going with Eddy, you may be inclined to answer: 'He's not the way he used to be....'

This is an example of what is known as 'empathic learning': prediction errors gradually lead to the updating of our model of what we think about others, so that we can better predict their behaviour in future. Of course, this also explains why we are better able to predict the behaviour of people we have known for a long time than the behaviour of people we have never met before.

The manner in which people with autism deal with prediction errors in the sensory world is also reflected in their approach to prediction errors in the social world. Autistic brains respond to prediction errors absolutely and do not adjust the importance they attach to these errors to take account of the context. In the case of Eddy, this means that even if a person with autism knows about the baby's sleeping problems, he/she will be more surprised by Eddy's behaviour than a person without autism. As a result, this stronger reaction to Eddy's behaviour may provoke a revision of the person with autism's general opinion of Eddy. He will no longer be seen as Mr Nice Guy but as Mr Moody. It is not unusual for people with autism to categorise people in this absolute way: the good and the bad (and in my case probably the ugly as well!). If you know someone with autism who has a tendency to categorise people in this 'black or white' manner and if you are currently fortunate enough to be in this person's good books, you need to be aware that a single unexpected 'negative' action on your part may be enough to see you moved into that person's bad books in the twinkling of an eye. People with autism find it difficult to view others in relative terms and are often unable to place variations in the behaviour of these others in their proper context. As a result, these variations are a source of great confusion for people with autism.

Another possible scenario is that the person with autism will attempt to define his model of Eddy more precisely. Eddy is good-natured, but not if the baby has kept him awake during the night. Eddy is funnier on Monday than on Tuesday. Eddy is optimistic about the future of the company up to and including the year 2043. As we saw earlier with sensory expectations, the model of Eddy will eventually become so specific that it will lead to more – many more – prediction errors, rather than fewer. It is possible that Eddy might be funnier on Tuesday than Monday. Or that he occasionally says something negative about the company's future. In this way, Eddy will increasingly become an unpredictable colleague for the person with autism. Empathic learning in people with autism, especially amongst those who are highly gifted, often results in an empathic model that is so precise and so detailed that it is unusable in any practical sense. So although people with autism are certainly capable of empathic learning, it needs to be borne in mind that their empathic models are absolute, rather than relative and context-sensitive.

❝The manner in which people with autism deal with prediction errors in the sensory world is also reflected in their approach to prediction errors in the social world. Autistic brains respond to

prediction errors absolutely and do not adjust the importance
they attach to these errors to take account of the context.**"**

Because people with autism deal absolutely with prediction errors, also when
making predictions in social situations, it is very hard for them to generalise. As far
as their brains are concerned, normal variations in the behaviour of other people
are prediction errors to which they need to devote attention. This means that for
them every social situation is a new situation, because no two social situations are
ever exactly the same. It takes a great deal of repetition and clarification before an
autistic brain can start to see certain similarities underlying the variations, so that
it can also start to predict (more or less) what is going to happen. Instead of trying
to teach people with autism new skills, what we really need to do is give them
more time to learn how to identify patterns of human behaviour in a context that
is relevant for them, including the most common variations in that behaviour.

In a nutshell:

- The social world is an open system. It is not possible to predict human
  behaviour on the basis of fixed and absolute laws and rules. People are
  even more unpredictable than bouncing tennis balls.
- That being said, it is still necessary to attempt to predict this behaviour, if
  we wish to respond quickly and effectively to others. Social interactions
  take place so rapidly that there is no time to first analyse the behaviour of
  others and then attempt to understand it.
- For this reason, the human brain has learnt how to unconsciously make
  use of context in order to make the social world more predictable.
  o   On the basis of context, we predict how people will move. This is
      useful to prevent us from constantly bumping into each other.
  o   On the basis of context, we guess what people are going to do and say.
      This is useful to avoid unpleasant surprises.
  o   On the basis of context, we estimate what other people want, think and
      feel. This is known as Theory of Mind, but is actually Prediction of Mind.
      It can be useful for tricking someone. Or for comforting someone.
- This predictive process largely takes place unconsciously. It is fast and intuitive.
  Conscious thought is scarcely involved. The predictions are not intended to
  be exact. They are simply expectations of what might happen.
- People with autism can also predict behaviour and mental states, such as
  emotions, but they are not able to do this quickly, intuitively and unconsciously. They need more time and, above all, more training and repetition.
- If it is pointed out to them, people with autism can also make use of context to predict human behaviour, but they have a tendency to approach
  the predictive process in absolute terms. They can learn social rules, but
  apply them very strictly. They also find it difficult to distinguish between
  what is important in the context and what is not important. The ability

to do this is necessary to be able to know if a social rule is applicable and whether or not you need to apply it.

- Ordinary variations in the behaviour and emotions of other people confuse people with autism. They give too much weight to these variations. This hinders their learning of flexible and generalisable empathic models.

- Because of their tendency to think absolutely, the social world is full of prediction errors for people with autism. Dealing with other people confuses them and costs them a great deal of energy. Social interaction is hard work for the autistic brain.

- We can support the social functioning of people with autism if we:
  o Press the context button, in order to clarify the context and the elements in it that are important.
  o Help them to learn how to deal with contextual variations in social rules and how people react in social situations.
  o Compensate for their reduced ability to predict human behaviour by making our own behaviour more predictable.

DID YOU KNOW?

It is easy to accept that subtle differences in facial expression can be ambiguous. After all, this is the basis of an argument that has been raging for centuries about Leonardo da Vinci's famous painting of 'Mona Lisa.' Is her smile sad? Or not? That being said, even the facial expressions of people who are experiencing powerful emotions can be misleading. This was amply demonstrated in an experiment conducted by the Israeli researcher Hillel Aviezer.[143] He showed his test subjects photographs of people who were either excessively proud and happy or else were extremely disappointed and sad. When the test subjects were only shown faces, it was almost impossible for them to say whether they were looking at a powerfully positive or powerfully negative emotion. Surprisingly, however, this was no longer a problem once they were able to see bodies instead of faces (which were covered in this second set of photos). Aviezer decided not to use the kind of photos that are normally used in experiments of this kind – which are primarily 'Ekman' photos, in which actors simulate emotions – but preferred instead to use photos from real life. And the real life setting he chose was... tennis! He used the facial expressions and body language of tennis players who had just either won or lost one of the most important games of their life. It looks as though tennis is slowly becoming the central theme in this book!

5 The predictive brain and communication

Believe it or not, the most commonly used metaphor for conducting a good conversation is… tennis! And indeed, in many respects a conversation is a bit like a game of tennis. Or that, at least, was the well-known opinion of Margery Wilson, a famous American author, actress and film director in the first half of the 20th century. After her film career, Wilson went on to specialise in coaching actors and actresses in pronunciation and communication skills.

According to her, a conversation, like a game of tennis, begins with a serve: a first someone says something or asks something. The intention is that someone else sees this serve and returns the ball back to where it came from: they say or ask something relevant in reply. Relevance is important: if you say something not relevant, it is like hitting the ball onto a different tennis court. In contrast to a real tennis game, it is not the intention that you should hit the ball where the other play cannot reach it. Instead, you want him (or her) to be able to reach it easily, so that he can hit it back to you again. A good conversation contains long rallies, where the ball is repeatedly hit back and forth in this same manner. What's more, there is no winner or loser. Like a good and exciting game of tennis, the real winner is tennis itself.

But if a conversation is really like a game of tennis, this means that the conversation partners will also require a good deal of predictive ability. Linguistic scientists have known this for decades. For example, since the 1980s it has been common knowledge that both talking and listening can only work well if people can anticipate what is going to be said. In short, processing language is largely a predictive activity.[144] This insight is now regarded as being so important that in 2015 the respected scientific journal *Cortex* devoted an entire issue to this very subject.

Once again, this means that the old computer-based metaphor for communication needs to be jettisoned. In this old model, communication was supposed to work as follows:

DOI: 10.4324/9781003340447-6

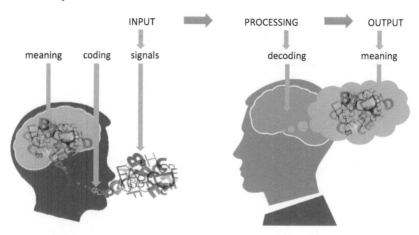

INPUT ➡ PROCESSING ➡ OUTPUT

meaning   coding   signals   decoding   meaning

But that is not how it works at all. In order to understand what someone is saying, we do not need to wait until all the external input has been received by our brain. Our processing of speech does not begin at the moment when someone comes to the end of a sentence or stops talking. Processing information in this way would be highly inefficient, especially in conversations. Conversations move forward at a fast pace and, in contrast to written communication, you cannot stop and look back at what has just been said.

> *'If a conversation is really like a game of tennis, this means that the conversation partners will also require a good deal of predictive ability.'*

During conversations we predict a number of different things:[145] whether or not someone will speak, when someone will speak, and what he or she will say. If we were not able to predict these things, we would never know when it is our turn to speak. Just as we would never know when to stop talking, once we have started. Most important of all, we would not immediately know what to say. Without predictions, the fluent back-and-forth transfer of information would be impossible. For example, if we cannot predict when someone is going to stop talking, conversations would be filled with long and uneasy silences. When the brain gets the signal that it is our turn to speak, it takes on average between 500 and 700 milliseconds – slightly more than half a second – before our mouth starts to form the necessary words. Various studies have shown that in natural conversation the time between the moment when one person stops talking and the other person starts talking is between 0 and 200 milliseconds.[146] This means that the gaps in conversation between each partner taking his/her turn to talk are shorter than the time it takes for our brain to activate our mouth for speech. This proves conclusively that we already know when our conversation partner is going to stop talking before he/she actually does it, which allows us to activate our speech processes before this moment arrives.

The cognitive linguistic scientist Jan P. de Ruiter has been fascinated for years by the rapid exchange of speech in natural conversations. He discovered that we know *when* someone's turn to speak will come to an end because we know *how* that turn will come to an end.[147] We can anticipate this moment of transfer because we know what the other person is going to say.

In other words, communicating and understanding language are both predictive activities, which work as follows:

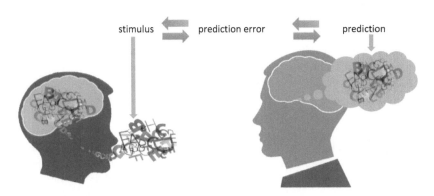

For example, you can see clearly that we have the ability to predict what people are going to say if you watch a conversation with someone who stutters. If the stutterer gets stuck on a word, the conversation partner will nearly always say the word for him or her, so that the conversation can get back on track. Similarly, we often finish the sentences of our conversation partners as a tactic for taking over the conversation and knocking the ball (tennis again!) back into their court:

He: 'Look, we've been sitting inside all day and I've been wrestling with this damned text on the predictive brain and autism for hours. What I really need…'

She: '… is a breath of fresh air. Good idea, but I haven't finished answering my mails yet. Let's say another ten minutes?'

Being able to predict what someone is going to say ensures that we are not continually confused by the imperfection of the sounds that reach our ears. When we are listening to someone speak, there are usually other sounds around as well. This means that our ears pick up a mixture of different sounds, some of which can overpower speech sounds, so that words or sentences are sometimes only partially heard. Fortunately, our predictions are usually able to fill in the gaps. Similarly, background noise and/or the huge variations in human pronunciation can also distort certain speech sounds or even whole words. For example, for some people a 'b' sounds like a 'p', whereas for others it is the other way around. Such distortions are not usually a problem in complete sentences, where you can predict what the person is trying to say, but it is not quite so easy when single words are spoken.

Once again, context plays an important role in all of this. A study conducted by Dutch researchers[148] discovered that context is crucial when people pronounce words unclearly or incompletely. The Dutch often have the habit when speaking in their dialects of truncating the ends of their words. For example, in the Dutch words *'eigenlijk,' 'moeilijk'* or *'vreselijk'* they hardly pronounce the *'-lijk'* sound, so that what people actually hear is *'eigek,' 'moeiek'* or *'vreesek,'* with the 'l'-sound being almost entirely absent. With the word *'natuurlijk,'* some Dutchmen and women take this shortening process a step further, so that the end result is something like *'tuuek.'* Even so, most people from different parts of the Netherlands still manage to understand each other most of the time, providing the shortened words form part of a context; in other words, a full sentence. Without this context, the word (or what is left of it) becomes unintelligible. Of course, similar examples can be found in almost every other language. Think, for example, of the Cockney pronunciation used in London: *'appen* instead of *happen; bruver* instead of *brother; nooze* instead of *news,* etc.

Perhaps surprisingly, the distortion or omission of sounds in words does not generally lead to prediction errors, although it can in some circumstances. Yet again, it is all dependent on the level of (un)certainty that the brain has about its own predictions. Research has shown that older people, even those with no loss of hearing, find it more difficult to correctly interpret shortened or mispronounced sounds or words that have been partially drowned out by background noise. As a result, they have to ask more frequently what someone has said. It seems that this might be due to a reduced inability to predict words as the brain gets older. This leads in turn to more prediction errors, which in a kind of snowball effect leads on to even greater predictive uncertainty. The predictions become therefore become less robust and less accurate, so that words are less easily recognisable when the quality of the component sounds is not optimal. This same lack of confidence and reduced predictive ability is something that you can also experience when attempting to communicate in a foreign language that you have not fully mastered.

> **❝**Being able to predict what someone is going to say ensures that we are not continually confused by the imperfection of the sounds that reach our ears.**❞**

On a few occasions I have had the pleasure of giving lectures to an Indian audience. Until 1947, India was a British colony. As a result, many Indians can still speak good English. But if their knowledge of the language is good, their pronunciation of it is sometimes, to say the least, 'atypical.' For example, they pronounce the English word 'tuition' as 'toosjun' instead of 'too-i-sjun.' For them, 'important' is 'impaartant,' while picture loses its 'c' to become 'piture.' On other occasions, they pronounce sounds that should not be pronounced, so that 'receipt,' which should be spoken as 'reciet' regains its 'p' when an

Indian is talking. Not surprisingly, when I get to question time at the end of my lectures, I often have to ask my questioners to repeat certain words (or sometimes even whole sentences) that I have not understood! However, I have noticed that my fellow-lecturers who come from English-speaking countries, like Australia, the United States or the United Kingdom, have far fewer problems in this respect. For them, the curious Indian way of speaking seems to hold few secrets. Why? Because English is their mother tongue, which means that they can better predict than I can what they are likely to expect. Because my knowledge of English is more limited, my brain has less confidence in its own predictions. Consequently, I attach greater weight to the sensory input of my ears, so that the Indian pronunciation of English words that I know leads to an increased number of prediction errors. And as I described in the chapter on sensory experiences, this process is one of interaction. Because the Indian pronunciation of many words is unknown and therefore unexpected for me, my brain becomes more uncertain when it needs to predict what am going to hear. After a while, this makes conversing with people who use a variant of standard English extremely exhausting for me. And I am not just talking about Indians. I can still remember my first taxi ride in Scotland, from the airport in Edinburgh to the town of Alloa, where I was doing a workshop. The taxi driver was one of those people who like to talk. And talk. And talk. In fact, he filled the entire 45-minute drive without me hardly having to say a word. Even so, by the end of the journey I was again exhausted. Although his talk was hardly rocket science – it was all football, the weather and the delights of Scotch whisky – trying to decipher his accent and dealing with the resulting prediction errors demanded huge amounts of energy from my brain (although he was right about the whisky!).

❝The fact that our brain predicts words does not mean that it knows exactly the words that other people will use. Just as in tennis a player does not know exactly where his opponent is going to hit the ball, but through prediction can seriously reduce the number of options.❞

At a congress in Singapore, a colleague and friend of mine, who also regularly conducts workshops in India, once told me that he no longer even noticed the curious Indian pronunciation of certain English words: the Indian variant of English had become part of the typical variation that his brain expected. This is similar to the situation in Belgium (and no doubt in other countries as well), where the different pronunciations in regional accents no longer lead to prediction errors, because over time they have become so familiar. Unless, of course, the pronunciation and its associated accent is particularly strong or obscure. In this way, for example Scousers from Liverpool often have trouble understanding Cockneys from London (and vice versa). In the Netherlands, people from Amsterdam still scratch their heads once people from Friesland start talking in dialect. And in Belgium everyone has problems with the West Flanders accent!

Our ability to predict does much more than simply allow us to recognise sounds and make them meaningful. Predicting what we are going to hear or read also makes it possible to quickly recognise entire words. When we hear the first sounds or read the first letters of a word, a super-fast rapid game of elimination takes place in the brain. If you hear or read a 'b,' you know that only the words starting with this letter are still in contention. Which, of course, is still a lot. If you then move on to 'ba,' you can reduce your list further. With 'bal,' yet further still. Eventually, you will work your way down to a very small number of possibilities from which to predict. Even so, this selection process involves a huge amount of work for the brain. So much so that the brain has developed a quicker and easier way of doing it. As a result, the brain can now recognise words *before* we have perceived all the relevant sounds and letters. And to make this mental *tour de force* possible, the brain makes use of its old ally: context. On the basis of context, a preselection of possible words is made.[149] Consider the following sentence: 'The clerk asked Emily to fill in her name and address. He handed her a pen and a sheet of pap...' Your brain is already thinking of 'paper' before you have heard or read the entire word. But in the sentence 'John likes his spaghetti spicy, so he always put in plenty of pap...' Your brain will quickly select 'paprika' as the best candidate.

Every word that we hear or read automatically limits the number of possible words that can follow it. This makes it possible to deal with the rapid flow of words that is inherent in communication. And it also saves the brain lots of work and energy. Studies involving eye tracking[150] have revealed that we read predictable words in a text faster than we read the unpredictable ones. In some circumstances, we even have a tendency to skip over predictable words. Which is only logical: why should the brain waste energy on things it already knows?

The fact that our brain predicts words does not mean that it knows exactly the words that other people will use. After all, we are not clairvoyants! Once again, however, the situation is not dissimilar to tennis. A tennis player never knows exactly where the ball travelling in his direction will arrive, but he can reduce the number of possibilities by selecting the most likely options. And it is the same when predicting language.

Karen: 'What did you eat at lunchtime?' *Tom:* 'It was delicious! I ordered...'

Of course, Karen has no idea what Tom will answer. If she did, it would be pointless to ask the question. But Karen knows what kind of words are likely to follow; above all, words that are associated with food. Karen's brain is therefore semi-prepared for what Tom will say. It is far more likely that he will use words like 'chicken' or 'salad' than words like 'tennis ball' or 'deckchair.'[151] Generally, we do not predict specific words; we predict categories of words.

And as we have seen on a number of occasions earlier in the book, this process is more a form of educated but unconscious guesswork than precise and conscious forecasting.

Brain research has shown that the brain can be surprised by unexpected twists and turns in language, and increases its level of activity as a result.[152] And again as we have already seen on a number of previous occasions, there are peaks in certain kinds of brain potential when prediction errors occur. For language and communication, these errors can be identified in the N400, which was discovered in 1980 by Marta Kutas and Steven Hillyard in their laboratory at the University of California.[153] The N400 is a negative wave on an EEG (electro-encephalogram) that is seen roughly 400 milliseconds after the start of a word that is not expected in the sentence in which it occurs.

People who took part in Kutas' research[154] were shown written sentences such as:

> Tourists in the Netherlands stare in amazement at the row upon row of dazzling colour. They wished that they could also live in a country where tulips are grown.

In this sentence, the word 'tulip' is an expected word. Sometimes, however, the participants were also shown sentences containing a word that was not expected, but was at least in the same 'floral' category:

> Tourists in the Netherlands stare in amazement at the row upon row of dazzling colour. They wished that they could also live in a country where roses are grown.

The word 'rose' belongs to a category you might expect – namely, flowers – but in the context of 'the Netherlands' and 'row upon row,' it is a word that we expect less or not at all.

Some participants were also shown sentences containing a word that was not expected from a category that was not expected:

> Tourists in the Netherlands stare in amazement at the row upon row of dazzling colour. They wished that they could also live in a country where palm trees are grown.

The N400 wave was most pronounced with this last kind of sentence, because this created the greatest level of surprise: the brain was expecting a word from the 'flower' category, but instead was confronted with a word from the 'tree' category. The N400 wave was lower when the word belonged to a category that was expected, as was the case with rose, because this generated a smaller and less dramatic prediction error.

Edward Wlotko and Kara Federmeier of the University of Illinois were interested to find out what might make the prediction of words in sentences easier or more difficult. With this in mind, they repeated Marta Kutas' experiment, but varied the speeds at which the words in the sentences were shown.[155] When the pauses between the words were longer, the peaks in the N400 were larger than when the words followed each other in rapid succession. These suggested that the brain needs more time to make its predictions accurately – although, of course, it needs to be remembered that we are talking here about fractions of a second, not seconds or minutes. One of the more remarkable results was noted when the test subjects who had first been through the slow version of the experiment were still surprised by unexpected words when they went through the fast version. On the basis of the first version, the brain had learnt that unexpected words would probably also appear in the second version. When the brain expects prediction errors, it moves into a higher gear to make its predictions. In this respect, the brain also predicts its own working: 'Watch out! Expect the unexpected!' The research findings of Wlotko and Federmeier provide strong evidence for the flexibility of the brain and its ability to adapt quickly to different contexts.

In various other studies,[156] the N400 reaction was investigated in people with autism. When children with autism, who were listening to a series of words for animals (cow, dog, bird, etc.), suddenly heard a word that did not belong to this category (table, car, house, etc.), their brains were less surprised than the brains of children without autism.[157] An experiment conducted by Judith Pijnacker and her colleagues at Radboud University in Nijmegen[158] concluded that in comparison to people without autism, the brains of people with autism were less surprised by unexpected words at the end of a sentence, such as 'The climbers finally reached the top of the tulip' or 'George wanted to go ice skating and so he caught the bus to the beach.' Correspondingly, the difference in the reaction in the N400 between predictable and unpredictable sentence endings was less great for people with autism than for people without autism, a finding that has also been confirmed by comparable studies.[159] This seems to suggest that people with autism make less use of the context of the sentence to predict how the sentence is likely to end. However, Pijnacker and her colleagues also reached another conclusion that was equally worthy of note. Although the N400 of people with autism was less active, the measurement of their brain potential – which is only activated at a slightly later stage[160] – indicated that unexpected words at the end of a sentence did, nevertheless, attract their attention. In other words, their brain only seemed to notice that a word is unexpected after it had been seen or heard. In other words, what we saw earlier in relation to human behaviour – first see, then believe – also seems to apply for language: first hear (or read), then process. This means that an autistic brain is capable of reacting to the unusual and the unpredictable, but is not so good at anticipating these things. The unpredictable first needs to happen, so that the brain can become aware of it, before it realises that something out of the ordinary has occurred. As was previously evident in connection with predictions in the social world, it is clear that fast, intuitive and unconscious predictions in relation to language and communication are not a strong point of people with autism. That being said, if they are given sufficient time and space for conscious processing, they are more than capable of using context to distinguish between the predictable and the unpredictable.

The fact that people with autism need more time to process language was also the conclusion of a research study carried out at the University of Southampton.[161] Predicting which words are likely is not done solely on the basis of the words we have already heard or read. When compiling a list of candidate words, we also take account of what we know about the world.

> To allow his player to practice returning balls with topspin, the tennis trainer decided to use a ball cannon. This cannon can fire off a total of 150 balls. At the end of the training session, the court was covered with ..... coloured balls.

In this sentence, there is no single word that limits or helps to specify the possibilities for the missing colour (represented by the dots). Only people with knowledge of tennis and the colour of balls traditionally used will be able to fill in the word after 'coloured.' Philippa Howard and her colleagues at Southampton wanted to know if the reduced capacity of the autistic brain to anticipate words was connected with a reduced sensitivity for the context of sentences or with a reduced ability to convert their knowledge of the world into predictions. To find this out, Howard asked her test subjects to read sentences like the ones below. During the reading, the research team tracked their eye movements and also the time it took them to complete the reading. Afterwards, the test subjects were questioned about the sentences they had read.

> Walter used a knife to chop the large carrots into pieces.
> Walter used an axe to chop the large carrots into pieces.
> Walter used a pump to blow up the large carrots.

Using a knife to chop up carrots is possible and also highly likely. Blowing up carrots with a pump is impossible. Using an axe to chop up carrots is also possible, but is less likely than using a knife. Processing the prediction error in this sentence demands a certain knowledge of cooking and the use of kitchen equipment. Moreover, the error is also more subtle than the obvious error with the pump. During the post-test question session, all the test subjects – both with and without autism – noticed that there was something wrong with this 'axe' sentence and also knew what it was. However, people with autism needed more time to read sentences of this kind, with possible but less likely combinations. The registration of eye movements revealed that people without autism hesitated when they came to the error in both the sentences with a possible but unlikely combination and the sentences with an impossible combination. In other words, they had immediately spotted the prediction error. In contrast, the people with autism did not hesitate but simply carried on reading. Once they had reached the end of the sentence, they went back to the beginning and read it again. This seems to suggest that during the first reading they sensed that something was wrong, but had insufficient confidence in their knowledge of the world and their resulting predictions to immediately notice the curious choice of words. Once again, this is very similar to something we have mentioned on more than one occasion earlier in the book: an autistic brain gives too little weight to its own predictions and seems to be less willing to trust itself in certain situations. It is only when it has all the necessary information and details that an autistic brain comes to the same conclusion as a non-autistic brain. This does not mean that people with autism are slower. It simply means that they are uncertain and want to check everything properly. And that takes time. This uncertainty among the test subjects with autism was also evident during the question session: several participants reported that they were anxious to answer questions about some of the sentences they had just read.

This is a strong argument in favour of giving people with autism more processing time when we are communicating with them. Such communication should be as relaxed and unhurried as possible. This is also one of the reasons why it is so often recommended to focus on visual forms of communication when interacting with people with autism: written texts, drawings, diagrams, photos, visual schedules such as a mindmap, etc. In contrast to spoken language, visual communication is not transient. Words disappear once they have been spoken; words on paper remain. This not only gives people with autism more processing time, but also allows them to look at the words more than once, if they feel the need to do so. Visual communication also places much less strain on the working memory, which is beneficial for people who are unable to process language and start making predictions until everything has been said or shown.

> **❝People with autism are not slower. They are (unconsciously) uncertain and want to check everything properly. And that takes time.❞**

Even so, it needs to be remembered that visual communication is only autism-friendly if people with autism are given sufficient processing time. Why? Because the difficulties experienced by people with autism when predicting what they are going to hear are also experienced when they need to predict what they are going to see.

Researchers at the University of Vermont[162] asked themselves whether the weak N400 recorded for people with autism when confronted with unexpected words and phrases would also apply in visual communication. To assess this, they decided to use the famous cartoon strips of *Peanuts*, with Charlie

Brown and his dog Snoopy, created and drawn by Charles Schulz. They used both a written and a drawn version of the strips. Here is one example:

> Charlie Brown taught Snoopy how to fetch. He threw a ball and Snoopy had to bring it back.
> By accident, Charlie Brown hit Snoopy with the ball.

Expected end to the story:

> Snoopy was angry and ran away from the ball.

Unexpected end to the story:

> Snoopy was angry and ran away from the wall.

Did you also have the idea that the last sentence was identical to the sentence with the expected end? Some people need to read the sentence twice to see that 'wall' is there, rather than the word you expect: 'ball.' This is proof of the predictive capability in language.

The results of the experiment showed that in both cases – with the written *and* the drawn version of the cartoon – the N400 for the unexpected ending was weaker in adults with autism than in adults without autism. Brazilian researchers noted comparable results in children with autism.[163] This demonstrates that people with autism are not only less proficient at predicting what they are going to hear or read, but also what they are going to see. Consequently, this means that with visual forms of communication or visually supported communication we also need to give people with autism more time to do their mental processing.

But if giving more time is necessary, it is not enough by itself to help people with autism communicate effectively. More time helps them to develop predictions about what will be said or shown, but this does not mean that these predictions will be correct. Because when processing language, the autistic brain once again has the tendency to view things in absolute terms and with insufficient context-sensitivity.

> *⁶This is a strong argument in favour of giving people with autism more processing time when we are communicating with them. Such communication should be as relaxed and unhurried as possible.⁹*

Imagine that you are watching a documentary about the day-to-day life of top players in the tennis world. You see Serena Williams sitting at a breakfast table. The voice of the commentator says: 'After her breakfast, it is time for Serena to do some condition training. She picks up a towel and her swimming costume and sets off for...' Before the commentator has spoken the next words, you know that he will say 'swimming pool' and not 'tennis court.'

Although the sight of Serena will have activated the 'tennis' category of words in your brain, so that you are initially primed to expect words from this category to be used, in the above example your brain will nonetheless predict words that have nothing to do with tennis, because this is what the circumstances strongly suggest. In other words, your brain is able to flexibly adjust its predictions to take account of the context. People with autism are less talented at this.

Context-sensitive anticipation is particularly important in language processing, because most words do not have a single fixed meaning. For example, the word 'root' can have the following different meanings:

- The part of a plant under the ground ('the roots of the tree go very deep').
- The part of a tooth in the gum socket ('the dentist said he needed root canal treatment').
- The cause of something ('money is the root of all evil').
- A quantity taken an indicated number of times as an equal factor ('2 is the fourth root of 16').
- A person's origin ('his family's roots are in Italy').

This phenomenon is known as polysemy, a word with a Greek root(!), derived from *poly* meaning 'many' and *sema* meaning 'sign.' When we attempt to anticipate during the processing of language, it is not enough simply to predict a word or category of words; we also need to select the most likely meaning of the word in relation to the given context from the many possible meanings it can have. Once again, this is not something we know consciously and with precision; it is a fast and unconscious 'best guess.' This means that when you hear the question 'Helen, have you found the root yet?' in a maths lesson, you will have a different 'root' in mind than if you were to hear the same question in a dentistry or biology lesson.

Getting to grips with polysemy is a hard nut for an autistic brain to crack. People with autism, providing they do not have an intellectual impairment, are perfectly capable of learning the meanings of words. Their vocabulary is just as large as people without autism and might even be larger, if they have a particular interest in language and literature. In other words, it is not the number of words that causes people with autism problems; it is the different meanings that those words can have. In this respect, one of the most ambiguous and serious challenges for people whose brains are less context-sensitive is presented by homonyms and homographs. Homonyms are words that sound the same but are spelt and written differently; for example, 'write' and 'right.' Homographs are words that look the same and are spelt the same, but mean something different; for example, the noun 'lead' (a heavy metal) and the verb 'lead' (to show the way). In normal circumstances, the context of the sentence will suggest how you should pronounce a homograph. However, research has shown that if a homograph occurs at the start of a sentence, people make more mistakes than if it occurs at the end of the sentence: "'Lead is dangerous. Lead me to the lead mine!" he ordered.'

❛It is not the number of words that causes people with autism problems; it is the different meanings that those words can have.❜

Different studies[164] have shown that people with autism, even those who are highly gifted, have difficulty in normal circumstances finding the right pronunciation for homographs. But if you press the context button, so that their context-sensitivity is activated, they perform just as well as people without autism. In this respect, Canadian researchers[165] were able to establish that children with autism were able to correctly pronounce homographs when they were preceded by a so-called 'prime.' A prime is a word that is related to one of the meanings of a homograph and therefore serves as a precursor to its meaning and pronunciation. For example, 'near' and 'shut' are both primes for the different meanings of the homograph 'close.' When a prime was used in the Canadian experiment, children with autism pronounced a series of homographs with the same level of accuracy as children without autism. In a second phase, the children were shown the same homographs again, but this time with a different prime for a different meaning. On this occasion, the children with autism made more mistakes than their non-autistic counterparts. It was almost as if the children with autism had remained 'locked' in the first meaning that they had been primed to choose and were unable to adjust to the next context suggested by the new prime.

This fixation on the first-learnt or dominant connection is something that is often seen in people with autism. As a rule, they do not have many problems with the dominant and (for them) most obvious meanings of words. In fact, it is something they generally do very well. It is the spontaneous and flexible adjustment of meanings to match contexts that really gives them trouble. Rhonda Booth and Francesca Happé[166] asked groups of people with and without autism to complete sentences like the following:

The sea tastes of salt and ...
You can go hunting with a knife and ...
The night was black and ...

In contrast to the people without autism, the people with autism often fell into the trap of relying on what they had learnt as their dominant connections, so that they failed to take account of the context. As a result, they filled in the sentences as follows:

The sea tastes of salt and pepper.
You can go hunting with a knife and fork.
The night was black and white.

Learned meanings and linguistic connections would therefore seem to be fixed and absolute in an autistic brain, which is less context-sensitive.

However, this is by no means a new discovery. More than 75 years ago, Leo Kanner already noted in children with autism the steadfast linking of meanings to words and the poor flexibility in handling those links. In his pioneering article published in 1943, Kanner wrote about John, one of the 11 children he was trying to help: 'His father said something about pictures they have at home on the wall. This disturbed John somewhat. He corrected his father: "We have them near the wall." ('on' apparently meaning to him 'above' or 'on top of').' John clearly applied the meaning of the word 'on' absolutely. The fact that 'on' can also mean 'against' or 'in contact with' was something that his brain could not accept. Similarly, when Kanner asked Donald, another of the 11 children, in a non-specific way to put something down, he immediately put whatever it was on the floor – and not on a desk or in a cupboard or somewhere else – because the only meaning he had learnt for the words 'put it down' was 'on the floor.'

This kind of absolute association of meanings with words leads to much confusion in the communication of people with autism. For most people, the verb 'to climb' can be used both for 'climb up' and 'climb down,' but this is a difficult distinction for people with autism to make. When an Irish mother saw that her autistic son had made his way right to the very top of a tall tree, she shouted to him to climb down at once. He replied that what she asked was impossible: for him climbing only meant one way, and that way was 'up.' In his mind, coming down by climbing was therefore a logical absurdity.

Here is a further example. 'Work' is another word that has many different meanings. When a psychologist says that he will 'work with you' to solve whatever problem you might be having, most people immediately know that what he means is talking together during your consultation sessions until the problem is resolved. This meaning is made clear by the context in which it is given: a conversation in the psychologist's therapy room. But this is not quite so evident for people with autism – like Robin. When he was told by a psychologist that they would work together, he completely failed to understand the context and so asked the psychologist: 'And what clothes will I need to wear?' Robin associated 'work' with physical labour, of the kind he was used to in the factory where he was employed and where he always needed to wear overalls and a safety helmet. It did not occur to him that this might seem out of place in a psychologist's office!

This kind of absolute thinking – the application of fixed associations in all circumstances – is not always easy to notice in people with autism. It can be easier if you know the nature of a person's first experience with a particular word – and that is true in almost every language in the world.

In some parts of Belgium close to the French border, a number of French words have been absorbed into the local Flemish language. One such word is *chapeau*, which in France is the word for 'hat,' but in Flanders is used as a congratulatory term to express 'well done' or, if you prefer, 'hats off!' Not a problem in most circumstances, you might think. But that was not the case for one young boy, who was asked to write down the translated names of articles of clothing as part of a French test! Alongside the word *chapeau* he wrote down 'well done.' When the amused teacher was later correcting the tests, she immediately realised what had happened. She often used the word *chapeau* in the Flemish sense of the word to praise her pupils when they had done something well. And this was now the context with which her autistic pupil now most associated the word. He had simply been unable to adjust this meaning flexibly to the different context of the French test. Fortunately, the teacher decided not to deduct a mark for this unintentional error.

After the statement by a classmate that she 'learnt her lesson,' a student with autism asked, 'And what did you do wrong?' But, in fact, the girl meant literally that she had learnt her lesson.

In these anecdotes, the people with autism do the opposite of what you might normally expect of them: they do *not* take something literally, when that is precisely what the context demands. Such anecdotes are further proof that the problem is not a tendency to take things literally, but rather their inability to free themselves from their dominant or first-learnt associations when the context requires it. Their approach to the meaning of words is therefore absolute and not contextual. It was to deal with situations of this kind that the cognitive psychologist George Miller introduced the term 'contextual representation.' Contextual representation is the capacity when predicting words to estimate the likelihood of different word meanings in relation to the given context. This means that you do not make a fixed single connection between a word and its meaning, but attach different meanings to a single word and then predict the most appropriate of these many meanings to match the context in which the word is used. You know, for example, that the word 'miss' will mean something different when you are talking about a train than when you are talking about a rifle range. People who are less context-sensitive – as is usually the case for people with autism – will more frequently understand things a-contextually. Like the rifle-shooting man who was going away on a business trip and was asked by his wife 'Will you miss me?' To which he replied: 'I sure as hell won't – if I ever get the chance…'

Sometimes you need to have an intuitive feel for autistic thinking if you want to recognise the more subtle examples of the absolutist approach that people with autism use when processing language. Rory Hoy, a popular British DJ, once made an amusing video about his own autism: *Autism & Me*. One of the stories he told was about a school test in which the teacher told the class: 'Write down on a sheet of paper the days of the week.' So Rory did exactly what he was asked. When the teacher marked the test, he was surprised to see that Rory's sheet bore no more than the words 'the days of the week'! 'Of course,' said Rory, 'all my other classmates had written down Monday, Tuesday, Wednesday, Thursday, Friday, Saturday, Sunday, etc.' I often show this video during lectures and courses, but most people fail to notice Rory's tiny addition of 'etc.' From a linguistic perspective, that 'etc.' is not necessary.

We use 'etc.' – an abbreviation for *et cetera*, which is Latin for 'and the rest' – when we do not want to mention all the individual elements of a collection. For example: 'Ball sports are sports like, football, volleyball, tennis, cricket, etc.' But Rory's summary of the days of the week is complete: he has listed all seven. As a result, the 'etc.' is surplus to requirements. It seems that in this instance Rory's brain relied on an absolute association: 'summaries are concluded with etc.'

Fortunately, absolute thinking can sometimes lead to amusing situations. Like this one. A pupil and a teacher are playing a game of one-on-one basketball on the school playground. The pupil scores a basket. 'Well done!' says the teacher. 'You shouldn't say that,' says the pupil angrily. 'Why on earth not?' asks the teacher. 'Because I am your opponent. And you shouldn't support your opponent.'

Or what about this? A man enters a cafeteria just before six o'clock in the evening. The cafeteria is a social project, operated by people with special needs. The man walks up to the counter and asks the young woman who is standing behind it: 'Are you still open?' The woman, who has autism, replies: 'Yes.' The man sits down at an empty table, waits for a minute or two, and then returns to the counter. 'Can I order something, please?' 'No,' says the woman. 'Why not?' says the man. 'Because we are closed.' She turns and points to a notice on the wall: 'Hours of opening: 09.00 to 18.00.' The clock next to the notice shows one minute past six...

In a nutshell:

- In order to communicate effectively, the brain needs to make numerous predictions: is someone going to say something, what are they going to say, when will it be my turn to say something, etc.?
- Once again, making such predictions is not an exact science. We do not know precisely what someone is going to say, but we estimate what will probably be said or shown on the basis of the context.
- Because we can make these predictions, we are less troubled by the distortion of speech sounds in noisy situations or when someone pronounces words differently from what we are used to.
- These predictions also make it possible to answer a question directly or to respond almost instantly to what someone has said. Likewise, they allow us to read fluently, without the need to devote attention to each individual word.
- When our conversation partners use unusual turns of phrase or unexpected words, prediction errors will result. We are surprised by what has been said. People with autism are less surprised, which suggests that they make fewer predictions when communicating.
- When an autistic brain does predict and expects something in communication, it has a tendency to rely on the first or most dominant meaning it has learnt. An autistic brain applies these meanings absolutely and finds it difficult to anticipate different meanings that would allow it to select the most likely meaning in the context, especially when it is not easy to discern.

• That being said, at times the autistic brain is nevertheless able to free itself from its absolute approach and can show flexibility in language and communication, but only if we press the context button and give people with autism sufficient time to respond. In these circumstances, the autistic brain will need to think consciously, whereas a non-autistic brain works quickly, unconsciously and intuitively.

DID YOU KNOW?

Prediction errors don't always have to be serious. Sometimes they can make us laugh.[167] In fact, a great deal of humour, certainly in language, is a result of these errors. For example, many jokes have an AAB structure:[168] two or more similar elements, and then a third but very different element, to serve as a counterpoint. In a series of As, B suddenly makes a prediction error that causes everyone else amusement. In a joke, this is often referred to as the 'punchline,' the unexpected twist in the storyline that makes it funny.

Psychologist Richard Wiseman asked more than a million and a half people to assess thousands and thousands of jokes. The following was selected as the winner, the best joke in the world:

> Two hunters are out in the woods when one of them collapses. He doesn't seem to be breathing and his eyes are glazed. The other guy whips out his phone and calls the emergency services. He gasps, 'My friend is dead! What can I do?' The operator says, 'Calm down. I can help. First, let's make sure he's dead.' There is a silence; then a gunshot is heard. Back on the phone, the guy says, 'OK, now what?'

Scientists think that this very unexpected twist – a serious prediction error, if ever there was one! – is the reason why so many people find this funny. The unexpected often makes us laugh.

The following sentences, as they stand, are not particularly funny:

Pat Cash about Lleyton Hewitt: 'His two greatest strengths are his legs.'
Interviewer: 'What is Pete Sampras' weakness?'
Andre Agassi to Andy Roddick: 'Let's see what you've got, big boy.'

What you don't expect – and what (hopefully) makes them funny – is the way these sentences continue or are answered:

Pat Cash about Lleyton Hewitt: 'His two greatest strengths are his legs, his speed, his agility and his competitiveness.' (Four things!)
Interviewer: 'What is Pete Sampras' weakness?' Michael Chang: 'He can't cook.'
Andre Agassi to Andy Roddick: 'Let's see what you've got, big boy.' Roddick: 'Hair.' (By then, Agassi was bald!)

An inability to predict accurately can also lead to humour. Anyone who has a smartphone with an auto-prediction and spelling correction function will know exactly what I mean. One of my grandchildren is called Ciriel. To begin with, my smartphone always wanted to correct this to 'cirkel,' the Dutch word for 'circle.' You will have to take my word for it that in Dutch this often led to amusing WhatsApp exchanges, along the lines of: 'Here you can see Circle, going round the class to hand out cupcakes on his birthday!' Not so smart of my smartphone, if you ask me! If you like this kind of thing, you can now find countless amusing auto-corrections on the internet

6 The predictive brain and autism

What now?

Like every other brain, the autistic brain does its very best to anticipate what is likely to happen, both to it and to the body it controls. However, it is not as good at performing this task as a non-autistic brain. It requires more time and more conscious thought before it can make its predictions. It also has less confidence in its own predictive powers, as a result of which it gives far too much attention to all kinds of sensory information that a non-autistic brain ignores, because it knows that these stimuli are not relevant for its models of the world. In contrast, an autistic brain gets bogged down in absolute, over-precise and overspecific models of the world. This leads autistic brains to make more prediction errors, to which they then need to devote even more thought and effort.

> *‘Like every other brain, the autistic brain does its very best to anticipate what is likely to happen, both to it and to the body it controls.’*

An autistic brain is confronted with a world that is far more VUCA – volatile, uncertain, complex and ambiguous – than it is for the brains of people without autism. People with autism therefore live in a world that for them is highly uncertain.

In recent articles and presentations about autism, you increasingly read and hear the term ‘intolerance of uncertainty.’[169] I am still in two minds about this term. The word ‘intolerance’ is used here in the same sense as it is used in terms like lactose-intolerance or nut-intolerance. In this medical context, the word ‘intolerance’ refers to a bodily reaction to a particular component of food. The word is also more generally used to describe a negative reaction to situations, opinions or people, as in phrases like ‘intolerance towards people of a non-average sexual orientation.’ An intolerance for uncertainty, as is the case for people with autism, belongs in the first category, but not in the second. It is possible that a misconception could be created that people with autism have a particular dislike or

DOI: 10.4324/9781003340447-7

even hate for uncertainty. As far as I am concerned, this is not the case. In my opinion, people with autism fundamentally have no greater hatred for uncertainty than the rest of the population. Surely we all prefer certainty to uncertainty? For people with autism, it is their different way of thinking that leads them to experience far *more* uncertainty than others, but this is not the same as saying they dislike or hate uncertainty any more than anyone else. For this reason, I am not a big fan of 'intolerance for uncertainty.' Instead, I prefer the term 'uncertainty stress.'.When your brain finds it difficult to predict the world and deals in an absolute manner with all the countless trivial variation in that world, your brain is confronted time after time after time with prediction errors. If that doesn't make you uncertain and stressed...

Whichever term we choose to use, various studies have now shown that uncertainty makes people anxious, even afraid.[170] And we also know that anxiety and depression are never far away for people with autism. The likelihood that they will experience mental health problems is significantly greater than for people without autism. If we wish to reduce this likelihood, we will have to do more than is currently the case to create a world that is safer, more certain and more predictable. In the well-known pyramid of human needs, first developed by the American clinical psychologist Abraham Maslow, safety is the second most basic of these needs, preceded only by the satisfaction of physiological needs (food, drink, sex, etc.). There is no reason to assume that this pyramid applies less or differently to people with autism. Perhaps their brain works in a different way, but their fundamental needs are the same as those for people without autism. This, of course, is only logical: people with autism are also people.

You often hear it said that people with autism have a greater need for predictability than people without autism. I do not agree. The needs of people with autism are human, and therefore no different from anyone else's. There is certainly a difference between different people with regard to the strength of their need for certainty and predictability, but in my opinion autism is not the cause of that difference. I have two children and there is a huge disparity between their respective needs for certainty and predictability – and neither of them has autism. I have also seen similarly large variations in the need for certainty and predictability in the many people with autism whom I have met during the past 35 years. Conclusion: people with autism do not have a greater need for certainty and predictability than people without autism.

‘People with autism live in a world that for them is highly uncertain.’

What is different is this: the brains of people with autism are less able to make the world predictable and therefore are also unable to reduce the number of prediction errors they make. That is why others need to make the world more predictable for them. We can significantly improve the quality of life for people with autism by offering them greater certainty, clarity and predictability or by giving them the necessary time to adjust their mental models of the world in such a way that their number of prediction errors is drastically reduced. Because that is the most important task of the human brain: minimising prediction errors.

Another of the things you often hear said today is that being 'autism-friendly' means creating a stimulus-free or at least a low-stimulation environment. This one-liner is a massive oversimplification of what autism-friendliness really involves. As we saw earlier in the book, the important thing is not to reduce the number of stimuli, but to control their flow in a predictable and controllable sensory environment. But if one-liners are the only way to encourage people to greater autism-friendliness, I would suggest the following: autism-friendliness is 90% certainty and predictability, and 10% good, old-fashioned friendliness. It should also be remembered that offering certainty and predictability requires almost no time and no effort. You don't need to follow an expensive training course to be able to do it. In fact, anyone can do it. And you can do it anywhere. What's more, it benefits everyone, and not just people with autism.

There is no doubt that offering predictability and certainty to people with autism can enhance their quality of life. More certainty means less stress. Less stress means more resilience to deal with an increasingly VUCA world. In addition, less stress through more certainty also makes it possible for people with autism to develop and thrive. When we feel comfortable and safe, we are able to blossom.[171] We are also more open to new things and new challenges, allowing us to learn more and more. And the more a person with autism is able to learn, the better the internal models in his/her brain will become, making it easier to predict the world with greater accuracy and flexibility. In life, it is feeling good that leads to success, and not the other way around.[172] And that applies equally to success in predicting the vagaries of the world.

I already discussed this point briefly in the chapter on sensory problems in autism, but I want to emphasise again that working to improve the well-being and self-esteem of people with autism is the first key step in improving their predictive ability. People who feel good about themselves are better able to cope with unexpected turns of events and have less need of absolute and overspecific models of the world. For everyone who wants to 'tinker' with autism or to 'treat' it, I have the following message: start by trying to improve the 'feel good' factor in the lives of the people with autism with whom you live and work. People with autism who are feeling good display fewer of the characteristics of autism. Are you flexible, sociable and communicative on days when you are feeling rotten? No? Well, people with autism are no different. An autistic brain that feels good has fewer problems with the 'intolerance of uncertainty.' Well-being is the best remedy there is against uncertainty stress.

In my own practice, I decided some years ago to resolutely play the 'well-being' card in all my interactions with people with autism.[173] No more social skills training, no more interventions that are designed to compensate for autistic 'shortcomings.' I am not saying that people with autism do not need to learn (social) skills. We all need to do that. But learning these skills will only be successful when we have the necessary space inside our head and the necessary energy in our body. And that can only happen when you are feeling good.

When, in my first book, I characterised autism as a reduced ability to think coherently, I was immediately asked by numerous people: so how exactly can you improve the coherence of people with autism?

After the publication of my second book on autistic thinking – the title was *Autism as context blindness* – the most frequently asked question was: so how exactly can you improve the context-sensitivity of people with autism?

As soon as this book appears, I predict that the most popular question will be: so how exactly can you improve the predictive capacity of people with autism? If you have read the previous pages carefully, you will already know my answer: first help them to feel good, in the first place about themselves.

> ‘*You often hear it said that people with autism have a greater need for predictability than people without autism. I do not agree. The needs of people with autism are human, and therefore no different from anyone else's.*’

Of course, to increase the opportunities for people with autism to lead a successful and meaningful life takes more than just a good feeling. So what else is required?

This book has been devoted almost in its entirety to the difficulties experienced by autistic brains when it comes to making predictions and the absolute way in which they deal with such predictions and the resulting prediction errors. If you want, you can see this as a shortcoming, a limitation or even a disorder. But that would be a very one-dimensional approach. The different way of thinking that typifies an autistic brain is just one of the many different expressions of neurodiversity. There is no such thing as an ordinary, average or normal brain. It simply does not exist, being no more than a statistical construction. No one has a brain that falls exactly in the middle for all the many different measurements of all the many different functions of the brain. Brains come in many different varieties and autism is just one of those varieties. And although it can be sometimes hard to find your way through life with such a brain, absolute thinking nevertheless also has its positive side.

In my very first book about autistic thinking – *This is the title* (1996) – I added a table (p. 112) which made a comparison between the respective strong points of people with and without autism. Since then, this table has undergone many transformations and has been used by numerous other authors and organisations. For nostalgia's sake, I reproduce it in its original form below:

Strong points of people with autism	Strong points of people without autism
Understand things literally	*Understand the sense of things*
Analytical thinking	Integrated thinking
An eye for detail	*An eye for the bigger picture*
Serial processing of information	Parallel processing of information
Dealing with concrete matters	*Dealing with abstract matters*
Dealing with formal, logical rules	Dealing with illogical things
Living according to the rules	Living between the lines of the rules
Facts	*Ideas*
Laws	Exceptions to laws
Images	*Imagination*
Calculating	Intuitive
Similarities	Analogies
Absolute	Relative
Objectivity	Subjectivity
Straightforward, honest	Difficult to pin down: lying and cheating
Perfectionism	Flexibility
Exterior	*Interior*
Deductive reasoning	Inductive reasoning

If I were to remake this list today, there are some things I would formulate differently and other things I would leave out altogether. These are the things marked in italics. We are now a quarter of a century further on and during that intervening period we have learnt a lot about the autistic brain. For example, we now know that people with autism do not always have an excellent eye for detail and that gifted people with autism find it harder to deal with concrete matters than with abstract ones. That being said, the majority of things have remained the same. What does surprise me, however, is that even back then I was already referring to autistic thinking as 'absolute.' There is nothing new under the sun…

Absolute thinking does have its benefits, which is why I included it as a strong point back in 1996. To survive in a world that is full of noise and constantly changing meanings, the ability to make context-sensitive, intuitive and super-fast predictions is of vital importance. But this contextual guessing does not always work in your favour. Sometimes it can lead to mistakes.

This was discovered as long ago as the 1970s by Daniel Kahneman, the man with whom we started this book. Together with his former colleague, Amos Tversky,[174] Kahneman investigated how people make decisions in situations where the outcome is uncertain. Like in the following scenario:

Imagine: you have 50 dollars. You must choose between two options:
A. *You make a bet. There is a 60% chance that you will keep your 50 dollars and a 40% chance that you will lose it.*
B. *You do not make a bet but opt for the certainty of keeping 20 dollars.*

Tversky and Kahneman also offered a second variant to their test subjects:

> *Imagine:* you have 50 dollars. You must choose between two options:
> A. *You make a bet. There is a 60% chance that you will keep your 50 dollars and a 40% chance that you will lose it.*
> B. *You do not make a bet but opt for the certainty of losing 30 dollars.*

Of course, in both situations the outcome is exactly the same. But option B is formulated differently. In the second scenario, the formulation is based on a perspective of money loss, whereas in the first scenario the perspective is one of money retention. No matter how strange it might seem, when faced with these two situations, the majority chose option B in the first scenario and option A in the second scenario. This showed that people are less rational than they think. They choose certainty when there is a prospect of gain or retention. But because loss hurts more than gain, they choose uncertainty when there is a prospect of possible loss, even though the chances of loss and gain, viewed objectively, are exactly the same. In the investment business, where profit and loss are the name of the game, this was big and important news – and one of the reasons why Kahneman's research won him the Nobel Prize for Economics in 2002.

British researchers[175] later carried out a variant of this experiment, using groups of more able people with and without autism. As in the original Tversky and Kahneman study, the majority of the test subjects without autism made different A/B choices in the different scenarios. When the prospect of loss was proposed, they preferred to gamble, significantly more than when the prospect of partial retention or gain was proposed. However, this contextual effect was far less evident among the group with autism: in both scenarios the majority opted for certainty in preference to taking a gamble. Moreover – and in contrast to the participants without autism – there was no difference in their emotional reaction to the different scenarios, as measured by skin conductance measurement. This study therefore showed that people with autism are often much more logical, consistent and rational when it comes to making decisions. Or to express it in slightly different terms: logical thinking, where it is beneficial not to be distracted or deceived by many different kinds of variable and contextual factors, is something that people with autism do well. In fact, it is one of the characteristics of people with autism that is most widely noticed and admired. True, to survive in a VUCA world it is often better to rely on fast, unconscious and context-sensitive guessing than on logical and rational thinking, but this does not detract from the fact that there are other situations in which the sober, logical and rational approach works best. So if you are faced with a situation of the latter kind, it is better to ask the advice of someone with autism.

‘People with autism are often much more logical, consistent and rational when it comes to making decisions.’

What people without autism refer to as 'noise,' 'interference' or 'random variation,' to which they generally devote no attention, is interpreted by an absolute brain as serious prediction errors. And as we have seen throughout this book, this leads to a number of difficulties for people with autism, such as sensory hyperreactivity and generalisation problems. Once again, however, the tendency to always identify prediction errors instead of mentally 'brushing them under the carpet' can be useful in performing many different tasks, where chance variations, however minor, can be important and do need to be taken seriously. Think, for example, of software testing or quality control functions, or the proofreading of texts. In tasks of this kind, which demand high levels of attentiveness and accuracy, people with autism are often far superior to their non-autistic colleagues. This is one of the reasons why Brussels Airport employs autistic people to carry out security checks, where conscientious attention to detail and giving weight to prediction errors can quite literally be a matter of life and death. Instead of relying on the prediction based on the experience that forbidden items are rare, an autistic brain that gives more weight to sensory input than on its own predictions will treat every suitcase as a new experience. It will scan every suitcase like it's the very first time it has to scan suitcases. This makes the autistic brain less vulnerable to overlooking forbidden items than a non-autistic brain. Of course, we should not be blind to the fact that it remains a challenge to find a proper place for absolute thinking in today's society where it can prove its worth, but as we have already mentioned, it takes all kinds of brains to make a world and all are equally valuable.[176]

Autistic brains are less good at predicting human behaviour. This has its disadvantages and makes social interaction a stressful challenge. But – as you have probably already guessed! – even this can have its advantages. The autistic principle of 'first see, then believe' means that people with autism are far less inclined to make a priori assumptions about people than people without autism. An a priori assumption is, of course, just another way of saying 'bias': the tendency to judge or expect that a person is going to behave in a particular manner, before you have seen the person in question do anything to support your supposition. Not that there is anything wrong per se with bias or assumptions: they are both the product of the predictive brain just doing its work. Your brain has models about other people and uses them to generate expectations about their behaviour. Assumptions help to make other people and their actions predictable. Even so, this can lead to problems when your assumptions are wrong or your model is not accurate enough. In the first chapter we saw how a predictive brain adjusts and updates its models when the facts contradict its predictions (prediction errors). However, we also saw that while people without autism generally have a tendency to give more weight to their own models when striking the right balance between these models and sensory data, people with autism have a tendency to do the opposite: they attach greater weight to the input they receive from the various senses. As a result, people with autism have less confidence in their own expectations, whereas people with autism perhaps have too much. This means in turn that people without autism are inclined to devote their attention primarily to information that confirms their own ideas and predictions.[177] They are less open to information that challenges or undermines their thinking. When this happens, their expectations can actually become a limiting factor in their dealings with others.

This is not the case for people with autism. If they make fewer a priori assumptions, so that they only reach conclusions after they have seen a person's behaviour, this means that they are less likely to pin particular labels on people that may not necessarily be accurate. They 'lock' other people less in assumptions and do not fill in your behaviour in advance. Because of this, you are given a more honest chance to be who you are and to do what you want to do. In short, people with autism are less prone to making stereotypical and biased judgements about others. And although I am not aware of any scientific research to confirm this, it is also my experience that people with autism are less likely to impose their assumptions and expectations on others. This is evident, for example, in their communication. They will almost never try to complete someone else's sentence, because their lack of confidence in their predictive ability means that they have to wait to hear what is said, rather than trying to guess what will be said. In some circumstances, this makes them much better listeners than people without autism. And, in my opinion, they are also better observers. Why? Because an autistic brain has a tendency to give more weight to sensory data and will therefore perceive what someone else says or does more objectively, more accurately and with fewer preconceptions.

Will the insights that I have written in this book contribute towards an improvement in the quality of life for people with autism? That I cannot say: the predictive powers of my brain, sadly, do not stretch that far. But if I cannot predict, at least I can hope. And dream. What's more, you can also help to realise that dream of making the world a more autism-friendly place. You have already made a good start by reading my book right through to the end, for which you have my heartfelt thanks. How you take things further from here is up to you.

Notes

1. Pellicano & Burr (2012).
2. The brain predicts, corrects and re-predicts throughout the entire day. Column by Heleen Slagter in *Trouw* on 1 February 2020.
3. To immediately give an example of where and how I have simplified things: Bayesian logic plays a prominent role in the story of the predictive brain, but I have chosen not to explain this kind of logic in this book, nor have I used it in my explanation of how a brain works.
4. For computer-nerds: when I say that the computer is a bad metaphor for the brain, I am talking about computers that process information on the basis of rules and algorithms programmed by people. At the present time, more and more use is being made of machine learning, which attempts to imitate the functioning of the human brain. Like the working of the brain, machine learning is based on evolving cycles of predictions and the processing of prediction errors, so that the programme improves (itself) step by step by evaluating the outcomes of its own predictions.
5. If you really want to know: 108,000 kilometres per hour.
6. I can strongly recommend his book: Kahneman, D. (2011). *Thinking, fast and slow*
7. For the work of Wuhazet – Henryk Żychowski, https://commons.wikimedia.org/w/index. php?curid=11910967
8. Frith (2007).
9. Anil Seth: Your brain hallucinates your conscious reality. TED Talk, April 2017. Seth: 'And when we agree about our hallucinations, that is what we call "reality."' https://www.ted.com/talks/anil_seth_your_brain_hallucinates_your_conscious_reality
10. The illustration is based on the work of cmglee, hong227, used on the Wikipedia page about the Hollow-Face illusion, where you can see an animated version: https://en.wikipedia.org/wiki/Hollow-Face_illusion If you want to experience another dynamic version of this illusion, using Charlie Chaplin, check out the following video: http://www.richardgregory.org/experiments/video/chaplin.htm
11. Van den Hurk, Van Baelen, & de Beeck (2017).
12. Barrett (2017b).
13. Brain scientists borrowed the term 'predictive coding' from communication engineers. In the 1950s, these engineers were searching for ways to limit the amount of information that communication devices could transmit and receive to the absolute minimum of what was essential. One of the conclusions they reached was that if only the discrepancies were transmitted/received instead of all data, this would significantly reduce the burden on the communications network. This is exactly what the human brain does: it does not process all data; it only processes prediction errors or discrepancies between its expectations and incoming data.
14. This limited technical explanation is a gross simplification of a complex interaction of processes that takes place with regard to the brain's management of its own functions, which involves both chemical and electrical activity.

15. Scientists refer to this as the free energy principle, first developed by Karl Friston at University College, London. The free energy principle explains how embodied cognition operates within self-organising biological systems, and not only in people. For those who would like more information on this fascinating subject, I refer with pleasure to the following highly accessible article written by Karl Friston: Friston, K. (2010). The free-energy principle: a unified brain theory? *Nature Reviews Neuroscience, 11*(2), p. 127–138.

16. In more technical terms: what we perceive, the data or pieces of information in our brain, in not *generated* by external sensory information, but only *modulated*. (Eagleman, 2011).

17. I have limited myself here to a simplified version of what really happens. We can also be aware of the environment even when there are no prediction errors. Think, for example, of mindfulness. Equally, the updating of the model as a result of prediction errors is not always a conscious process. A distinction is made between unconscious updating (perceptual learning) and conscious updating (active learning). My example with chocolate is an example of active learning. However, most learning activity in the brain is unconscious, as you will read further in this book. In other words, we are not constantly, consciously and actively occupied in dealing with prediction errors throughout the day.

18. Eagleman (2011).

19. Lotto (2017), p. 2.

20. Botvinick & Cohen (1998).

21. For the cognoscenti: we are dealing here with what the scientific literature refers to as the Bayesian brain. Thomas Bayes was an English priest and mathematician who lived in the 18th century. He developed a statistical formula that made it possible to predict the probability of an event in uncertain circumstances. This probability is based on how plausible the event is, in the light of the (new) information you receive. The brain uses Bayesian logic to minimise its prediction errors, a logic that is very efficient at dealing with volatile, uncertain and far from coherent input.

22. The technical term is the 'precision-weighting of prediction errors.' A high degree of precision means that the brain attaches significant importance to what deviates from the prediction.

23. Hohwy (2013), p. 63.

24. A reference list of all the scientific books relating to the predictive brain and autism that were known at the time of publication are included in a bibliography at the end of the book.

25. In my book *Autism as context blindness,* I devoted an entire chapter – entitled 'Context and knowledge' – to the importance of context in conceptual development and how this differs in people with autism. There is no room in this book for a more detailed discussion, but suffice it to say that concepts are not something fixed: they are not stored somewhere in your brain. On the contrary, concepts are highly flexible and constructed on an ad hoc basis and in this book can be seen as a synonym for expectation or prediction. In essence, they are our models of the world on which we base our predictions.

26. Grandin (2009).

27. Grandin (2000).

28. Qian & Lipkin (2011), p. 9.

29. Pellicano & Burr (2012).

30. Pellicano and Burr use the term *hypo priors*.

31. Sinha et al. (2014).

32. Van de Cruys et al. (2013).

33. Van de Cruys uses the acronym HIPPEA: High, Inflexible Precision of Prediction Errors in Autism.

34. The technical term is 'overfitting.'

35. Van de Cruys et al. (2014).

36. Lawson, Rees, & Friston (2014).

37. Palmer, Paton, Kirkovski, Enticott, & Hohwy (2015).
38. Qian & Lipkin, 2011, p. 7.
39. Gomot & Wicker, 2012, p. 245.
40. Van de Cruys et al., 2013, p. 97.
41. Lawson, Friston, & Rees, 2015.
42. Palmer, Lawson, & Hohwy, 2017, abstract.
43. The theory of autism and context-blindness as outlined in my book *Autism as context blindness* only needs to be slightly modified to take account of the conceptual framework of predictive coding. In the book, I defined context-blindness as 'a reduced capacity to use the context spontaneously to give meaning to stimuli'. I would now reformulate that definition as 'a reduced capacity to use the context spontaneously to predict the world and deal with prediction errors'. Apart from the chapter on perception, which I then based on the outdated computer metaphor, the validity of the rest of the book's content has not been affected by the latest insights.
44. Quotation taken from George Musser, 7 March 2018: https://www.spectrumnews .org/ features/deep-dive/autism-may-stem-problems-prediction/
45. Cascio et al. (2012). See also: Paton, Hohwy, & Enticott (2012) and Palmer et al. (2013).
46. Mitchell et al. (2010).
47. © Lbeaumont; https://commons.wikimedia.org/wiki/File:Shepards_Table_Illusion .jpg
48. Loth, Gómez, & Happé (2010); Van de Cruys et al. (2018).
49. Król & Król (2019).
50. Allenmark et al. (2020).
51. Lawson, Mathys, & Rees (2017).
52. Above all, the P300 and the N400. But also MMN: mismatch negativity.
53. Amongst others: Kleinhans et al. (2009); Gomot et al. (2011); Goris et al. (2018); Utzerath et al. (2018); Tikir, Crosse, & Molholm (2019); Sapey-Triomphe, Timmermans, & Wagemans (2020).
54. Arthur et al. (2020).
55. Eric Schopler and Robert Reichler were already talking about hyperreactivity and hyporeactivity at a conference in April 1968. It took almost another half century before the terms were included in the official criteria for autism.
56. Nowadays, there are numerous variants. Amongst the most widely used is the Sensory Profile™ devised by Winnie Dunn, for which a Dutch translation has been available since 2013 (Sensory Profile – NL), and the Sensory Profile Checklist by Olga Bogdashina.
57. Schulz & Stevenson (2020).
58. No people with autism took part in this research.
59. Lucker (2013).
60. Kuiper, Verhoeven, & Geurts (2019).
61. Van de Cruys et al. (2014), p. 661.
62. For a more scientific explanation, see Blakemore, Wolpert, & Frith (2000).
63. Van Laarhoven et al. (2019).
64. Grandin & Panek (2014), p. 69.
65. This became apparent from the fact that the brain potential P2, which follows the N1, also registered a lower peak for them. A weaker P2 reaction indicates a 'belated' awareness that a sound that directly follows the pressing of a button is self-generated.
66. Van Laarhoven et al. (2020).
67. Sapey-Triomphe, Leiros Costa, & Wagemans (2019).
68. Here, we are again dealing with bottom-up signals that systematically have a too high level of precision, signals that should be ignored as noise. This results in overspecific, overfitted models, which in turn generate major predictive errors.
69. © Free after Utzerath et al. (2018).

70. Utzerath et al. (2018).
71. Goris et al. (2018). They used a hierarchical auditory *oddball task*, in which a strange tone is inserted in a series of identical tones.
72. Again for the cognoscenti: the mismatch negativity (MMN). This component becomes evident after 150 to 200 milliseconds and is pre-attentive.
73. Various studies have since demonstrated the link between certainty, anxiety and sensory hyperreactivity. See, amongst others: Wigham et al. (2015); Neil, Olsson, & Pellicano (2016); Green et al. (2019); MacLennan et al. (2019). A link between anxiety, sensory hyperreactivity and sub-optimal predictions has even been established at the level of the neurotransmitters; more concretely, in a link between GABA (gamma- aminobutyric acid) and tactile hyperreactivity: Sapey-Triomphe et al. (2019).
74. Remington et al. (2019).
75. Audiologists use different kinds of noise tailored to the requirements of individual patients. Sometimes natural noises – such as rain – are used.
76. The predictive coding framework is also used in cases of tinnitus. See, amongst others, Sedley et al. (2016); Hullfish, Sedley, & Vanneste (2019).
77. As far as acute pain is concerned, there is usually bodily damage or dysfunction. This generates a prediction error and this in turn results in a high level of precision for bodily signals. It is different with chronic pain. In this case, minor variations in the interoceptive input (the signals coming from the body) are not seen as noise that should be ignored, but as signals of bodily damage or dysfunction. See: Ongaro & Kaptchuk (2019) and Hoskin et al. (2019).
78. This is after Dimsdale & Dantzer (2007).
79. Bayer et al. (1998).
80. Lorimer Moseley: Why things hurt (2011).
81. Moseley et al. (2002).
82. Büchel et al. (2014).
83. Moseley, Parsons, & Spence (2008).
84. Hoffman et al. (2004).
85. Sharvit, Vuilleumier, & Corradi-Dell'Acqua (2019).
86. At least in the central and frontal areas of the insula.
87. See, amongst others, Geers et al. (2008) and Goodin & Bulls (2013).
88. Van de Cruys, Friston, & Clark (2020) refer to this as 'controlled optimism'.
89. Glass & Singer (1972). 84. Glass et al. (1973).
90. Glass et al. (1973).
91. Geer, Davison, & Gatchel (1970).
92. Robertson & Simmons (2015).
93. This is known as allostasis (Sterling, 2012). The brain does not seek to achieve a state of balance with the body (homeostasis), but wishes to prepare the body to the maximum possible extent to deal with the world and the events that it expects.
94. Barrett (2017b).
95. Noel et al. (2018); Quattrocki & Friston (2014).
96. Garfinkel et al. (2016). Garfinkel compared the results of people with autism against the results of people without autism. She discovered that the interoceptive accuracy (the ability to detect bodily signals) of people with autism was lower and their interoceptive sensitivity (how well they think they can detect bodily signals) was higher than the control group. The measurements of these criteria are expressed as the Interoceptive Trait Prediction Error (ITPE).
97. In this connection, it must be said that research involving children (Schauder et al., 2015) has shown different results: they were slightly better able than the control group to monitor their own heart rate, possibly because they were also better able to focus on the task. It is also possible that interoceptive accuracy declines with ageing (Palser et al., 2018), because the brain has learnt that bodily signals have little predictive value.

Research into interoception in autism is still in its infancy and contradictory results are characteristic of this kind of early phase.

98. In her book *How emotions are made* (2017b), Lisa Feldman Barrett explains this in detail: interoception is the basis of Theory of Mind and emotional intelligence. Together with my colleagues and good friend Kelly Mahler, author of the *Interoception Curriculum*, I have been arguing for some time that we should be learning Theory of Own Mind, before we try to make further progress with Theory of Mind.
99. Williams (1996), p. 120.
100. Quattrocki & Friston (2014).
101. Hohwy (2013); Barrett (2017a).
102. Hample, Mahler, & Amspacher (2020).
103. It was John Lawson (2003), an associate of Simon Baron-Cohen, who first applied the difference between open and closed systems to social difficulties in autism.
104. Zalla et al. (2010).
105. Pijnacker et al. (2009).
106. Baez et al. (2012); Baez & Ibanez (2014).
107. Frith & Frith (2008).
108. Jones, DeBrabander, & Sasson (2021). This explains why developing greater autism-friendliness requires more than a few awareness posters, articles, blogposts and video submissions on the annual World Autism Day (2 April).
109. Jones et al. (2011).
110. Cusack, Williams, & Neri (2015).
111. Tewolde, Bishop, & Manning (2018).
112. Amoruso et al. (2019).
113. Amoruso et al. (2019).
114. Amoruso, Finisguerra, & Urgesi (2018).
115. Chambon et al. (2017).
116. Von Der Lühe et al. (2016).
117. http://www.researchgate.net/figure/Examples-of-point-light-display-and-stimulus-display-and-stimulus- display-Panel-a-The-schematic-depiction-of_fig1_236106484
118. Sato et al. (2010).
119. Sometimes the direction of gaze was predictive, sometimes it was not. The researchers studied the difference in reaction times to valid and invalid cues. To make it more understandable, I have simplified the description of the experiment.
120. Schuwerk, Sodian, & Paulus (2016).
121. Paulus (2012).
122. Ganglmayer et al. (2020).
123. Schuwerk, Vuori, & Sodian (2015). They used two explicit Theory of Mind taken: the Strange Stories of Francesca Happé and the Reading the Mind in the Eyes (RME) test developed by Simon Baron-Cohen and his team. In addition, they also used an implicit Theory of Mind test, based on the one designed by Atsushi Senju in 2009: an animation film in which the behaviour of a person must be predicted on the basis of a false belief.
124. A European research group under the leadership of Joshua Balsters et al. (2017) demonstrated a clear connection between a disruption in the predictive brain (at the neurological level: brain signals that indicate prediction errors) and social shortcomings and difficulties in autism.
125. Fletcher-Watson et al. (2014).
126. Koster-Hale & Saxe (2013).
127. See, amongst others: Barrett, Mesquita, & Gendron (2011); Hassin, Aviezer, & Bentin (2013); Aviezer, Ensenberg & Hassin (2017).
128. Carroll & Russell (1996).

129. Context determines the level of brain potential that is active in facial recognition; namely, the N170 (Righart & De Gelder, 2006; 2008b). The N170 is a form of top-down modulation. Deviations in the activation of the N170 have been noted in people with autism: see Dawson et al. (2005) and Harms et al. (2010) for a summary of the neurological studies of facial recognition in people with autism.
130. Green et al. (2008).
131. Righart & De Gelder (2008a). Moreover, it is not a question of how accurately we can read emotions in others. It is more about whether our expectation of how someone feels and is going to behave aligns with the experience and intentions of the other person. In my opinion, we speak incorrectly about the ability to discover 'rightly' or 'wrongly' what other people are thinking, feeling and wanting. Social interaction is not a quiz with right and wrong answers.
132. Photo by: azerbaijan_stockers.
133. Tell & Davidson (2015).
134. Da Fonseca et al. (2009).
135. The only exception was the drawing for anxiety. A boy with a happy face surrounded by a swarm of bees was seen by seven of the ten children as being anxious. Even so, 15% saw the boy as being happy.
136. Speer et al. (2007).
137. Amongst others, Hanley et al. (2013) and Sasson et al. (2016).
138. Balconi, Amenta, & Ferrari (2012); Ramachandran, Mitchell, & Ropar (2010); Wright et al. (2008).
139. Loth, Gómez, & Happé (2008).
140. Grandin & Barron (2005).
141. Jankowski & Pfeifer (2021); Schreiter & Beste (2020).
142. Loth, Gómez, & Happé (2011).
143. Aviezer, Trope, & Todorov (2012).
144. Federmeier (2007); Kutas, DeLong, & Smith (2011).
145. See, amongst others: Gambi, Cop, & Pickering (2015); Garrod & Pickering (2015); Kuperberg & Jaeger (2016).
146. Stivers et al. (2009).
147. De Ruiter, Mitterer, & Enfield (2006); Magyari & De Ruiter (2012).
148. Ernestus, Baayen, & Schreuder (2002); Kemps et al. (2004).
149. The technical term is lexical priming: giving primacy to word candidates in a cohort. According to the cohort model of William Marslen-Wilson (1990), speech input activates a large number of word candidates, referred to as a cohort. That cohort therefore originates bottom-up and also contains a number of word candidates that are incompatible with the context. It is on the basis of context that these candidates will be eliminated (top-down selection). Once again, we can here see the predictive brain in action: it weighs sensory input against expectations.
150. For example, Rayner et al. (2011).
151. The technical term for this phenomenon is semantic priming. Exact lexical priming (the predicting of specific works) does not happen very often, but the expectation of certain sematic categories and characteristics is a standard part of the processing of language.
152. See, amongst others: Laszlo & Federmeier (2009) and – for a more recent overview – Kutas, DeLong, & Smith (2011).
153. Kutas & Hillyard (1980). For a recent summary of the situation relating to the N400: Kutas & Federmeier (2011).
154. Federmeier & Kutas (1999).
155. Wlotko & Federmeier (2015).
156. See, amongst others: McCleery et al. (2010); O'Connor (2012); O'Rourke & Coderre (2021).
157. Dunn & Bates (2005).

158. Pijnacker et al. (2010).
159. See, amongst others: Braeutigam, Swithenby, & Bailey (2008).
160. For the cognoscenti: the late positive component; a similar reaction in the P600 was also found in other studies.
161. Howard, Liversedge, & Benson (2017).
162. Coderre et al. (2018).
163. Manfredi et al. (2020).
164. Frith & Snowling (1983); Snowling & Frith (1986); Happé (1997); Jolliffe & Baron-Cohen (1999); Lopez & Leekam (2003).
165. Hala, Pexman, & Glenwright (2007).
166. Booth & Happé (2010).
167. Van de Cruys (2017).
168. Rozin et al. (2006).
169. See, amongst others: Hodgson et al. (2017) and Vasa et al. (2018).
170. For a summary article on the subject of the connection between uncertainty intolerance and anxiety, see: Jenkinson, Milne, & Thompson (2020).
171. Fredrickson & Losada (2005).
172. Lyubomirsky, King, & Diener (2005).
173. For those who would like to read more, I would refer you with pleasure to my website (www.petervermeulen. be), where you can find information about my H.A.P.P.Y. project, a psycho-educational programme for improving happiness among people with autism.
174. Tversky & Kahneman (1974).
175. De Martino et al. (2008).
176. For those who would like to read more, I would refer you with pleasure to my book *Autisme is niet blauw, de smurfen wel* (Autism is not blue, smurfs are), in which I look more closely at neurodiversity and neuroharmony.
177. This is known as confirmation bias.

References

Allenmark, F., Shi, Z., Pistorius, R. L., Theisinger, L. A., Koutsouleris, N., Falkai, P., ... & Falter-Wagner, C. M. (2020). Acquisition and use of 'priors' in autism: Typical in deciding where to look, atypical in deciding what is there. *Journal of Autism and Developmental Disorders*. https://doi.org/10.1007/s10803-020-04828-2.

Amoruso, L., Finisguerra, A., & Urgesi, C. (2018). Autistic traits predict poor integration between top-down contextual expectations and movement kinematics during action observation. *Scientific Reports, 8*(1), 1–10.

Amoruso, L., Narzisi, A., Pinzino, M., Finisguerra, A., Billeci, L., Calderoni, S., ... & Urgesi, C. (2019). Contextual priors do not modulate action prediction in children with autism. *Proceedings of the Royal Society B, 286*(1908), 20191319.

Arthur, T., Vine, S., Brosnan, M., & Buckingham, G. (2020). Predictive sensorimotor control in autism. *Brain, 143*(10), 3151–3163.

Aviezer, H., Ensenberg, N., & Hassin, R. R. (2017). The inherently contextualized nature of facial emotion perception. *Current Opinion in Psychology, 17*, 47–54.

Aviezer, H., Trope, Y., & Todorov, A. (2012). Body cues, not facial expressions, discriminate between intense positive and negative emotions. *Science, 338*(6111), 1225–1229.

Baez, S., & Ibanez, A. (2014). The effects of context processing on social cognition impairments in adults with Asperger's syndrome. *Frontiers in Neuroscience, 8*, 270.

Baez, S., Rattazzi, A., Gonzalez-Gadea, M. L., Torralva, T., Vigliecca, N., Decety, J., ... & Ibanez, A. (2012). Integrating intention and context: Assessing social cognition in adults with Asperger syndrome. *Frontiers in Human Neuroscience, 6*, 302.

Balconi, M., Amenta, S., & Ferrari, C. (2012). Emotional decoding in facial expression, scripts and videos: A comparison between normal, autistic and Asperger children. *Research in Autism Spectrum Disorders, 6*(1), 193–203.

Balsters, J. H., Apps, M. A., Bolis, D., Lehner, R., Gallagher, L., & Wenderoth, N. (2017). Disrupted prediction errors index social deficits in autism spectrum disorder. *Brain, 140*(1), 235–246.

Barrett, L. F. (2017a). The theory of constructed emotion: An active inference account of interoception and categorization. *Social Cognitive and Affective Neuroscience, 12*(1), 1–23.

Barrett, L. F. (2017b). *How emotions are made: The secret life of the brain.* Houghton Mifflin Harcourt.

Barrett, L. F., Mesquita, B., & Gendron, M. (2011). Context in emotion perception. *Current Directions in Psychological Science, 20*(5), 286–290.

Bayer, T. L., Coverdale, J. H., Chiang, E., & Bangs, M. (1998). The role of prior pain experience and expectancy in psychologically and physically induced pain. *Pain, 74*(2–3), 327–331.

Blakemore, S. J., Wolpert, D., & Frith, C. (2000). Why can't you tickle yourself? *Neuroreport*, *11*(11), R11–R16.

Booth, R., & Happé, F. (2010). "Hunting with a knife and… fork": Examining central coherence in autism, attention deficit/hyperactivity disorder, and typical development with a linguistic task. *Journal of Experimental Child Psychology*, *107*(4), 377–393.

Botvinick, M., & Cohen, J. (1998). Rubber hands "feel" touch that eyes see. *Nature*, *391*, 756.

Braeutigam, S., Swithenby, S. J., & Bailey, A. J. (2008). Contextual integration the unusual way: A magnetoencephalographic study of responses to semantic violation in individuals with autism spectrum disorders. *European Journal of Neuroscience*, *27*(4), 1026–1036.

Büchel, C., Geuter, S., Sprenger, C., & Eippert, F. (2014). Placebo analgesia: A predictive coding perspective. *Neuron*, *81*(6), 1223–1239.

Carroll, J. M., & Russell, J. A. (1996). Do facial expressions signal specific emotions? Judging emotion from the face in context. *Journal of Personality and Social Psychology*, *70*(2), 205.

Cascio, C., McGlone, F., Folger, S., Tannan, V., Baranek, G., Pelphrey, K. A., & Essick, G. (2008). Tactile perception in adults with autism: A multidimensional psychophysical study. *Journal of Autism and Developmental Disorders*, *38*(1), 127–137.

Cascio, C. J., Foss-Feig, J. H., Burnette, C. P., Heacock, J. L., & Cosby, A. A. (2012). The rubber hand illusion in children with autism spectrum disorders: Delayed influence of combined tactile and visual input on proprioception. *Autism*, *16*(4), 406–419.

Cascio, C. J., Moana-Filho, E. J., Guest, S., Nebel, M. B., Weisner, J., Baranek, G. T., & Essick, G. K. (2012). Perceptual and neural response to affective tactile texture stimulation in adults with autism spectrum disorders. *Autism Research*, *5*(4), 231–244.

Chambon, V., Farrer, C., Pacherie, E., Jacquet, P. O., Leboyer, M., & Zalla, T. (2017). Reduced sensitivity to social priors during action prediction in adults with autism spectrum disorders. *Cognition*, *160*, 17–26.

Clark, A. (2013). Whatever next? Predictive brains, situated agents, and the future of cognitive science. *Behavioral and Brain Sciences*, *36*(03), 181–204.

Coderre, E. L., Cohn, N., Slipher, S. K., Chernenok, M., Ledoux, K., & Gordon, B. (2018). Visual and linguistic narrative comprehension in autism spectrum disorders: Neural evidence for modality-independent impairments. *Brain and Language*, *186*, 44–59.

Cusack, J. P., Williams, J. H., & Neri, P. (2015). Action perception is intact in autism spectrum disorder. *Journal of Neuroscience*, *35*(5), 1849–1857.

Da Fonseca, D., Santos, A., Bastard-Rosset, D., Rondan, C. Poinso, F., & Deruelle, C. (2009). Can children with autistic spectrum disorders extract emotions out of contextual cues? *Research in Autism Spectrum Disorders*, *3*(1), 50–56.

Dawson, G., Webb, S. J., & McPartland, J. (2005). Understanding the nature of face processing impairment in autism: insights from behavioral and electrophysiological studies. *Developmental Neuropsychology*, *27*(3), 403–424.

De Martino, B., Harrison, N. A., Knafo, S., Bird, G., & Dolan, R. J. (2008). Explaining enhanced logical consistency during decision making in autism. *The Journal of Neuroscience*, *28*(42), 10746–10750.

De Ruiter, J. P., Mitterer, H., & Enfield, N. J. (2006). Projecting the end of a speaker's turn: A cognitive cornerstone of conversation. *Language*, *82*(3), 515–535.

Den Ouden, H. E., Kok, P., & de Lange, F. P. (2012). How prediction errors shape perception, attention, and motivation. *Frontiers in Psychology*, *3*, 548.

Dimsdale, J. E., & Dantzer, R. (2007). A biological substrate for somatoform disorders: Importance of pathophysiology. *Psychosomatic Medicine*, *69*(9), 850.

Dunn, M. A., & Bates, J. C. (2005). Developmental change in neural processing of words by children with autism. *Journal of Autism and Developmental Disorders, 35*(3), 361–376.

Eagleman, D. (2011). *Incognito: The secret lives of the brain.* Pantheon.

Ernestus, M., Baayen, H., & Schreuder, R. (2002). The recognition of reduced word forms. *Brain and Language, 81,* 162–173.

Federmeier, K. D. (2007). Thinking ahead: The role and roots of prediction in language comprehension. *Psychophysiology, 44*(4), 491–505.

Federmeier, K. D., & Kutas, M. (1999). A rose by any other name: Long-term memory structure and sentence processing. *Journal of Memory and Language, 41*(4), 469–495.

Feldman Barrett, L. (2017). *How emotions are made. The secret life of the brain.* Hoghton Mifflin Harcourt.

Fletcher-Watson, S., McConnell, F., Manola, E., & McConachie, H. (2014). Interventions based on the theory of mind cognitive model for autism spectrum disorder (ASD). *Cochrane Database of Systematic Reviews, 2014*(3), CD008785. https://doi.org/10.1002 /14651858.CD008785.pub2.

Fredrickson, B. L., & Losada, M. F. (2005). Positive affect and the complex dynamics of human flourishing. *American Psychologist, 60*(7), 678.

Friston, K. (2010). The free-energy principle: A unified brain theory? *Nature Reviews Neuroscience, 11*(2), 127–138.

Friston, K. (2016). The Bayesian savant. *Biological Psychiatry, 80,* 87–89.

Frith, C. (2007). *Making up the mind: How the brain creates our mental world.* Wiley-Blackwell.

Frith, C. D., & Frith, U. (2008). Implicit and explicit processes in social cognition. *Neuron, 60*(3), 503–510.

Frith, U., & Snowling, M. (1983). Reading for meaning and reading for sound in autistic and dyslexic children. *Journal of Developmental Psychology, 1,* 329–342.

Gambi, C., Cop, U., & Pickering, M. J. (2015). How do speakers coordinate? Evidence for prediction in a joint word-replacement task. *Cortex, 68,* 111–128.

Ganglmayer, K., Schuwerk, T., Sodian, B., & Paulus, M. (2020). Do children and adults with autism spectrum condition anticipate others' actions as goal-directed? A predictive coding perspective. *Journal of Autism and Developmental Disorders, 50*(6), 2077–2089.

Garfinkel, S. N., Tiley, C., O'Keeffe, S., Harrison, N. A., Seth, A. K., & Critchley, H. D. (2016). Discrepancies between dimensions of interoception in autism: Implications for emotion and anxiety. *Biological Psychology, 114,* 117–126.

Garrod, S., & Pickering, M. J. (2015). The use of content and timing to predict turn transitions. *Frontiers in Psychology, 6,* 751.

Geer, J. H., Davison, G. C., & Gatchel, R. I. (1970). Reduction of stress in humans through nonveridical perceived control of aversive stimulation. *Journal of Personality and Social Psychology, 16*(4), 731.

Geers, A. L., Wellman, J. A., Helfer, S. G., Fowler, S. L., & France, C. R. (2008). Dispositional optimism and thoughts of well-being determine sensitivity to an experimental pain task. *Annals of Behavioral Medicine, 36*(3), 304–313.

Glass, D. C., & Singer, J. E. (1972). Behavioral aftereffects of unpredictable and uncontrollable aversive events: Although subjects were able to adapt to loud noise and other stressors in laboratory experiments, they clearly demonstrated adverse aftereffects. *American Scientist, 60*(4), 457–465.

Glass, D. C., Singer, J. E., Leonard, H. S., Krantz, D., Cohen, S., & Cummings, H. (1973). Perceived control of aversive stimulation and the reduction of stress responses. *Journal of Personality, 41,* 4, 577–595.

Gomot, M., Blanc, R., Clery, H., Roux, S., Barthelemy, C., & Bruneau, N. (2011). Candidate electrophysiological endophenotypes of hyper-reactivity to change in autism. *Journal of Autism and Developmental Disorders, 41,* 705–714. https://doi.org/10.1007/s10803-010-1091-y.

Gomot, M., & Wicker, B. (2012). A challenging, unpredictable world for people with autism spectrum disorder. *International Journal of Psychophysiology, 83*(2), 240–247.

Gonzalez-Gadea, M. L., Chennu, S., Bekinschtein, T. A., Rattazzi, A., Beraudi, A., Tripicchio, P., ... & Sigman, M. (2015). Predictive coding in autism spectrum disorder and attention deficit hyperactivity disorder. *Journal of Neurophysiology, 114*(5), 2625–2636.

Goodin, B. R., & Bulls, H. W. (2013). Optimism and the experience of pain: Benefits of seeing the glass as half full. *Current Pain and Headache Reports, 17*(5), 329.

Goris, J., Braem, S., Nijhof, A. D., Rigoni, D., Deschrijver, E., Van de Cruys, S., ... & Brass, M. (2018). Sensory prediction errors are less modulated by global context in autism spectrum disorder. *Biological Psychiatry: Cognitive Neuroscience and Neuroimaging, 3*(8), 667–674.

Grandin, T. (2000). My mind is a web browser: How people with autism think. In Geneva Centre for Autism (Ed.), *International symposium on autism 2000: November 8, 9, 10, 2000. Conference proceedings* (pp. 37–44). Toronto.

Grandin, T. (2009). How does visual thinking work in the mind of a person with autism? A personal account. *Philosophical Transactions of the Royal Society B, 364,* 1437–1442.

Grandin, T., & Barron, S. (2005). *The unwritten rules of social relationships.* Future Horizons.

Grandin, T., & Panek, R. (2014). *The autistic brain.* Random House.

Green, M. J., Waldron, J. H., Simpson, I., & Coltheart, M. (2008). Visual processing of social context during mental state perception in schizophrenia. *Journal of Psychiatry and Neuroscience, 33*(1), 34–42.

Green, S. A., Hernandez, L., Lawrence, K. E., Liu, J., Tsang, T., Yeargin, J., ... & Bookheimer, S. Y. (2019). Distinct patterns of neural habituation and generalization in children and adolescents with autism with low and high sensory overresponsivity. *American Journal of Psychiatry, 176*(12), 1010–1020.

Greene, R. K., Zheng, S., Kinard, J. L., Mosner, M. G., Wiesen, C. A., Kennedy, D. P., & Dichter, G. S. (2019). Social and nonsocial visual prediction errors in autism spectrum disorder. *Autism Research, 12*(6), 878–883.

Haker, H., Schneebeli, M., & Stephan, K. E. (2016). Can Bayesian theories of autism spectrum disorder help improve clinical practice? *Frontiers in Psychiatry, 7*(107). https://doi.org/10.3389/fpsyt.2016.00107.

Hala, S., Pexman, P. M., & Glenwright, M. (2007). Priming the meaning of homographs in typically developing children and children with autism. *Journal of Autism and Developmental Disorders, 37,* 329–340.

Hample, K., Mahler, K., & Amspacher, A. (2020). An interoception-based intervention for children with autism spectrum disorder: A pilot study. *Journal of Occupational Therapy, Schools, & Early Intervention, 13*(4), 339–352.

Hanley, M., McPhillips, M., Mulhern, G., & Riby, D. M. (2013). Spontaneous attention to faces in Asperger syndrome using ecologically valid static stimuli. *Autism, 17*(6), 754–761.

Happé, F. G. E. (1997). Central coherence and theory of mind in autism: Reading homographs in context. *British Journal of Developmental Psychology, 15*(1), 1–12.

Harms, M. B., Martin, A., & Wallace, G. L. (2010). Facial emotion recognition in autism spectrum disorders: A review of behavioral and neuroimaging studies. *Neuropsychology Review, 20*(3), 290–322.

Hassin, R. R., Aviezer, H., & Bentin, S. (2013). Inherently ambiguous: Facial expressions of emotions, in context. *Emotion Review, 5*(1), 60–65.

Hodgson, A. R., Freeston, M. H., Honey, E., & Rodgers, J. (2017). Facing the unknown: Intolerance of uncertainty in children with autism spectrum disorder. *Journal of Applied Research in Intellectual Disabilities, 30*(2), 336–344.

Hoffman, H. G., Richards, T. L., Coda, B., Bills, A. R., Blough, D., Richards, A. L., & Sharar, S. R. (2004). Modulation of thermal pain-related brain activity with virtual reality: Evidence from fMRI. *Neuroreport, 15*(8), 1245–1248.

Hohwy, J. (2013). *The predictive mind.* Oxford University Press.

Hohwy, J., & Palmer, C. (2014). Social cognition as causal inference: Implications for common knowledge and autism. In M. Gallotti & J. Michael (Eds.). *Perspectives on social ontology and social cognition* (pp. 167–189). Springer Netherlands.

Hoskin, R., Berzuini, C., Acosta-Kane, D., El-Deredy, W., Guo, H., & Talmi, D. (2019). Sensitivity to pain expectations: A Bayesian model of individual differences. *Cognition, 182*, 127–139.

Howard, P. L., Liversedge, S. P., & Benson, V. (2017). Investigating the use of world knowledge during on-line comprehension in adults with autism spectrum disorder. *Journal of Autism and Developmental Disorders, 47*(7), 2039–2053.

Hullfish, J., Sedley, W., & Vanneste, S. (2019). Prediction and perception: Insights for (and from) tinnitus. *Neuroscience & Biobehavioral Reviews, 102*, 1–12.

Jankowski, K., & Pfeifer, J. (2021). Exploring the subjective experience and neural correlates of self-conscious emotion processing in autistic adolescents: Over-reliance on learned social rules during heightened perspective-taking demands may serve as compensatory strategy for less reflexive mentalizing. *Journal of Autism and Developmental Disorders.* Advance online publication. https://doi.org/10.1007/s10803-020-04808-6

Jenkinson, R., Milne, E., & Thompson, A. (2020). The relationship between intolerance of uncertainty and anxiety in autism: A systematic literature review and meta-analysis. *Autism, 24*(8), 1933–1944.

Jolliffe, T., & Baron-Cohen, S. (1999). A test of central coherence theory; linguistic processing in high-functioning adults with autism or Asperger's syndrome: Is local coherence impaired? *Cognition, 71*, 149–185.

Jones, C. R., Swettenham, J., Charman, T., Marsden, A. J., Tregay, J., Baird, G., ... & Happé, F. (2011). No evidence for a fundamental visual motion processing deficit in adolescents with autism spectrum disorders. *Autism Research, 4*(5), 347–357.

Jones, D. R., DeBrabander, K. M., & Sasson, N. J. (2021). Effects of autism acceptance training on explicit and implicit biases toward autism. *Autism.* https://doi.org/10.1177/1362361320984896.

Kahneman, D. (2011). *Thinking, fast and slow.* Farrar, Straus and Giroux.

Kanner, L. (1951). The conception of wholes and parts in early infantile autism. *American Journal of Psychiatry, 108*(1), 23–26.

Karvelis, P., Seitz, A. R., Lawrie, S. M., & Seriès, P. (2018). Autistic traits, but not schizotypy, predict increased weighting of sensory information in Bayesian visual integration. *ELife, 7*, e34115.

Kemps, R., Ernestus, M., Schreuder, R., & Baayen, R. H. (2004). Processing reduced word forms: The suffix restoration effect. *Brain and Language, 90*, 117–127.

Kleinhans, N., Johnson, L., Richards, T., Mahurin, R., Greenson, J., Dawson, G., & Aylward, E. (2009). Reduced neural habituation in the amygdala and social impairments in autism spectrum disorders. *American Journal of Psychiatry, 166*, 467–475. https://doi.org/10.1176/appi.ajp.2008.07101681.

Kok, P., & de Lange, F. P. (2015). Predictive coding in sensory cortex. In B. U. Forstmann & E. J. Wagenmakers (Eds.), *An introduction to model-based cognitive neuroscience* (pp. 221–244). Springer.

Koster-Hale, J., & Saxe, R. (2013). Theory of mind: A neural prediction problem. *Neuron*, *79*(5), 836–848.

Król, M., & Król, M. (2019). The world as we know it and the world as it is: Eye-movement patterns reveal decreased use of prior knowledge in individuals with autism. *Autism Research*, *12*(9), 1386–1398.

Kuiper, M. W., Verhoeven, E. W., & Geurts, H. M. (2019). Stop making noise! Auditory sensitivity in adults with an autism spectrum disorder diagnosis: Physiological habituation and subjective detection thresholds. *Journal of Autism and Developmental Disorders*, *49*(5), 2116–2128.

Kuperberg, G. R., & Jaeger, T. F. (2016). What do we mean by prediction in language comprehension? *Language, Cognition and Neuroscience*, *31*(1), 32–59.

Kutas, M., DeLong, K. A., & Smith, N. J. (2011). A look around at what lies ahead: Prediction and predictability in language processing. In M. Bar (Ed.), *Predictions in the brain: Using our past to generate a future* (pp. 190–207). Oxford University Press.

Kutas, M., & Federmeier, K. D. (2011). Thirty years and counting: Finding meaning in the N400 component of the event-related brain potential (ERP). *Annual Review of Psychology*, *62*, 621–647.

Kutas, M., & Hillyard, S. A. (1980). Reading senseless sentences: Brain potentials reflect semantic incongruity. *Science*, *207*(4427), 203–205.

Laszlo, S., & Federmeier, K. D. (2009). A beautiful day in the neighborhood: An event-related potential study of lexical relationships and prediction in context. *Journal of Memory and Language*, *61*(3), 326–338.

Lawson, J. (2003). Depth accessibility difficulties: An alternative conceptualisation of autism spectrum conditions. *Journal for the Theory of Social Behaviour*, *33*(2), 189–202.

Lawson, R. P., Friston, K. J., & Rees, G. (2015). A more precise look at context in autism. *Proceedings of the National Academy of Sciences*, *112*(38), E522.

Lawson, R. P., Mathys, C., & Rees, G. (2017). Adults with autism overestimate the volatility of the sensory environment. *Nature Neuroscience*, *20*(9), 1293–1299.

Lawson, R. P., Rees, G., & Friston, K. J. (2014). An aberrant precision account of autism. *Frontiers in Human Neuroscience*, *8*, 302.

Lopez, B., & Leekam, S. R. (2003). Do children with autism fail to process information in context? *Journal of Child Psychology and Psychiatry*, *44*(2), 285–300.

Loth, E., Gómez, J. C., & Happé, F. (2008). Event schemas in autism spectrum disorders: The role of theory of mind and weak central coherence. *Journal of Autism and Developmental Disorders*, *38*(3), 449–463.

Loth, E., Gómez, J. C., & Happé, F. (2010). When seeing depends on knowing: Adults with autism spectrum conditions show diminished top-down processes in the visual perception of degraded faces but not degraded objects. *Neuropsychologia*, *48*, 1227–1236.

Loth, E., Gómez, J. C., & Happé, F. (2011). Do high-functioning people with autism spectrum disorder spontaneously use event knowledge to selectively attend to and remember context-relevant aspects in scenes? *Journal of Autism and Developmental Disorders*, *41*(7), 945–961.

Lotto, B. (2017). *Deviate: The science of seeing differently*. Hachette Books.

Lucker, J. R. (2013). Auditory hypersensitivity in children with autism spectrum disorders. *Focus on Autism and Other Developmental Disabilities*, *28*(3), 184–191.

Lyubomirsky, S., King, L., & Diener, E. (2005). The benefits of frequent positive affect: Does happiness lead to success? *Psychological Bulletin*, *131*(6), 803.

MacLennan, P., Tavassoli, T., Roach, L., Englezou, F., & Daniels, C. R. (2019). Sensory reactivity symptoms are related to specific anxiety symptomology in autistic children. Poster presented at INSAR meeting, Montréal, Friday 3 May 2019.

Magyari, L., & De Ruiter, J. P. (2012). Prediction of turn-ends based on anticipation of upcoming words. *Frontiers in Psychology*, *3*, 376.

Mahler, K. (2019). *The interoception curriculum: A step-by-step guide to developing mindful self-regulation*. Mahler.

Manfredi, M., Cohn, N., Mello, P. S., Fernandez, E., & Boggio, P. S. (2020). Visual and verbal narrative comprehension in children and adolescents with autism spectrum disorders: An ERP study. *Journal of Autism and Developmental Disorders*, *50*(8), 2658–2672.

Marslen–Wilson, W. D. (1990). Activation, competition, and frequency in lexical access. In G. T. M. Altmann (Ed.), *Cognitive models of speech processing: Psycholinguistic and computational perspectives* (pp. 148–172). MIT Press.

McCleery, J. P., Ceponiene, R., Burner, K. M., Townsend, J., Kinnear, M., & Schreibman, L. (2010). Neural correlates of verbal and nonverbal semantic integration in children with autism spectrum disorders. *Journal of Child Psychology and Psychiatry*, *51*, 277–286.

Mitchell, P., Mottron, L., Soulieres, I., & Ropar, D. (2010). Susceptibility to the Shepard illusion in participants with autism: Reduced top-down influences within perception? *Autism Research*, *3*(3), 113–119.

Moseley, G. L., Parsons, T. J., & Spence, C. (2008). Visual distortion of a limb modulates the pain and swelling evoked by movement. *Current Biology*, *18*(22), R1047–R1048.

Moseley, J. B., O'Malley, K., Petersen, N. J., Menke, T. J., Brody, B. A., Kuykendall, D. H., ... & Wray, N. P. (2002). A controlled trial of arthroscopic surgery for osteoarthritis of the knee. *New England Journal of Medicine*, *347*(2), 81–88.

Neil, L., Olsson, N. C., & Pellicano, E. (2016). The relationship between intolerance of uncertainty, sensory sensitivities, and anxiety in autistic and typically developing children. *Journal of Autism and Developmental Disorders*, *46*, 1962–1973.

Noel, J. P., Lytle, M., Cascio, C., & Wallace, M. T. (2018). Disrupted integration of exteroceptive and interoceptive signaling in autism spectrum disorder. *Autism Research*, *11*(1), 194–205.

O'Connor, K. (2012). Auditory processing in autism spectrum disorder: A review. *Neuroscience and Biobehavioral Reviews*, *36*(2), 836–854.

Ongaro, G., & Kaptchuk, T. J. (2019). Symptom perception, placebo effects, and the Bayesian brain. *Pain*, *160*(1), 1.

O'Rourke, E., & Coderre, E. L. (2021). Implicit semantic processing of linguistic and non-linguistic stimuli in adults with autism spectrum disorder. *Journal of Autism and Developmental Disorders*, *51*(8), 2611–2630.

Palmer, C. J., Lawson, R. P., & Hohwy, J. (2017). Bayesian approaches to autism: Towards volatility, action, and behavior. *Psychological Bulletin*, *143*(5), 521–542.

Palmer, C. J., Paton, B., Hohwy, J., & Enticott, P. G. (2013). Movement under uncertainty: The effects of the rubber-hand illusion vary along the nonclinical autism spectrum. *Neuropsychologia*, *51*(10), 1942–1951.

Palmer, C. J., Paton, B., Kirkovski, M., Enticott, P. G., & Hohwy, J. (2015). Context sensitivity in action decreases along the autism spectrum: A predictive processing perspective. *Proceedings of the Royal Society of London B: Biological Sciences*, *282*(1802), 20141557.

Palmer, C. J., Seth, A. K., & Hohwy, J. (2015). The felt presence of other minds: Predictive processing, counterfactual predictions, and mentalising in autism. *Consciousness and Cognition, 36,* 376–389.

Palser, E. R., Fotopoulou, A., Pellicano, E., & Kilner, J. M. (2018). The link between interoceptive processing and anxiety in children diagnosed with autism spectrum disorder: Extending adult findings into a developmental sample. *Biological Psychology, 136,* 13–21.

Palser, E. R., Fotopoulou, A., Pellicano, E., & Kilner, J. M. (2020). Dissociation in how core autism features relate to interoceptive dimensions: Evidence from cardiac awareness in children. *Journal of Autism and Developmental Disorders, 50*(2), 572–582.

Paton, B., Hohwy, J., & Enticott, P. G. (2012). The rubber hand illusion reveals proprioceptive and sensorimotor differences in autism spectrum disorders. *Journal of Autism and Developmental Disorders, 42*(9), 1870–1883. https://doi.org/10.1007/s10803-011-1430-7.

Paulus, M. (2012). Action mirroring and action understanding: An ideomotor and attentional account. *Psychological Research Psychologische Forschung, 76,* 760–767. https://doi.org/10.1007/s0042-6-011-0385-9.

Pellicano, E., & Burr, D. (2012). When the world becomes 'too real': A Bayesian explanation of autistic perception. *Trends in Cognitive Sciences, 16*(10), 504–510.

Pijnacker, J., Geurts, B., Van Lambalgen, M., Buitelaar, J., & Hagoort, P. (2010). Exceptions and anomalies: An ERP study on context sensitivity in autism. *Neuropsychologia, 48*(10), 2940–2951.

Pijnacker, J., Geurts, B., van Lambalgen, M., Kan, C. C., Buitelaar, J. K., & Hagoort, P. (2009). Defeasible reasoning in high-functioning adults with autism: Evidence for impaired exception-handling. *Neuropsychologia, 47*(3), 644–651.

Qian, N., & Lipkin, R. M. (2011). A learning-style theory for understanding autistic behaviors. *Frontiers in Human Neuroscience, 5,* 77.

Quattrocki, E., & Friston, K. (2014). Autism, oxytocin and interoception. *Neuroscience & Biobehavioral Reviews, 47,* 410–430.

Ramachandran, R., Mitchell, P., & Ropar, D. (2010). Recognizing faces based on inferred traits in autism spectrum disorders. *Autism, 14*(6), 605–618.

Rayner, K., Slattery, T. J., Drieghe, D., & Liversedge, S. P. (2011). Eye movements and word skipping during reading: Effects of word length and predictability. *Journal of Experimental Psychology: Human Perception and Performance, 37*(2), 514.

Remington, A., Hanley, M., O'Brien, S., Riby, D. M., & Swettenham, J. (2019). Implications of capacity in the classroom: Simplifying tasks for autistic children may not be the answer. *Research in Developmental Disabilities, 85,* 197–204.

Righart, R., & de Gelder, B. (2006). Context influences early perceptual analysis of faces. An electrophysiological study. *Cerebral Cortex, 16,* 1249–1257.

Righart, R., & de Gelder, B. (2008a). Facial expressions and emotional scene gist. *Cognitive, Affective, & Behavioural Neuroscience, 8*(3), 264–272.

Righart, R., & de Gelder, B. (2008b). Rapid influence of emotional scenes on encoding of facial expressions. An ERP study. *Social Cognitive and Affective Neuroscience, 3,* 270–278.

Robertson, A. E., & Simmons, D. R. (2015). The sensory experiences of adults with autism spectrum disorder: A qualitative analysis. *Perception, 44*(5), 569–586.

Rosenberg, A., Patterson, J. S., & Angelaki, D. E. (2015). A computational perspective on autism. *Proceedings of the National Academy of Sciences, 112*(30), 9158–9165.

Rozin, P., Rozin, A., Appel, B., & Wachtel, C. (2006). Documenting and explaining the common AAB pattern in music and humor: Establishing and breaking expectations. *Emotion, 6*(3), 349–355.

Sapey-Triomphe, L. A., Lamberton, F., Sonié, S., Mattout, J., & Schmitz, C. (2019). Tactile hypersensitivity and GABA concentration in the sensorimotor cortex of adults with autism. *Autism Research.* https://doi.org/10.1002/aur.2073.

Sapey-Triomphe, L. A., Leiros Costa, T., & Wagemans, J. (2019). Sensory sensitivity in autism mostly depends on contextual predictions. *Cognitive Neuroscience, 10*(3), 162–164.

Sapey-Triomphe, L. A., Timmermans, L., & Wagemans, J. (2020). Priors bias perceptual decisions in autism, but are less flexibly adjusted to the context. *Autism Research.* https://doi.org.10.1002/aur.2452.

Sasson, N. J., Pinkham, A. E., Weittenhiller, L. P., Faso, D. J., & Simpson, C. (2016). Context effects on facial affect recognition in schizophrenia and autism: Behavioral and eye-tracking evidence. *Schizophrenia Bulletin, 42*(3), 675–683.

Sato, W., Uono, S., Okada, T., & Toichi, M. (2010). Impairment of unconscious, but not conscious, gaze-triggered attention orienting in Asperger's disorder. *Research in Autism Spectrum Disorders, 4*(4), 782–786.

Schauder, K. B., Mash, L. E., Bryant, L. K., & Cascio, C. J. (2015). Interoceptive ability and body awareness in autism spectrum disorder. *Journal of Experimental Child Psychology, 131*, 193–200.

Schopler, E. (1965). Early infantile autism and receptor processes. *Archives of General Psychiatry, 13*(4):327–335.

Schopler, E., & Reichler, R. J. (1968). *Psycholobiological referents for the treatment of autism.* Paper presented at Indiana University Colloquium on Infantile Autism, Indiana University Medical Center, Indianapolis, Indiana, April, 1968.

Schreiter, M. L., & Beste, C. (2020). Inflexible adjustment of expectations affects cognitive-emotional conflict control in adolescents with autism spectrum disorder. *Cortex, 130*, 231–245.

Schulz, S. E., & Stevenson, R. A. (2020). Differentiating between sensory sensitivity and sensory reactivity in relation to restricted interests and repetitive behaviours. *Autism, 24*(1), 121–134.

Schuwerk, T., Sodian, B., & Paulus, M. (2016). Cognitive mechanisms underlying action prediction in children and adults with autism spectrum condition. *Journal of Autism and Developmental Disorders, 46*(12), 3623–3639.

Schuwerk, T., Vuori, M., & Sodian, B. (2015). Implicit and explicit theory of mind reasoning in autism spectrum disorders: The impact of experience. *Autism: The International Journal of Research and Practice, 19*(4), 459–468.

Sedley, W., Friston, K. J., Gander, P. E., Kumar, S., & Griffiths, T. D. (2016). An integrative tinnitus model based on sensory precision. *Trends in Neurosciences, 39*(12), 799–812.

Sharvit, G., Vuilleumier, P., & Corradi-Dell'Acqua, C. (2019). Sensory-specific predictive models in the human anterior insula. *F1000Research, 8*, 164.

Sinha, P., Kjelgaard, M. M., Gandhi, T. K., Tsourides, K., Cardinaux, A. L., Pantazis, D., … & Held, R. M. (2014). Autism as a disorder of prediction. *Proceedings of the National Academy of Sciences, 111*(42), 15220–15225.

Skewes, J. C., & Gebauer, L. (2016). Brief report: Suboptimal auditory localization in autism spectrum disorder: Support for the Bayesian account of sensory symptoms. *Journal of Autism and Developmental Disorders.* https://doi.org/10.1007/s10803-016-2774-9.

Skewes, J. C., Jegindø, E. M., & Gebauer, L. (2015). Perceptual inference and autistic traits. *Autism, 19*(3), 301–307.

Snowling, M., & Frith, U. (1986). Comprehension in 'hyperlexic' readers. *Journal of Experimental Child Psychology, 42*, 392–415.

Speer, L. L., Cook, A. E., McMahon, W. M., & Clark, E. (2007). Face processing in children with autism: Effects of stimulus contents and type. *Autism*, *11*(3), 265–277.

Sterling, P. (2012). Allostasis: A model of predictive regulation. *Physiology & Behavior*, *106*(1), 5–15.

Stivers, T., Enfield, N. J., Brown, P., Englert, C., Hayashi, M., Heinemann, T., … & Levinson, S. C. (2009). Universals and cultural variation in turn-taking in conversation. *Proceedings of the National Academy of Sciences*, *106*(26), 10587–10592.

Tell, D., & Davidson, D. (2015). Emotion recognition from congruent and incongruent emotional expressions and situational cues in children with autism spectrum disorder. *Autism*, *19*(3), 375–379.

Tewolde, F. G., Bishop, D. V., & Manning, C. (2018). Visual motion prediction and verbal false memory performance in autistic children. *Autism Research*, *11*(3), 509–518.

Tikir, S., Crosse, M. J., & Molholm, S. (2019). Predictive processing in changing environments in autism: Electrophysiological, pupillometric and behavioral assays. Poster presentation at INSAR 2019 Annual Meeting, Montreal, Québec, Saturday, May 4, 2019.

Tversky, A., & Kahneman, D. (1974). Judgment under uncertainty: Heuristics and biases. *Science*, *185*, 1124–1131.

Utzerath, C., Schmits, I. C., Buitelaar, J., & de Lange, F. P. (2018). Adolescents with autism show typical fMRI repetition suppression, but atypical surprise. *Cortex*, *109*(25), e3–4.

Van de Cruys, S. (2017). Affective value in the predictive mind. In T. Metzinger & W. Wiese (Eds.), *Philosophy and predictive processing: 24*. MIND Group. https://doi.org/10 .15502/9783958573253.

Van de Cruys, S., de-Wit, L., Evers, K., Boets, B., & Wagemans, J. (2013). Weak priors versus overfitting of predictions in autism: Reply to Pellicano and Burr (TICS, 2012). *i-Perception*, *4*(2), 95.

Van de Cruys, S., Evers, K., Van der Hallen, R., Van Eylen, L., Boets, B., de-Wit, L., & Wagemans, J. (2014). Precise minds in uncertain worlds: Predictive coding in autism. *Psychological review*, *121*(4), 649.

Van de Cruys, S., Friston, K., & Clark, A. (2020). Reply to Sun and Firestone on the dark room problem. *Trends in Cognitive Sciences*, *24*(9), 1–2.

Van de Cruys, S., Perrykkad, K., & Hohwy, J. (2019). Explaining hyper-sensitivity and hypo-responsivity in autism with a common predictive coding-based mechanism. *Cognitive Neuroscience*, *10*(3), 164–166.

Van de Cruys, S., Van der Hallen, R., & Wagemans, J. (2017). Disentangling signal and noise in autism spectrum disorder. *Brain and Cognition*, *112*, 78–8.

Van de Cruys, S., Vanmarcke, S., Van de Put, I., & Wagemans, J. (2018). The use of prior knowledge for perceptual inference is preserved in ASD. *Clinical Psychological Science*, *6*(3), 382–393.

Van den Hurk, J., Van Baelen, M., & de Beeck, H. P. O. (2017). Development of visual category selectivity in ventral visual cortex does not require visual experience. *Proceedings of the National Academy of Sciences*, *114*(22), E4501–E4510.

Van Laarhoven, T., Stekelenburg, J. J., Eussen, M. L., & Vroomen, J. (2019). Electrophysiological alterations in motor-auditory predictive coding in autism spectrum disorder. *Autism Research*, *12*(4), 589–599.

Van Laarhoven, T., Stekelenburg, J. J., Eussen, M. L., & Vroomen, J. (2020). Atypical visual-auditory predictive coding in autism spectrum disorder: Electrophysiological evidence from stimulus omissions. *Autism*, *24*(7), 1849–1859.

Vasa, R. A., Kreiser, N. L., Keefer, A., Singh, V., & Mostofsky, S. H. (2018). Relationships between autism spectrum disorder and intolerance of uncertainty. *Autism Research*, *11*(4), 636–644.

Vermeulen, P. (1996). *Dit is de titel. Over autistisch denken*. Berchem: EPO. (English version: Vermeulen, P. (2001). *Autistic thinking: this is the title*. London: Jessica Kingsley Publishers.)

Vermeulen, P. (2012). *Autism as context blindness*. Overland Park, KS: Autism Asperger Publishing Company.

Vermeulen, P. (2017). *Autisme is niet blauw. Smurfen wel*. Kalmthout: Pelckmans Pro. (Not translated into English.)

Von Der Lühe, T., Manera, V., Barisic, I., Becchio, C., Vogeley, K., & Schilbach, L. (2016). Interpersonal predictive coding, not action perception, is impaired in autism. *Philosophical Transactions of the Royal Society B: Biological Sciences*, *371*(1693), 20150373.

Wigham, S., Rodgers, J., South, M., McConachie, H., & Freeston, M. (2015). The interplay between sensory processing abnormalities, intolerance of uncertainty, anxiety and restricted and repetitive behaviours in autism spectrum disorder. *Journal of Autism and Developmental Disorders*, *45*(4), 943–952.

Wlotko, E. W., & Federmeier, K. D. (2015). Time for prediction? The effect of presentation rate on predictive sentence comprehension during word-by-word reading. *Cortex*, *68*, 20–32.

Wright, B., Clarke, N., Jordan, J., Young, A. W., Clarke, P., Miles, J., Nation, K., Clatke, L., & Williams, C. (2008). Emotion recognition in faces and the use of visual context in young people with high-functioning autism spectrum disorders. *Autism*, *12*(6), 607–626.

Zalla, T., & Korman, J. (2018). Prior knowledge, episodic control and theory of mind in autism: Toward an integrative account of social cognition. *Frontiers in Psychology*, *9*, 752–752.

Zalla, T., Labruyère, N., Clément, A., & Georgieff, N. (2010). Predicting ensuing actions in children and adolescents with autism spectrum disorders. *Experimental Brain Research*, *201*(4), 809–819.

Index

Interoceptive Trait Prediction Error (ITPE) 146n94
intolerance of uncertainty 135–136
ITPE (Interoceptive Trait Prediction Error) 146n94

juvenile retinoschisis 16

Kahneman, D. 10, 139–140
Kanner, L. 46–48, 130
Kopernik, N. 9
Kutas, M. 123

language *see* communication
language processing 125–131
Lawler, P. 66
Lawson, R. 36, 37, 43
learned meanings 130–131
learning 24; context-dependent learning 33; emphatic learning 114
learning styles 32–33, 36, 42
lexical priming 148n145; 148n147
Lipkin, R. 32–34
logical thinking 10, 140
Loth, E. 110, 112
low-stimulation 62–63, 69, 76, 137; *see also* autism-friendly
Lucker, J. 51–53

machine metaphors 9
Mahler, K. 85
Maslow, A. 136
McNeil, C. 13
meaning 11, 17–18, 39, 65, 84, 86, 91, 103, 118, 128-132, 139
mental health problems 136
mental shrinking 68
metaphors for the brain 9–10
Miller, G. 131
minimisation of prediction errors 30
mis-firings 83–84
Mooney, C. 39
Mooney image 39, 44
Moseley, L. 67–68
movement: eye movement *see* eye movement; point light displays 97–98; predicting 93–95
Muller, J. P. 12

N100 56, 58
N170 147n125
N400 123–124
Necker, L. A. 26
Nijmegen experiment 60

noise 141; hypersensitivity 51–54; as interference 28–29; perception of sounds 58; silence 58; urban stress 76
noise experiments 51–54, 60, 76
noise hypersensitivity 51–54
noise-cancelling headphones 63–64

oddities 47–48, 51
open systems 89, 111, 115
optimism 73, 86, 113
over-firings 83
overstimulation 61 *see also* sensory overload

pain 49, 65–69, 73, 146n74
Palmer, C. 36
Palser, E. 82
passive relaxation 76
Patterson, J. S. 68, 76
Pellicano, L. 34
perception 4, 10, 15, 18, 24, 36, 57–58
Pijnacker, J. 90, 124
placebo effects 67–68
point light displays 97–98
polysemy 128
precision-weighting of prediction errors 144n19
predictability 43, 55–57, 65, 70–72, 136–138
predicting behaviour 89–91, 96; apple/cup experiment 94–96
predicting movement 93–95; point light displays 97–98
predicting what someone will say *see* communication
prediction errors 23, 28–29, 42, 45, 56, 133; minimisation of prediction errors 30; precision-weighting of 144n19; reducing 70; social relationships 113–115
predictions 21–27, 34–35
predictive ability, impairment in 37–38
predictive coding 20, 143n10, 145n40, 146n73
pre-programmed information 15–16
priori assumptions 141–142
Prizant, B. 2
processing 9; communication 125–128; language 125–131
pronunciation 120–121; homographs 129
puzzle experiments 77

Qian, N. 32–34

random variation 141
reactivity 50; *see also* hyperreactivity

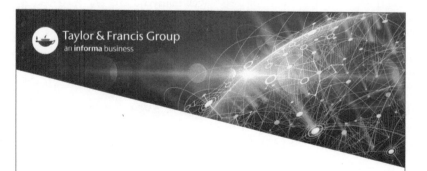